Langenscheidt

Reading Business

Englische Wirtschaftstexte
lesen und verstehen

von Gerald und Helga Williams

Langenscheidt

Berlin · München · Wien · Zürich · New York

Herausgegeben von der Langenscheidt-Redaktion
Autoren: Gerald und Helga Williams
Beratung: Birgit Abegg, Sprachprüferin, IHK, Düsseldorf;
Cover-Design: Independent Medien-Design
Layout: Ute Weber
Bildnachweis: Photo Alto S. 21; PhotoDisc S. 10, 82, 149;
John Fox S. 108, 118, 129

Umwelthinweis:
Gedruckt auf chlorfrei gebleichtem Papier

© 2003 by Langenscheidt KG, Berlin und München

Satz: Typodata GmbH, München
Druck: Druckhaus, Langenscheidt, Berlin
Bindung: Schoneberger Buchbinderei, Berlin

Printed in Germany
ISBN 3-468-21915-6
www.langenscheidt.de

Vorwort

Reading Business?

Welcher Geschäftsmann oder welche Geschäftsfrau heute, welcher Abteilungsleiter oder welche Abteilungsleiterin, welcher oder welche Angestellte wird nicht täglich mit einer scheinbar unendlichen Flut von unterschiedlichen Dokumenten konfrontiert? Briefe, Aktennotizen, Berichte, Artikel aus Zeitungen oder Fachzeitschriften, Verträge, Internet-Websites, Werbetexte, Rechnungen, Reklamationen – ob als traditioneller Brief gestaltet oder per E-Mail zugestellt – die Liste scheint in der Tat endlos zu sein.

Und je größer die Zahl, desto kürzer die Zeit, die einem für die Lektüre und Analyse zur Verfügung steht.

Hier ist es wichtig, Strategien zu entwickeln, die uns helfen, in kurzer Zeit das Wesentliche in den verschiedensten Texten und Dokumenten zu erkennen und zu verstehen. Diese Strategien beim Lesen müssen selbstverständlich auch geübt werden, was das Ziel dieses Buches ist.

Umso wichtiger ist es also, dass Sie nicht nur den Inhalt solcher Dokumente verstehen, sondern auch imstande sind, schnell zu erkennen, ob das Schriftstück wirklich wichtig ist, und dass Sie dessen Inhalt schnell und korrekt erfassen, um dann entsprechend darauf reagieren zu können. So vermeiden Sie unnötigen Leerlauf oder – noch schlimmer – das Risiko einer folgenschweren Fehlentscheidung aufgrund eines „Missverständnisses".

Diese überaus unterschätzte Fertigkeit des schnellen Erkennens ist in der eigenen Muttersprache schon wichtig genug, umso wichtiger ist sie aber heute in der internationalen Sprache der Geschäftswelt geworden – im Englischen.

Große und kleine Firmen aus aller Welt korrespondieren, faxen, emailen in der *lingua franca* unserer Zeit. Die USA haben einen enormen Einfluss auf die Weltökonomie. Die großen Finanzzentren der Welt in London, New York und Tokio sind englischsprachig, und auch sonstwo in der Welt, in Asien, Afrika oder Australien kommt man ohne Englischkenntnisse nicht sehr weit.

Umso sinnvoller ist es also für nicht englischsprachige Muttersprachler geworden, sich mit den verschiedenen Arten von Dokumenten und Texten aus der englischsprachigen Geschäftswelt auseinander zu setzen und die schnelle Analyse der darin enthaltenen Informationen zu üben – nicht nur der Fakten, sondern auch der Sprache und der dahinter liegenden Kommunikationsabsichten.

Der Leseverstehensprozess

Im muttersprachlichen Bereich wird das Leseverhalten durch folgende Bedingungen geprägt:
- Der Leser ist im Besitz von einigen Vorinformationen.
- Bilder, Überschriften oder Schlagzeilen in Texten weisen auf Inhalte und Absichten hin.
- Der Text wird zur Erfassung seines Inhaltes meistens sehr schnell und leise gelesen, ohne lange auf die genaue Bedeutung sämtlicher Wörter und Begriffe zu achten.
- Der Text wird nicht gelesen, um ihn nach genauer Analyse wortgetreu wiederholen zu können, sondern um ihm bestimmte wesentliche Informationen zu entnehmen.

Bei Texten in einer Fremdsprache weiß man noch weniger, worum es geht! Umso wichtiger kann es also sein, Arbeitstechniken anzuwenden, die einige Probleme lösen helfen. Solche Techniken können sich auf folgende Gesichtspunke konzentrieren:
- wie man sich auf einen Text vorbereiten kann,
- wie man Überschriften und Schlagzeilen für das Textverständnis nutzen/auswerten kann,
- wie man einem Text durch schnelles Lesen wesentliche Informationen entnimmt,
- wie man schwierige Wörter erschließt,
- wie man einen Text gezielt nach Detailinformationen durchsucht,
- wie man wesentliche Punkte zusammenfasst und sich als Gedächtnisstütze Notizen macht.

Dieses Buch will Ihnen helfen, solche Arbeitstechniken zu entwickeln. Es ist für Selbstlerner konzipiert und nimmt Rücksicht auf die praktischen Belange und Bedürfnisse des zeitgeplagten Privatmenschen. Die Gestaltung und die Formulierungen sind deshalb bewusst knapp, aber dennoch präzise, ohne lange wissenschaftliche Erklärungen oder Exkurse, die unter anderen Umständen sicher ihren Platz im Lernprozess hätten.

Zugrunde gelegt werden folgende bewährte Lesestrategien, die sich in den Übungssequenzen des Buches wiederfinden und Ihnen helfen werden, aus jedem englischen Text das Optimale herauszuholen und dadurch nicht nur Ihre allgemeinen Englischkenntnisse zu verbessern, sondern auch Ihre Kommunikations- und Reaktionsfähigkeiten.

Erste Bewusstmachung
(Looking at headings or general context)

- Worum geht es im Text eigentlich?
- Was weiß ich darüber?

Schnelles Durchlesen (Skimming)

- sehr schnelles Durchlesen
- Gibt es jetzt schon Antworten auf meine Fragen?
- Welche weiteren Informationen habe ich gefunden?
- Welche sind die zentralen Punkte?
- Habe ich diese wirklich verstanden?

Genaueres Durchlesen (Scanning)

- nochmaliges Lesen
- die Bedeutung neuer oder unbekannter Wörter erraten
- Schlüsselbegriffe identifizieren
- die Bedeutung aus dem Kontext erschließen
- Welche Funktion hat das Wort/der Begriff im Satz?
- Wie ist das Wort/der Begriff gebildet?

- Passt die aktuelle Bedeutung des Wortes/ Begriffes in den Textzusammenhang?

Interpretation
(Reading between the lines)

- Hintergrund und Absicht des Textes/ der Textinformationen verstehen
- zwischen den Zeilen lesen
- Was wird zwar nicht gesagt, wird aber gemeint?
- aktive Umsetzung der rezeptiven Fertigkeit Lesen
- Notizen über die wichtigsten Fakten machen
- kurze schriftliche Zusammenfassung anfertigen
- Umsetzung der Lesekompetenz in schriftliche Form

Der Aufbau des Buches

Reading Business enthält 15 typische Lesetexte – Dokumente, die zum Arbeitsalltag gehören: Anzeigentext, Brief, Homepage einer Firma, Artikel aus Fachzeitschriften und Zeitungen, Aktennotiz, Vertrag, Finanzbericht, Sitzungsprotokoll... Anhand der dazu passenden Aufgaben und Übungen, die in fünf Abschnitte oder Sequenzen mit steigendem Schwierigkeitsgrad aufgeteilt und in der praktischen Umsetzung speziell für Selbstlerner konzipiert sind, lernen Sie diese Texte inhaltlich und sprachlich zu analysieren. Sie werden aber auch dazu ermuntert, sich nicht nur dem einfachen Lesen zu widmen, sondern auch zwischen den Zeilen zu lesen, den wahren Anlass für den jeweiligen Text herauszufinden und die Gedanken des Verfassers zu erforschen, damit Sie später vielleicht Ihre neu gewonnene Lesekompetenz umsetzen und einen ähnlichen Text selber schreiben können.

Die Übungssequenzen
Übungssequenz 1: *Before you read*

Diese Aufgabe dient einer ersten Bewusstmachung bzw. einer Reaktivierung Ihrer Vorkenntnisse. Zu jedem Thema wissen Sie bereits etwas, vermutlich sogar eine ganze Menge. In dieser Phase werden Sie aufgefordert, darüber nachzudenken, Ihre Gedanken auf das Thema zu fokussieren. Der folgende Text wird dadurch umso leichter für Sie verständlich, denn Sie werden nun schon wissen, worum es in diesem geht.

Übungssequenz 2: *Reading for Gist*

„Gist" heißt so etwas wie „grobes Verständnis". Sie werden in diesem Abschnitt also nach dem allgemeinen Inhalt des Textes gefragt, ohne dass Sie sich an Details erinnern müssen. Umso leichter werden die späteren Detailfragen dann sein, wenn Sie sich vergewissert haben, dass Sie den Textinhalt im Großen und Ganzen gedanklich erfasst haben.

Übungssequenz 3: *Reading for Language*

Hier geht es um die ersten Details. Wichtig ist natürlich, dass Sie zunächst den themenspezifischen Wortschatz und die relevanten Redewendungen verstehen bzw. lernen. Aber auch die korrekte Umsetzung von grammatischen Regeln wird Ihnen helfen, später mit komplexen Inhalten besser zurechtzukommen.

Übungssequenz 4:
Reading for Understanding

In diesem Abschnitt werden Sie gebeten, über den Textinhalt nachzudenken, aus dem Text heraus Fakten oder Aussagen miteinander zu vergleichen, eine eigene Interpretation zu versuchen, damit Sie sich schließlich nicht nur zum Inhalt, sondern auch zum Zusammenhang eine eigene Meinung bilden können.

Übungssequenz 5: *Over to you*

Zum krönenden Abschluss dürfen Sie nun kreativ sein und Ihre Lesekompetenz mit dem frisch gewonnenen Wissen in die Tat umsetzen. Die Art der Aufgabe ändert sich hierbei zwangsläufig, da es sich nun logischerweise um die aktive Umsetzung der rezeptiven Fertigkeit Lesen handelt. Sie werden eingeladen, zum Inhalt der Unit ein „Produkt" in schriftlicher Form zu erstellen. Die Übungsanweisung erfolgt nun zum größten Teil auf Englisch Eine eindeutige „Lösung" so wie bei den vorausgegangenen Übungen gibt es nicht. Hier ist Ihre persönliche Ansicht/Vorstellung gefragt. Und Sie dürfen sich auch hinterher selbst beurteilen.

Alle sonstigen Anweisungen werden auf Deutsch gegeben, damit Sie sich auf das Wesentliche konzentrieren können, nämlich die englischen Texte und die entsprechenden Aufgaben. Nach jedem Text folgt eine Auflistung der wichtigsten und schwierigsten Wörter in chronologischer Reihenfolge zusammen mit ihren deutschen Übersetzungen. Im alphabetisch geordneten englisch-deutschen Glossar am Ende des Buches können Sie die Ihnen unbekannten englischen Begriffe jederzeit schnell und leicht nachschlagen.

Ebenfalls im Anhang am Ende des Buches finden Sie einen Übungsschlüssel mit den Lösungen zu allen Aufgaben in den Übungssequenzen *Reading for Gist*, *Reading for Language* und *Reading for Understanding*. So können Sie Ihre Fortschritte selbst überprüfen.

Autoren und Verlag wünschen Ihnen viel Erfolg mit diesem Buch.
Remember: reading business is easy – when you know how.

Inhalt

Vorwort 3

Unit 1
Company Research 9

Unit 2
Recruitment 19

Unit 3
Meeting 29

Unit 4
Marketing 39

Unit 5
Contracts 49

Unit 6
Invoices 61

Unit 7
Company Finance 71

Unit 8
Stock Markets 81

Unit 9
Takeovers 91

Unit 10
Trade Fairs 99

Unit 11
International Business Relations 107

Unit 12
Multinationals 117

Unit 13
New Technologies 127

Unit 14
Environmental Issues 137

Unit 15
Taxation 147

Lösungen 159

Glossar 164

Im Buch verwendete Abkürzungen

abbrev.	abbreviation	Abkürzung
adj.	adjective	Adjektiv
adv.	adverb	Adverb
n.	noun	Substantiv, Hauptwort
p.p.	past participle	Partizip Perfekt
pr.p.	present participle	Partizip Präsens
prep.	preposition	Präposition
v.	verb	Verb, Zeitwort

Unit 1

Company Research

Ein weltbekannter Großkonzern hat eine neue Niederlassung in Ihrer Stadt. Sie haben viel über eine neue, anscheinend sehr erfolgreiche kleine Firma in Ihrer Nähe gehört. Sie haben auch in manchen Zeitungen und Zeitschriften etwas über verschiedene andere Firmen gelesen. Vielleicht suchen Sie einen neuen Job – und es wäre bestimmt nicht schlecht, wenn Sie ein paar Fakten in Erfahrung bringen könnten? Information ist alles. Hier sind zwei kurze Texte, die typisch sind für das, was man in Fachzeitschriften oder auf einer Website im Internet finden könnte.

Das folgende Übungsmaterial wird Ihnen helfen, die Texte zu verstehen, sowohl sprachlich als auch inhaltlich. Es wird Ihnen auch vielleicht helfen, zu erkennen, warum diese oder jene Ausdrucksweise verwendet wird, welche Absichten der Verfasser dabei hatte und schließlich, ob Sie das alles glauben können, was geschrieben wurde!

Aber bevor Sie die Texte lesen, machen Sie diese kurze Aufgabe „zum Aufwärmen"!

Before you read
Welche Vorstellung haben Sie von einer richtig „guten" Firma? Schreiben Sie fünf Punkte auf, die Sie für erforderlich halten, und ordnen Sie sie dann nach Wichtigkeit.

Jetzt lesen Sie die Texte.

Joystix Computers UK plc
Up-and-coming Whiz-Kids find the Recipe

Peter Jones

Founded in 1990 in Manchester, England as a subsidiary of the Joystix Computer Company of Los Angeles, Ca. by the now Managing Director John Grisedale, this small and energetic young firm has grown appreciably over the past decade and now has a total of 100 local employees.

Annual turnover was quoted at last week's AGM as having risen to £10 million sterling with a £2.2 million sterling pre-tax profit last year. Joystix seems to have made the big time - almost. What is their secret?

Employees like it at Joystix. Staff turnover has averaged out at four to five years. Ten employees have been with the firm since the start. 55% of staff are women. Internal candidates are given preference when new positions become available. Salaries are mid-range to good. Graduate trainees start at £12,000. £25,000 to £35,000 for managers with a company car as a typically British extra. Staff get 35 days annual holiday with a bonus of a four week sabbatical on full pay after six years. There is a generous company pension scheme, health insurance for everyone. and a profit-sharing scheme for managerial staff. Employees have their own personal computer and

printer for home use. No wonder that employees are happy here in Manchester. And there's more!

Joystix UK plc has modern air-conditioned offices in the centre of the city with its own underground carpark. It also has a subsidised canteen with a more than adequate choice of daily menues. Train and bus stations are no more than five minutes' walk away.

American-style high-pressure management is complemented by American-style informality: all staff use first names and use the same canteen. There is no dress code.

All the employees we talked to were unanimous: Joystix is a good firm to work for.

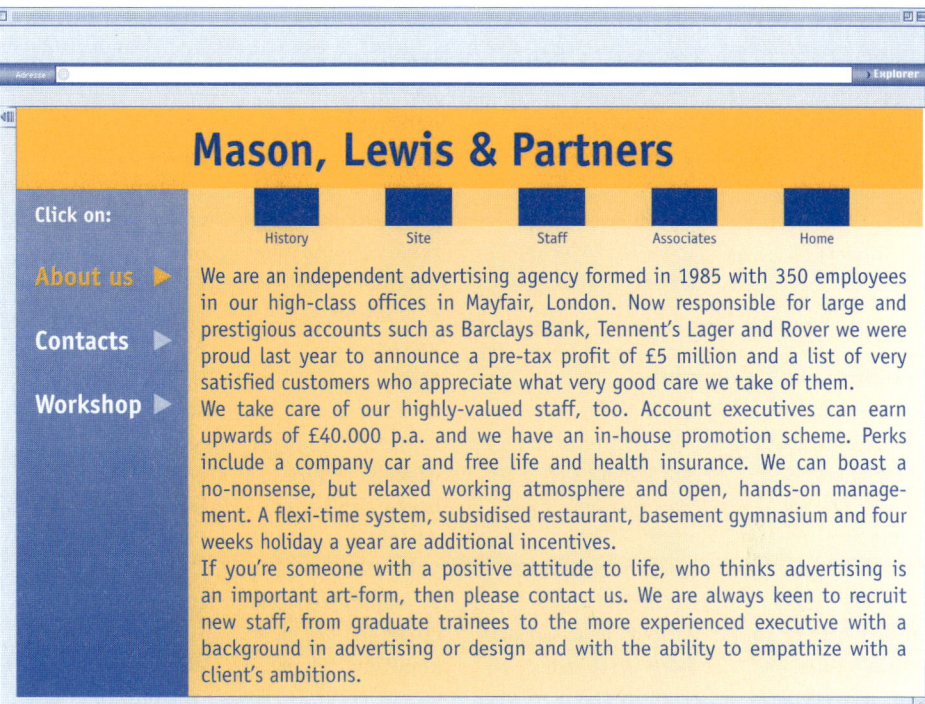

Vocabulary

Joystix

up-and-coming *(adj.)*	aufstrebend	to make the big time *(infml.)*	groß einsteigen
whiz-kid *(n.)*	Senkrechtstarter		
recipe *(n.)*	Rezept	to average *(v.)*	im Durchschnitt sein
to found *(v.)*	gründen	graduate trainee *(n.)*	Auszubildende(r) mit Hochschulabschluss
subsidiary *(adj.)*	Tochter-		
Managing Director *(n.)*	Generaldirektor, Firmenchef	company car *(n.)*	Firmenwagen
		annual *(adj.)*	jährlich
appreciably *(adv.)*	beträchtlich	sabbatical *(n.)*	Sonderurlaub, Beurlaubung
decade *(n.)*	Jahrzehnt		
employee *(n.)*	Angestellte(r)	generous *(adj.)*	großzügig
turnover *(n.)*	Umsatz	pension scheme *(n.)*	Pensionskasse
AGM *(abbrev.)* (Annual General Meeting)	Jahresversammlung	health insurance *(n.)*	Krankenversicherung
		profit sharing *(n.)*	Gewinnbeteiligung
		no wonder	kein Wunder
sterling *(n.)*	brit. Währung	air-conditioned *(adj.)*	mit Klimaanlage
pre-tax profit *(n.)*	Gewinn vor Steuer	underground carpark *(n.)*	Tiefgarage

1

subsidised *(adj.)*	subventioniert	p.a. (per annum) *(adv.)*	jährlich
adequate *(adj.)*	adäquat	in-house *(adj.)*	hausintern
daily menue *(n.)*	Tages(speise)karte	promotion *(n.)*	Beförderung
high-pressure *(adj.)*	Hochleistungs-, anspruchsvoll	perks *(n.)*	Vergünstigungen
		to boast *(v.)*	vorzeigen
to complement *(v.)*	ergänzen	no-nonsense *(adj.)*	sachlich
dress code *(n.)*	Kleidungsordnung	hands-on *(adj.)*	in direktem Kontakt
unanimous *(adj.)*	einer Meinung; sich einig	flexi-time *(n.)*	Gleitzeit
		basement *(n.)*	Untergeschoss, Keller
		gymnasium *(n.)*	Sport-, Fitnessraum
		incentive *(n.)*	Anreiz

Mason, Lewis & Partners

independent *(adj.)*	unabhängig	attitude *(n.)*	Haltung; Einstellung
advertising agency *(n.)*	Werbeagentur	art-form *(n.)*	Kunstform
prestigious *(n.)*	mit hohem Prestigewert	to recruit *(v.)*	rekrutieren
		experienced *(adj.)*	erfahren
proud *(adj.)*	stolz	background *(n.)*	Hintergrund
to announce *(v.)*	bekannt geben	design *(n.)*	Design; Kunstgewerbe
to appreciate *(v.)*	schätzen	ability *(n.)*	Fähigkeit
to take care of sb. *(v.)*	sich um jmd. kümmern	to empathize *(v.)*	sich einfühlen
highly valued *(adj.)*	hoch geschätzt	client *(n.)*	Klient
account executive *(n.)*	Projektleiter	ambition *(n.)*	Ambition, Ehrgeiz

Reading for Gist

1. True or false?
Sind die folgenden Sätze richtig oder falsch?

	True	False
Example: John Grisedale is the Managing Director of Joystix.	✓	☐
1. Joystix is a computer company in Manchester, England.	☐	☐
2. Joystix has become smaller over the last ten years.	☐	☐
3. The advertising agency is based in New York.	☐	☐
4. Both firms made a profit last year.	☐	☐
5. More than half the staff at Joystix are women.	☐	☐
6. Mason, Lewis & Partners deal with large advertising accounts.	☐	☐
7. Employees hate working at Joystix.	☐	☐
8. Both firms offer a number of incentives to employees.	☐	☐
9. The advertising agency made a bigger profit than the computer firm.	☐	☐
10. Mason, Lewis & Partners are always looking for new well-qualified staff.	☐	☐

2. Match them up
Welche Satzteile passen zusammen?

Example: 2 e
We take care of our highly valued staff.

1. This energetic young firm
2. We take care of our
3. We can boast a no-nonsense, but
4. There is a generous company pension scheme and
5. If you're someone with a positive attitude to life,
6. Staff turnover has averaged out
7. No wonder that employees
8. Ten employees have been
9. We are an independent
10. All staff use

a. relaxed working atmosphere.
b. a profit-sharing scheme for managerial staff.
c. has grown appreciably over the past decade.
d. then please contact us.
e. highly-valued staff.
f. are happy here in Manchester.
g. the same canteen.
h. advertising agency formed in 1985.
i. at four to five years.
j. with the firm since the start.

Reading for Language

1. True or false ?
Sind diese Aussagen richtig oder falsch?

Example:	True	False
A *daily menu* is what you eat every day.	✓	
1. A *Managing Director* is the boss.		
2. A *decade* is a period of twenty years.		
3. *Annual turnover* is the amount of money made in one year.		
4. A *graduate trainee* is someone with a university degree.		
5. A *sabbatical* can only take place on a Sunday.		
6. *Sterling* is the name of the currency used in Britain.		

7. To *empathize* means to feel sorry for someone. ☐ ☐
8. *Unanimous* means that everyone is agreed. ☐ ☐
9. *Perk* is another word for incentive. ☐ ☐
10. To have a *dress code* means that you cannot always wear what you like. ☐ ☐

2. Fill in the gaps
Ergänzen Sie bitte folgende Sätze mit dem jeweils richtigen Wort.

| appreciate | company | employees | in-house | founded |
| recruit | advertising | dress code | subsidised | annual |

Example:
A .... car is considered a perk.   A <u>company</u> car is considered a perk.

1. Joystix was .... in Manchester in 1990.
2. Joystix now has 100 local .... in Manchester.
3. As an .... agency Mason, Lewis & Partners help their clients to sell their products.
4. Both firms have a............................ canteen.
5. Employees in both firms are provided with a .... car.
6. The customers at Mason, Lewis & Partners .... the service provided.
7. At Joystix employees can wear what they like, there is no ....
8. At last week's Joystix AGM the .... turnover was quoted at £10 million.
9. Mason, Lewis & Partners have an .... promotion scheme.
10. We are always keen to .... new staff.

3. Form sentences
Vervollständigen Sie bitte diese Sätze mit dem Passiv und der richtigen Zeitform.

Example:

At Joystix profits (to share) .... by managerial staff.
At Joystix profits <u>are shared</u> by managerial staff.

1. Joystix (to found) .... in 1990.
2. Turnover (to quote) .... last week at £10 million.

3. Company cars (to give) .... usually to managers.
4. High-pressure management (to complement) .... by informality every day.
5. Next week in the canteen first names (to use) .... by all staff.
6. 350 people (to employ) .... in the Mayfair offices at the moment.
7. Customers at Mason, Lewis & Partners (to satisfy) .... for a very long time now.
8. Upwards of £40,000 (to be able/to earn) .... by account executives each year.
9. The restaurant (to subsidise) .... for the past ten years.
10. Advertising today (to think of) .... as an art-form by Mason, Lewis & Partners.

4. Language alternatives
Wählen Sie die richtige Bedeutung für folgende Redewendungen.

Example:
Does subsidised canteen mean that the meals are **a.** cheaper or **b.** more expensive?   **a**

1. Does up-and-coming mean **a.** successful or **b.** expensive?
2. Is pre-tax profit **a.** the money a firm pays to the government or **b.** the money it earns before tax is deducted?
3. Does more than adequate mean **a.** very good or **b.** very bad?
4. Does unanimous mean **a.** no-one agrees or **b.** everyone has the same opinion?
5. Does highly-valued staff mean **a.** that employees are very well paid or **b.** that their employer thinks a lot of them?
6. Does in-house promotion mean **a.** that employees have the chance to get a better job within the firm or **b.** that employees have to do their own advertising?
7. Does no-nonsense but relaxed mean **a.** very formal and strict or **b.** pleasant and professional?
8. Does a flexi-time system **a.** allow employees to start and finish work at different times or **b.** require them to start work punctually?
9. Does hands-on management mean **a.** that employees hardly ever see the boss or **b.** that senior managers consult their colleagues regularly?
10. Does we are always keen to recruit new staff mean **a.** that no new employees will be taken on or **b.** that there is general interest in employing good people?

Reading for Understanding

1. Essential facts

Lesen Sie beide Texte noch einmal und listen Sie alle Merkmale auf, die die beiden Firmen anzubieten haben. Ordnen Sie diese Punkte unter den folgenden getrennten Überschriften. Vergleichen Sie die beiden Listen und notieren Sie die Unterschiede.

	Joystix	Mason, Lewis & Partners
Location		
Age		
Size		
Turnover		
Salaries		
Holidays		
Perks		
....		
....		

Jetzt beantworten Sie bitte folgende Fragen:

	Joystix	M, L & Partners
1. Which firm is based in London?	☐	☐
2. Which of the two firms is the older?	☐	☐
3. Which firm pays the higher salaries?	☐	☐
4. Which of the two firms has the greater number of employees?	☐	☐
5. Which firm made the higher profit?	☐	☐
6. Which firm has the longer holidays?	☐	☐
7. Which firm has American-style management?	☐	☐
8. Which firm has variable working hours?	☐	☐
9. Which text was written by a newspaper reporter?	☐	☐
10. Which firm doesn't mention its turnover?	☐	☐
11. Which firm does John Grisedale manage?	☐	☐
12. Which firm practises an in-house promotion scheme?	☐	☐
13. Which firm has a fitness centre?	☐	☐
14. Which firm designs and produces computer software?	☐	☐
15. Which firm doesn't mention a pension scheme?	☐	☐

2. Understanding the text

Versuchen Sie folgende Fragen zu beantworten.

Example:
Is Joystix
a. an independent   or   **b.** a subsidiary company? | *b* |

1. What is the main reason for Joystix's success?
   a. staff motivation   **b.** good food   **c.** help from America
2. How many female employees work at Joystix?
   a. 150   **b.** 10   **c.** 55   **d.** 90
3. Which firm makes the most money per person employed?
   a. Joystix   **b.** M, L & P
4. Which features are not offered or mentioned by Joystix?
   a. company car   **b.** health insurance
   c. canteen   **d.** flexi-time
5. Which features are not offered or mentioned by Mason, Lewis & Partners?
   a. in-house promotion scheme   **b.** home computer
   c. car park   **d.** gymnasium

3. What do you think?

Versuchen Sie beide Texte als Ganzes zu betrachten. Dann beantworten Sie folgende Fragen.

Example:
Which expression best describes the style of the Joystix text?
   a. up-beat positive journalism   **b.** factual sober report | *a* |

1. Which expression describes best the style of the Mason, Lewis & Partners text?
   a. modest understatement   **b.** persuasive rhetoric
2. Which text do you think is the more objective?
   a. Joystix   or   **b.** M, L & P
3. How do you recognise this?
   a. from the use of the first person   **b.** from the listing of facts
4. Why was the text about the advertising agency written and put on a website?
   a. to impress old clients   **b.** to attract new staff
5. Is the writer of the newspaper text impressed?
   a. Yes   **b.** No
6. Which of the two texts is more believable?
   a. Joystix   or   **b.** M,L & Partners
7. Do you believe everything in both texts?
   a. Yes   **b.** No

8. Which statement would you question as being very subjective?
   a. "our highly-valued staff"   **b.** "hands-on management"
9. Why do you think travel to work and accessibility are not mentioned in the M,L & P text?
   a. because it is irrelevant
   b. because travel in London is difficult and would have a negative effect
10. Why do you think M, L & P emphasize that they are looking for new staff with a positive attitude to life?
   a. because they don't want people who think negatively
   b. because they know that this flatters most people's self-image

Over to you

1. A short report
Schreiben Sie einen kurzen Bericht, um Ihre Lesekompetenz zu bestätigen.
Write a short report on your research into the two firms mentioned in the texts for your boss (who hasn't read either of them) stating the most important features. Say whether you think these features are good or whether you think they should be improved. Say what type of text you got the information from, whether you think the information is credible at first hand and if not, why not.

Start like this:

> *Report*
> *For the attention of. ....*
> *Researched into two firms: Joystix, Manchester and Mason, Lewis & Partners, London. My findings were as follows:*
> *Joystix: small firm producing computer software, 164 employees, very successful, excellent staff conditions in my view, seen favourably by the press in objective survey*
>
> *...*

2. Your own firm
Beschreiben Sie Ihre eigene Firma.

Write a short report about your own firm.

Unit 2

Recruitment

"Young, dynamic with x years experience in the field, willing to work hard in a mixed team, on negotiable salary? Join US, we are the firm you´re looking for ..."

Suchen Sie einen neuen interessanten und motivierenden Traumjob mit tollem Gehalt und Super-Aussichten? Sie kennen sich noch nicht so richtig aus mit dem Jargon der Stellenanzeigen und können noch nicht zwischen den Zeilen lesen bzw. wissen noch nicht, wie man auf Englisch einen Lebenslauf schreibt oder ein Bewerbungsschreiben verfasst?

In diesem Text lernen Sie, einen Anzeigentext zu analysieren und die Wortwahl und Ausdrucksweise für eine erfolgreiche Bewerbung.

"Ich bin der/die ideale Mitarbeiter/Mitarbeiterin für Sie! Auf mich haben Sie ja die ganzen Jahre gewartet ..."

Erhalten Sie als Personalchef oft solche Blindbewerbungen? Oder suchen Sie in der Tat immer wieder neue Leute für spezifische Aufgaben in Ihrer Firma? Dann müssen Sie auch wissen, was in einen Anzeigentext hineingehört und wie man in der darauf folgenden Flut von Bewerbungsschreiben die vielversprechendsten Kandidaten heraussucht. Diese Unit wird Ihnen helfen, zwischen den Zeilen zu lesen.

Before you read
Wenn Sie glauben, Ihre Traumfirma gefunden zu haben, welche fünf Fähigkeiten oder Eigenschaften bieten Sie mit Ihrer Person? Warum sollte die Firma Sie einstellen? Wenn Sie als Personalchef eine Wahl unter mehreren Kandidaten zu treffen haben, auf welche Eigenschaften legen Sie Wert?

Machen Sie eine kurze Liste.

Jetzt lesen Sie folgende Texte.

2

The Advertisement

Account executive

We are a large independent advertising agency based in central London with prestigious high-grade customers at home and abroad. We are looking for an **account executive / project manager** to help expand business in Europe. The successful applicant should be a university graduate preferably with some experience in advertising or journalism and be fluent in at least one other European language apart from English, preferably German or French. He or she should have excellent communication skills and be computer literate.

Applications should be sent in writing to:
Personnel Manager, **Thompson & Thompson**, PO Box 1349, London WC3 6XZ, England

The Letter of Application and CV

27b Lavender Avenue
Guildford GU9 5PF
Tel. 01545 3311

25th March 2003

To
Thompson & Thompson
Att. The Personnel Manager
P.O. Box 1349
London WC3 6XZ

Ref. Your advertisement in The Times 25.3.03

Dear Sir or Madam,
I am writing in response to your advertisement in today's edition of the The Times newspaper and would like to apply for a post as an account executive in your agency.

At present I am employed by Southern Newspapers as a freelance journalist but would very much like to move into advertising and a job with more responsibility and which could provide a greater challenge. I feel that Thompson & Thompson could give me exactly that opportunity.

I have no doubt that my experience in journalism together with my other skills are suited to the post you offer. I speak fluent German and some French, enjoy meeting people and have excellent computer skills. I enclose my CV.

I look forward to hearing from you and could come for an interview at any time.

Yours sincerely,

George Watts
George Watts

Curriculum Vitae

Name: George William Watts

Born: 12 March 1970 in Croydon

Parents: Henry and Susan Watts (née Gibson)

Education:
1981–1986 Croydon Comprehensive School
1987–1988 Croydon Sixth Form College
1989–1992 University of Southampton
1993–94 Guildford College of Journalism

Qualifications:
GCSE in 9 subjects
3 A-Levels in English and German (both Grade B) and Art (Grade C)
Diploma in Design Technology, University of Southampton
City & Guilds Certificate, Guildford College of Journalism

Employment:
1995–1997 copy editor for the Southampton Echo
1997–2000 junior reporter for the Southampton Echo
2000–2003 freelance journalist for Southern Newspapers

Special skills:
Fluent in German
Reasonable competence in French
PC-literate (Microsoft Word, Excel, Access)

Hobbies:
Photography
Sailing

2

The Invitation for an Interview

Thompson & Thompson
Barclay Place
London WC3 6XZ
United Kingdom

Make your business our business

Personnel Department
Geoffrey Squires

4th April 2003

Dear Mr Watts,

Thank you for your letter of 25th March in response to our advertisement in the Times newspaper. We would be pleased to invite you to come for an interview to our London office on Tuesday 10th April at 3p.m. Please let my PA Rebecca Pearson know by telephone if this is convenient. (Tel. 0208 7355 671). Please bring samples of your journalistic work with you. The interview will last about two hours.
We look forward to meeting you.
Yours sincerely,

G. Squires

Geoffrey Squires

Vocabulary

application *(n.)*	Bewerbung	**high-grade** *(adj.)*	hochwertig
recruitment *(n.)*	Einstellung, Rekrutierung	**to expand** *(v.)*	expandieren
		applicant *(n.)*	Bewerber(in)
advertisement *(n.)*	Anzeige	**university**	Hochschul-
account *(n.)*	Konto; hier: Auftrag	**graduate** *(n.)*	absolvent(in)
executive *(n.)*	Manager	**preferably** *(adv.)*	bevorzugt
independent *(adj.)*	unabhängig	**experience** *(n.)*	Erfahrung
advertising agency *(n.)*	Werbeagentur	**fluent** *(adj.)*	fließend
prestigious *(adj.)*	mit hohem Prestigewert	**at least** *(adv.)*	wenigstens
		apart from *(adv.)*	abgesehen von

communication skills *(n.)*	Kommunikationsfähigkeiten	comprehensive school *(n.)*	Gesamtschule
computer literate *(adj.)*	PC-erfahren	sixth form college *(n.)*	Oberstufe/Kollegstufe
		subject *(n.)*	hier: Schulfach
personnel manager *(n.)*	Personalchef	employment *(n.)*	bisherige Anstellungen
response *(n.)*	Antwort		
edition *(n.)*	Ausgabe	copy editor *(n.)*	Redakteur
to apply *(v.)*	sich bewerben	skill *(n.)*	Fähigkeit, Fertigkeit
post *(n.)*	Posten, Position	reasonable *(adj..)*	hier: einigermaßen
freelance *(adj.)*	freiberuflich	competence *(n.)*	Kompetenz
responsibility *(n.)*	Verantwortung	hobbies *(n.)*	Freizeitinteressen, Hobbys
challenge *(n.)*	Herausforderung		
opportunity *(n.)*	Gelegenheit	photography *(n.)*	Fotografieren
to suit *(v.)*	passen	sailing *(n.)*	Segeln
CV (curriculum vitae)	Lebenslauf	PA *(abbrev.)* **(Personal Assistant)** *(n.)*	Assistent(in), Sekretär(in)
née *(adj.)*	geborene		
education *(n.)*	Schulbildung	convenient *(adj.)*	passend, akzeptabel

Reading for Gist

1. True or false?
Sind die folgenden Aussagen richtig oder falsch?

Example:	True	False
Thompson & Thompson is an advertising agency.	✓	☐

	True	False
1. Thompson & Thompson are looking for a university graduate.	☐	☐
2. George Watts is a freelance journalist.	☐	☐
3. George Watts applies for the job without sending in a CV.	☐	☐
4. He is not prepared to go to London for an interview.	☐	☐
5. He has no academic qualifications.	☐	☐
6. George is accepted for an interview in London.	☐	☐
7. The advertising agency is based in Manchester.	☐	☐
8. They would prefer applicants without a university degree.	☐	☐
9. George is computer literate.	☐	☐
10. Rebecca Pearson is a PA in the Personnel Department.	☐	☐

2. Match them up

Setzen Sie bitte die richtigen Satzteile zusammen.

Example: 1 c
Thompson & Thompson are based in London.

1. Thompson & Thompson are
2. The successful applicant should be
3. Applications should be sent
4. At present George is employed
5. George would like to apply for a post

a. computer literate.
b. as an account executive.
c. based in London.
d. sent in writing.
e. as a freelance journalist.

Reading for Language

1. Fill in the gaps

Ergänzen Sie bitte folgende Sätze mit dem jeweils richtigen Wort.

| freelance | suited | fluent | competence | hobbies |
| prestigious | interview | personnel | graduate | challenge |

Example:
Thompson & Thompson is a large .... advertising agency.
Thompson & Thompson is a large *independent* advertising agency.

1. Their customers are high-grade and ....

2. The successful applicant should be .... in several languages.

3. George Watts sends his reply to the .... manager.

4. George Watts works as a .... journalist.

5. He speaks German and has reasonable .... in French.

6. He is looking for a new job which could provide a greater ....

7. Sailing is one of George´s ....

8. George is a .... of Southampton University.

9. He is prepared to go to London for an .... at any time.

10. He thinks his qualifications are .... to the post of account executive.

2. What does it mean?
Wählen Sie die richtige Bedeutung für folgende Redewendungen

Example:
Does the job of *account executive* mean that staff
a. manage customers and projects?   or   **b.** deal with bank accounts?   *a*

1. Does working freelance mean
   a. you are independent without a monthly salary?
   b. you are in permanent employment?

2. Does I enclose my CV mean
   a. I am sending a list of my qualifications and work experience?
   b. I will send proof of my identity later?

3. Does reasonable competence in French mean
   a. he can speak French very well?
   b. he can speak French quite well?

4. Does computer literate mean
   a. that you can write poetry on your computer?
   b. that you know how to work with a computer and use computer programs?

5. Is a Personal Assistant
   a. a secretary?   **b.** a machine?

3. Odd one out
Welches Wort passt nicht in die jeweilige Gruppe? Unterstreichen Sie es.

1. agency – executive – manager – business – sailing
2. to respond – to photograph – to apply – to suit – to expand
3. GCSE – challenge – A-Levels – Diploma – Certificate
4. fluent – competent – literate – employed – skilled
5. CV – reasonably – at least – apart from – preferably

4. Translate these words into German

1. advertising agency   ....
2. CV   ....
3. job application   ....

4. freelance ....
5. challenge ....
6. responsibility ....
7. copy editor ....
8. education ....
9. university graduate ....
10. opportunity ....

5. Crossword

Across
5 The ability to do something. (10)
6 Someone with a university degree. (8)

Down
1 Someone who works for themselves. (9)
2 What you get at school. (9)
3 What the agency calls a regular customer. (7)
4 Another word for manager. (9)

Reading for Understanding

1. Writing a letter of application
Welche der folgenden Bestandteile sollten in dem Brief **nicht** enthalten sein. Mark your answer with a cross in the appropriate box.

1. Your own address and telephone number
2. The date
3. Reference data
4. Salutation "Dear Sir or Madam"
5. Your reason for writing
6. A list of people you know
7. Complimentary close "Yours sincerely"
8. Salutation "Dear Friends"

2. Essential facts: which is correct?
Welche der folgenden Sätze sind richtig? Antworten Sie mit „Yes" oder „No".

	Yes	No
Example: George Watts wants a new story for his newspaper.	☐	☑
1. Thompson & Thompson are keen to expand their business in Europe.	☐	☐
2. George Watts has experience in the television industry.	☐	☐
3. Thompson & Thompson have famous and important customers.	☐	☐
4. It is advisable for applicants for the job to speak two languages.	☐	☐
5. George has worked for over ten years as a journalist.	☐	☐
5. George Watts is looking for an easier job.	☐	☐
7. George Watts has the basic qualifications.	☐	☐
8. Geoffrey Squires thinks that George may be suitable for the job.	☐	☐

3. What do you think?
Lesen Sie alle vier Textbestandteile als Einheit nochmals durch. Was meinen Sie jetzt dazu?

Example:
How many years experience has George Watts had in journalism?
a. ten　　　or　　　**b.** nearly eight　　　`b`

1. What qualifications give George the best chance of getting the job?
    a. languages and computer skills
    b. photography as a hobby

2. Why do Thompson & Thompson need well qualified staff?
    a. because of their important international clients
    b. because computers are important for business

3. Will George´s wish for more responsibility be seen
    a. positively?
    b. negatively?

4. George has worked in journalism and likes meeting people. Does this suggest he has
    a. no real ability to deal with people?
    b. relatively good communication skills?

5. George's curriculum vitae seems to be complete from school right up to the present day. Is this likely to be
   a. in his favour?
   b. seen as a disadvantage?

6. George´s application sounds
   a. very positive and confident?
   b. reserved and uncertain?

7. The reply from Thompson & Thompson sounds
   a. polite but negative?
   b. open and encouraging?

8. Why do you think Thompson & Thompson are asking for fluency in a foreign language?
   a. because they want their new executive to deal with European customers
   b. because everyone in the firm needs to speak German

9. Why do you think experience in journalism will help in the new job?
   a. Because the agency only wants to advertise in newspapers.
   b. Because in advertising writing good texts is important.

10. Why do you think Geoffrey Squires asks George to contact his PA?
    a. Because he doesn't want to speak to him personally.
    b. Because his PA probably has to coordinate his appointments.

Over to you

1. Writing a letter of application

Setzen Sie nun Ihre Lesekompetenz in die Tat um und schreiben Sie Ihren eigenen Bewerbungsbrief.
Imagine that you would like to apply for the same position as George Watts as advertised in the Times newspaper. Based on what you have learned in this unit, write your own letter accompanied by your own CV (Lebenslauf).

2. Writing an advertisement

Sie möchten eine Stelle in Ihrer Firma neu besetzen. Schreiben Sie einen Anzeigentext für eine Zeitung.

You are looking for a new employee. Carefully consider what sort of person you need and then write an advertisement for this job.

Unit 3

Meetings

Der ganz normale Business-Alltag: Meetings, Meetings, Meetings – Sitzungen, Besprechungen, Tagungen, Treffen – auch unter anderen Namen gehören sie zum täglichen Geschehen in kürzerer oder längerer Form.

Jede Besprechung sollte, um effektiv ablaufen und messbare Ergebnisse liefern zu können, möglichst gut vor- und nachbereitet werden. Hierfür gibt es zwei wichtige Werkzeuge: die Tagesordnung und das Protokoll.

In dieser Unit nehmen wir an einer Vorstandssitzung in einer amerikanischen Firma teil. Wir erfahren, welche Besprechungspunkte typischerweise auf einer Tagesordnung stehen und was danach im Protokoll besprochen und beschlossen wurde. Dabei ist die Art der Firma bzw. die Produktlinie dieser Firma relativ unwichtig. Es geht um Form und Ausdrucksweise solcher Dokumente. Aus beiden werden Informationen gewonnen, die im Business-Alltag für eine effektive Kommunikation zwischen Abteilungen und unter Kollegen und Kolleginnen und für einen zügigen Fortlauf von Entwicklungsarbeiten jeglicher Art unabdingbar sind.

Before you read
Ordnen Sie zunächst Ihre eigenen Gedanken zu diesem Thema. Sie haben sicherlich selbst schon an Dutzenden von Besprechungen teilgenommen. Waren sie effektiv? Was lief dabei nicht so gut? Wie hätte man den Ablauf vororganisieren sollen, um unnötige Reibungsverluste zu vermeiden? Denken Sie auch an die Art der Besprechung und die Art des Protokolls, das hinterher dazu passen würde. Sollte es ein ausführliches, detailliertes Protokoll sein oder eher nur eine knapp formulierte Liste von Stichpunkten für zeitgeplagte Manager? Welche Form passt zu welcher Art Meeting?

Board Meeting

December 9, 2003 in New York

Agenda

9 a.m. Boardroom

1. **Minutes and Action Points from Previous Meeting**
   November 17, 2003

2. **Business Review:**
   → Sales figures
   → New products 2003
   → Update on project approvals for 2004
   → Marketing strategy: effectiveness
   → Prognosis

3. **Project proposals**
4. **Licensing**
5. **Staff situation**
6. **A.O.B.**
   incl. date of next meeting
7. **Action Points**

Board Meeting
December 9, 2003, New York

Minutes

Participants: Chair: Roberta Freeman (RF), **Program Planning:** Peter Mason (PLM), **Finance:** David Schwartz (DS), **Marketing:** Gary Wilson (GSW) **Personnel:** Helen Johnson (HJ)

Members are referred to the Agenda and discussion papers prepared by Board members.

1. **Action Points from last meeting (Nov.17, 2003)**
   → Royalty agreement for use of CALL programmes approved. Details provided by GSW. License Dept. has provided contracts. Duly signed by RF and copies returned.
   → Further research into California communication breakdown revealed server error in LA office. Remedied but decision needed on future backup strategy.
   → PLM has provided new revised figures for Pluto project.(see below)
   Sample materials sent to Dwight Lansing in Atlanta for inspection. As yet no result. Terry Pitomski person to contact. PLM to invite to NY for discussions early February.

2. Business Review
→ Sales figures
To date annual improvement trend continues. Dec. turnover overall 3% above previous year. Positive result tempered by fluctuation in export figures. South America down appreciably. Offset by special deal with Shanghai.
Detailed figures provided by GSW per segment.

→ New products 2003
PLM reviews production status on new Trymore line. Behind schedule on template development. Production forewarned. Fallback policy switch 50% production to Atlanta. Decision dependent on status end of January.

→ Update on project approvals for 2004
PLM refers to new figures for Pluto project. DS finds unacceptable and recommends total revision of basic concept. GSW agrees.

→ Marketing strategy: effectiveness
GSW reports on advertising, mailing, demonstrations, TV coverage and sales reps' feedback. Recommends increase in expenditure for website presence. Overall less concrete feedback from direct mailing than previous year's campaigns. Analysis of address systems ongoing.

→ Prognosis
In general considered favorable. Nevertheless, staff should be warned against complacency. Review of Pluto project a.s.a.p. essential.

3. Project Proposals
PLM outlines ideas for new down-market range for Brazil and Argentina. Board approves in general and refers to marketing for further analysis.

4. Licensing
GSW reports on research into possible license agreements with Itech S.A. and Mazko Enterprises in Japan. Awaiting finance proposals from both corporations.

5. Staff Situation
Cf. Organigram: Reorganisation plans for department structure complete. Promotion of Kylie Moston and David Lewinski to Project Manager status approved with increase in responsibility for project guidance and quality control

6. A.O.B.
1. Competition: Increase in advertising activity from competitor group Intex observed in last quarter. Marketing to analyse for next meeting.

2. Complaints from various members of staff that regulation of flexi-time is taking too long thus making vacation plans difficult. HJ reports on malfunction of database and introduction of new more efficient system.
New backup strategy in case of server failure required.

3. Next meeting: January 15, 2004

7. Action Points
- DS and HJ to research and recommend computer backup.
- PLM to invite Terry Pitomski from Atlanta branch for discussions early Feb.2004
- PLM to prepare further revision of figures for Pluto project
- GSW to analyse customer address systems
- PLM to liaise with GSW on analysis of South American markets.
- GSW to analyse Intex activities.
- HJ to ensure introduction of database facility to monitor flexi-time.
- HJ to implement staff promotions.

12.10.03
GSW/pl

Vocabulary

board *(n.)*	Vorstand	**fluctuation** *(n.)*	Fluktuation, Varianz
agenda *(n:)*	Tagesordnung	**offset** *(p.p.)*	ausgeglichen, entgegengewirkt
boardroom *(n.)*	Konferenzraum		
minutes *(n.)*	Protokoll	**segment** *(n.)*	Segment, Bereich
action points *(n.)*	zu erledigende Punkte	**template** *(n.)*	Schablone, Muster
licensing *(n.)*	Lizenzgeschäfte	**to forewarn** *(v.)*	vorwarnen
staff situation *(n.)*	Personalstand	**fallback** *(n.)*	Notplan, Reserve
A.O.B. *(abbrev.)*		**policy** *(n.)*	Plan, Strategie
(Any Other Business)	sonstige Punkte	**to switch** *(v.)*	umstellen
participants *(n.)*	Teilnehmer	**update** *(n.)*	Aktualisierung
chair *(n.)*	Vorsitz	**effectiveness** *(n.)*	Effektivität
RF, PLM etc.	Initialien als Namenskürzel	**mailing** *(n.)*	Werbeaktion per Post, Mailing
royalty *(n.)*	Honorar	**coverage** *(n.)*	Abdeckung
agreement *(n.)*	Vertrag	**sales reps** *(n.)*	
license *(n.)* AE (BE licence)	Lizenz	**(representatives)** **feedback** *(n.)*	Außendienstmitarbeiter Rückmeldungen
duly *(adv.)*	entsprechend	**expenditure** *(n.)*	Ausgaben, Auslagen
breakdown *(n.)*	Panne, Fehler, Versagen	**ongoing** *(adj.)*	aktuell
error *(n.)*	Fehler	**prognosis** *(n.)*	Prognose, Vorhersage
backup strategy *(n.)*	Plan für den Notfall	**favorable** *(adj.)*	günstig
as yet *(adv.)*	bisher	**complacency** *(n.)*	Bequemlichkeit
to date *(adv.)*	bisher	**a.s.a.p.** *(abbrev.)* as soon as possible *(adv.)*	möglichst bald
turnover *(n.)*	Umsatz		
overall *(adj.)*	gesamt	**to outline** *(v.)*	umreißen
tempered *(p.p.)*	abgemildert	**proposal** *(n.)*	Vorhaben, Vorschlag

range (n.)	Reihe	regulation (n.)	Kontrolle
enterprises (n.)	Unternehmen (hier als Firmennamen)	flexitime (n.)	Gleitzeit
		malfunction (n.)	Fehlfunktion
organigram (n.)	Organigramm (Organisationsdiagramm)	failure (n.)	Versagen
		to liaise (v.)	kommunizieren, kooperieren
promotion (n.)	Beförderung		
guidance (n.)	Leitung, Beratung	to ensure (v.)	sicherstellen
increase (n.)	Zuwachs	database (n.)	Datenbank
advertising (n.)	Werbung	facility (n.)	Enrichtung
to observe (v.)	beobachten	to monitor (v.)	beobachten, registrieren
quarter (n.)	Quartal		
complaint (n.)	Beschwerde	to implement (v.)	bewerkstelligen

Reading for Gist

1. What's it all about?
Beantworten Sie folgende Fragen:

Example:
Where is the meeting?
a. in a New York boardroom   **b.** in a London conference room   `a`

1. Who takes the chair?
   a. Gary Wilson   **b.** Roberta Freeman
2. What's the first point on the agenda?
   a. staff situation   **b.** action points from last meeting
3. How many people were present?
   a. four   **b.** five
4. What was the main discussion point?
   a. annual business results   **b.** future investment
5. Was business during the year
   a. only at home?   **b.** international?
6. Were the results
   a. satisfactory in general?   **b.** disappointing?
7. Are these minutes
   a. a short summary?   **b.** a very detailed report?
8. What are action points?
   a. points talked about in the meeting   **b.** things still to be done
9. Will some members of staff be
   a. promoted?   **b.** given notice?
10. Staff had been complaining about
    a. computer sales?   **b.** flexi-time?

2. Match them up
Welche Sätze passen zu welcher Überschrift?

Example: 1 c
To date annual improvement trend continues = Sales figures

1. To date annual improvement trend continues.	☐	a. New products
2. Promotion to Project Manager status approved.	☐	b. Marketing
3. Analysis of address systems ongoing.	☐	c. Sales figures
4. Board approves in general.	☐	d. Staff
5. Behind schedule on development.	☐	e. Proposals

3. Odd one out
Welcher Punkt passt nicht zu der Überschrift?

Example: **a.** 4
Business Preview ≠ flexi-time

a. Business Review	b. Proposals	c. Licensing	d. Staff
1 figures ☐	1 outline ☐	1 vacation ☐	1 organigram ☐
2 update ☐	2 new range ☐	2 agreement ☐	2 minutes ☐
3 strategy ☐	3 complaint ☐	3 partner ☐	3 department ☐
4 flexi-time ☐	4 plans ☐	4 finance ☐	4 promotion ☐

4. True or false?
Sind diese Aussagen richtig oder falsch?

Example:	True	False
The action points from the last meeting are dealt with first.	✓	☐
1. The Board Meeting takes place in London.	☐	☐
2. The software licence contracts were not signed.	☐	☐
3. Sales figures have continued to improve.	☐	☐
4. The future of the Pluto project is uncertain.	☐	☐
5. The firm is looking to do business in Japan.	☐	☐
6. The firm has completed plans for reorganisation.	☐	☐
7. The firm has no worries at all about their competitors.	☐	☐
8. Employees are very happy with their hours of work.	☐	☐
9. The date for the next Board Meeting is left open.	☐	☐
10. The Action Points in the Minutes list what still has to be done.	☐	☐

Reading for Language

1. The right meaning
Wählen Sie bitte die passende Übersetzung.

Example:
Does *chair* in this context mean
a. Lehrstuhl b. Vorsitz **b**

1. Does *overall* in this context mean
   a. insgesamt? b. Arbeitskleidung?
2. Does *turnover* mean
   a. umdrehen? b. Umsatz?
3. Does *fallback* mean
   a. umfallen? b. Notplan?
4. Does *promotion* of staff mean
   a. Beförderung? b. Werbekampagne?
5. Does *to take a vacation* mean
   a. Urlaub nehmen? b. das Haus verlassen?
6. Does *feedback* mean
   a. Essensreste? b. Rückmeldungen?
7. Does *template* mean
   a. großer Teller? b. Schablone?
8. Does *malfunction* mean
   a. Funktionsfehler? b. anstreichen?
9. Does *facility* mean
   a. Einrichtung? b. einfache Sache?
10. Does *to date* in this context mean
    a. sich verabreden? b. bisher?

2. The right word
Setzen Sie das richtige Wort in die Lücke ein.

Example:
Members are referred to the .... and discussion papers.
Members are referred to the <u>Agenda</u> and discussion papers.

1. Marketing has provided revised .... for the project.
2. We are behind .... on development of the new project.
3. We need to increase .... for an improved website.

35

4. Our general .... is considered favorable.

5. Staff should be warned against ....

6. We are awaiting finance .... from both corporations.

7. Marketing is to .... our competitor's advertising activities.

8. A new more .... system for the regulation of flexi-time will be introduced.

9. The personnel department will .... staff promotions.

10. A new backup strategy is needed in case of computer ....

3. Translation
Welche Übersetzung passt zu den folgenden Wörtern und Begriffen?

Example: 1 e

1. boardroom
2. participants
3. minutes
4. template
5. complacency
6. increase
7. complaint
8. breakdown
9. chair
10. range

a. Schablone
b. Reihe
c. Panne
d. Beschwerde
e. Konferenzraum
f. Teilnehmer
g. Protokoll
h. Vorsitz
i. Bequemlichkeit
j. Zuwachs

4. Crossword

Across
1 The report on a meeting. (7)
7 All the latest facts. (6)
8 A plan for emergencies. (8)

Down
2 Something used as a model or example. (8)
3 Written permission. (7)
4 The people who work in a firm. (5)
5 Advertising by post. (7)
6 Another word for support. (6)

Reading for Understanding

1. Who or what?
Beantworten Sie folgende Fragen:

Example:
How long has it been since the last Board meeting?
a. six weeks **b.** three weeks | *b*

1. Who wrote the minutes?
   a. Gary Wilson **b.** Peter Mason
2. What do the initials HJ stand for?
   a. Roberta Freeman **b.** Helen Johnson
3. Who is the marketing expert?
   a. DS **b.** GSW
4. What does Peter Mason need to send to Atlanta?
   a. a license agreement **b.** sample materials
5. Who produced the worse export figures?
   a. Shanghai **b.** South America
6. What should staff be warned about?
   a. competition **b.** complacency

2. Why "action points"?
Warum sind die folgenden Punkte notiert worden? Ordnen Sie den *action point* dessen Begründung oder Ursache zu.

Example: 1 c
Research and recommend computer backup/In case of future computer failure

1. Research and recommend computer backup.
2. Discussions with Atlanta branch.
3. Revise figures on Pluto project.
4. Analyse customer addresses.
5. Liaise with marketing on markets in South America.
6. Analyse activities of competitors Intex.
7. Ensure the introduction of a new database.
8. Promote certain members of staff.

a. Because of complaints from staff.
b. Because of low export figures.
c. In case of future computer failure.
d. Because the Finance Dept. weren't happy with the concept.

- e. As a result of the decision to reorganise department structure.
- f. Because of an increase in their advertising.
- g. In case of a switch in production.
- h. Due to a drop in feedback from mailings.

Over to you

Preparing an agenda

Stellen Sie sich vor, Sie haben Besuch aus Amerika. Um Ihre Gäste zu informieren, müssten Sie eine monatliche Planungs- und Diskussionsrunde einberufen unter Beteiligung aller betroffenen bzw. relevanten Abteilungen Ihres Hauses. Es geht natürlich um Berichte über die wichtigsten Ereignisse des vergangenen Monats, um die Erläuterung von Problemen, neuen Ideen oder Vorschlägen.

Write an agenda for the meeting which reflects your wishes and plans, provides a framework for discussion and gives all departments adequate opportunity to voice their opinions. You may like to imagine one or two unexpected or unusual crises as points of discussion. Of course, you can also make several brilliant and innovative suggestions for improving the annual turnover or filling holes in the budget or for securing the export market.

Unit 4

Marketing

Über Qualität und Geschmack lässt sich lange hin und her diskutieren. Aber letzten Endes muss der Kunde entscheiden, denn er ist König. Aber was will der Kunde eigentlich? Weiß er das selber? Und wenn er das weiß, sagt er es auch ? Sagt er es so, dass man ihn verstehen kann? Und sagt er es auch rechtzeitig, damit der Produkthersteller darauf reagieren kann, bevor zu viel umsonst investiert wird? Werbung allein reicht nicht, um Kunden zu überzeugen, Produkte an den Mann zu bringen. Heutzutage reicht es nicht, einen Dollar für die Produktentwicklung und einen für Werbung à la Henry Ford auszugeben. Das wirklich erfolgreiche Unternehmen hat auch ein wirklich erfolgreiches Marketing-Konzept.

Marketing ist der alles umfassende Begriff für sämtliche Maßnahmen, die eine Firma einsetzt, um nicht nur die oben gestellten Fragen zu beantworten, sondern auch sicherzustellen, dass die Antworten richtig interpretiert und umgesetzt werden. Marketing hat sich heute zu einem Spezialgebiet für erfahrene Experten entwickelt – man könnte fast sagen zu einer Wissenschaft für sich. Folgender Text möchte dieser Wissenschaft auf den Grund gehen und die Verbindung zwischen Marktforschung, Produktentwicklung und Produktverkauf, die sich Marketing nennt, etwas erläutern.

Before you read
Wie würden Sie die Frage „Weiß der Kunde immer, was er will?" beantworten? Schreiben Sie kurz die Gründe für Ihre Antwort auf.

Marketing Measures

Take care of your customers and your customers will take care of you.

Thomas Smythe

In this age of the philosophy of self-assertion and self-fulfillment it must often be difficult for product developers locked into their own private and necessarily egocentric world of expert knowledge to accept any customer's dismissive verdict on the results of their painstaking work and adopt an altruistic view of customer-care. To ensure that this happens companies employ large numbers of marketing-executives whose job it is to circle the square made by research department, production, advertising and sales and provide the overall philosophy that unites them in a common aim.

To do this a large number of measures needs to be employed, grouped into three main areas: finding out what people want and need; developing the right products to satisfy those needs; determining the right price, the right place and the right time for promotion and distribution. In all three key areas the questions *what, when, where and how* form a useful guideline.

Market research
Analysis of the competition, feedback on previous products monitored from customers, questionnaires on specific ideas testing public opinion, focus groups invited to deal with the results and organize facts into concepts: what product do people need, when do they need it, where can they find it, how should it be presened?

Concept and product development
Constant liaison with production staff, test phases, analysis of feedback: what concept lies behind the product, when should it be produced, where can it be manufactured, how and in what form should it be packaged?

Promotion and distribution
Advertising in press and media, mailing, door-to-door leafleting, so-called "freebies", hard or soft sell, use of sales reps, placement with retailers: what kind and amount of promotion does the product require, when should it be implemented and the product launched, where should it take place, how should it be done?

These, in short, are the kind of questions marketing-executives are expected to answer. In doing so they speak of the "marketing mix" which, experts tell us, includes "the seven ps" or seven essential factors all beginning with the letter p – in itself a clever marketing-oriented ploy to help them remember!

- Product: a clear definition of the thing you want to sell
- Price: the amount of money research has told you customers will be prepared to pay
- Place: what segments of the markets you aim to cater for and where it will be distributed
- People: everyone involved at the various stages of planning, producing and selling

- **P**ackaging: the appearance and image of the product and the form it is sold in
- **P**hasing: making sure the timing is right
- **P**romotion: the most effective strategies for achieving advertising and market presence

The application of these "p" factors has resulted in some fascinating new words and phrases in the English language used to describe as briefly as possible the new phenomena being created to win over new customers in an ever-more competitive environment. *Freebie, infomercial, corporate identity, co-branding, follow-up, spam, re-launch, teaser ad, one-stop-shop, piggyback mailshot* are just some of them.

With the advent of the internet and the world wide web, opportunities for fast and easy access by customers to information have increased enormously, but the psychological barriers have changed since customers can please themselves when and where they "visit" a product anonymously. The inventiveness of the marketing-executive is now applied to contacting customers via email and thereby removing the anonymity. In the age of virtual reality the virtual customer needs to be real. In the back of every marketing-executive's mind lingers the hope of eventually achieving brand loyalty in the customer and of creating a new cash cow destined to provide easy income to help finance the next generation of products – when we find that once again marketing, as an economic principle, has not only turned full circle but also proved its worth as a result.

Vocabulary

measure *(n.)*	Maßnahme	**to ensure** *(v.)*	sicherstellen
age *(n.)*	Zeitalter, Ära	**to employ** *(v.)*	beschäftigen
self-assertion *(n.)*	Selbstbehauptung	**marketing executive** *(n.)*	Marketing-Manager
self-fulfillment *(n.)*	Selbstverwirklichung		
product developer *(n.)*	Produktentwickler	**to circle the square** *(v.)*	aus dem Quadrat einen Kreis zu machen
to lock into *(v.)*	einschließen, einsperren	**research department** *(n.)*	Forschungsabteilung
necessarily *(adv.)*	notwendigerweise		
egocentric *(adj.)*	egozentrisch	**to provide** *(v.)*	sorgen für, bereitstellen
expert knowledge *(n.)*	Fachwissen	**overall** *(adj.)*	übergreifend, umfassend
dismissive *(adj.)*	abweisend		
verdict *(n.)*	Urteil, Beurteilung	**to unite** *(v.)*	vereinen
painstaking *(adj.)*	sorgfältig, peinlich genau	**common aim** *(n.)*	gemeinsames Ziel
		to employ *(v.)*	einsetzen, anwenden
altruistic *(adj.)*	altruistisch	**to satisfy** *(v.)*	befriedigen, zufrieden stellen
customer-care *(n.)*	Kundenservice, -betreuung		
		needs *(n.)*	Bedürfnisse

to determine *(v.)*	bestimmen	application *(n.)*	Anwendung
promotion *(n.)*	Werbung, Werbemaßnahmen	fascinating *(adj.)*	faszinierend
		phenomena *(n.pl.)*	Phänomene
distribution *(n.)*	Vertrieb	competitive *(adj.)*	wettbewerbsbetont
key area *(n.)*	Schlüsselbereich	environment *(n.)*	Umgebung, Situation
guideline *(n.)*	Richtschnur, -linie	infomercial *(n.)*	Werbung mit Information (information und commercial)
analysis *(n.)*	Analyse		
competition *(n.)*	Konkurrenz		
feedback *(n.)*	Rückmeldung(en)	corporate identity *(n.)*	einheitliches Firmenimage
to monitor *(v.)*	registrieren, beobachten		
		co-branding *(n.)*	Partnerschaft zwischen Firmen
questionnaire *(n.)*	Fragebogen(aktion)		
focus group *(n.)*	Arbeitsgruppe	follow-up *(n.)*	Nachhakaktion
to deal with *(v.)*	bearbeiten, sich beschäftigen mit	spam *(n.)*	Werbung per E-Mail
		re-launch *(n.)*	neuer Versuch, ein Produkt auf den Markt zu bringen
liaison *(n.)*	Zusammenarbeit, Verbindung		
staff *(n.)*	Mitarbeiter (-innen)	teaser ad *(n.)*	Werbestrategie mit nur wenig Information, „Appetitanreger"
to manufacture *(v.)*	herstellen		
to package *(v.)*	präsentieren		
mailing *(n.)*	Werbesendung per Post	one-stop-shop *(n.)*	eine Firma, die alle Produkte für ein bestimmtes Marktsegment anbietet
door-to-door leafleting *(n.)*	Werbeblätter an alle Haushalte, Postwurfsendungen		
freebies *(n.)*	kostenlose Werbegeschenke	piggyback mailshot *(n.)*	eine Werbeaktion, die mit einer anderen größeren Aktion mitläuft
hard or soft sell *(n.)*	aggressive oder „weichere" Verkaufsmethoden		
		access *(n.)*	Zugang
		enormously *(adv.)*	enorm
sales reps *(n.)*	Außendienstmitarbeiter, Verkäufer im Außendienst	psychological *(adj.)*	psychologisch
		barrier *(n.)*	Barriere, Sperre
		anonymously *(adv.)*	anonym
		inventiveness *(n.)*	Einfallsreichtum
placement *(n.)*	hier: Vereinbarungen	to linger *(v.)*	bleiben, zurückbleiben
retailer *(n.)*	Einzelhändler	brand loyalty *(n.)*	Markentreue
to implement *(v.)*	bewerkstelligen	cash cow *(n.)*	Cash-Cow-Produkt, „Goldesel"
to launch *(v.)*	auf den Markt bringen		
essential *(adj.)*	wesentlich		
ploy *(n.)*	Trick, Strategie	destined to *(adj./p.p.)*	bestimmt für
segment *(n.)*	Segment	income *(n.)*	Einkommen
to cater for *(v.)*	betreuen	economic *(adj.)*	wirtschaftlich
appearance *(n.)*	Aussehen, Anmutung	principle *(n.)*	Prinzip
phasing *(n.)*	Zeitplanung	to turn full circle *(v.)*	sich im Kreis drehen
market presence *(n.)*	Marktpräsenz	worth *(n.)*	Wert

Reading for Gist

1. True or false?
Sind diese Aussagen richtig oder falsch?

	True	False
Example: It is always easy for product developers to accept customers' views.	☐	✓
1. Marketing measures can be grouped into three key areas.	☐	☐
2. All departments in a firm need to have a common marketing philosophy.	☐	☐
3. Market research does not include an analysis of the competition.	☐	☐
4. Test phases are no longer a part of product development.	☐	☐
5. The marketing-mix is the combination of all marketing measures.	☐	☐
6. Eight essential factors in marketing begin with the letter "t".	☐	☐
7. The internet has made it impossible for customers to get information quickly.	☐	☐
8. Packaging is the term used in marketing to cover transport costs.	☐	☐
9. Lots of new words have entered the language of marketing.	☐	☐
10. All marketing executives dream of customers loyal to their firm.	☐	☐

2. Match them up
Welche Satzteile passen zusammen?

Example: 1 g
Take care of your customers and your customers will take care of you.

1. Take care of your customers
2. A large number of measures
3. Market research involves
4. It's important to develop products
5. Concept development includes
6. Promotion of a product means
7. In marketing you need a clear definition
8. New phenomena are being created
9. With the advent of the internet
10. A cash cow provides easy income

a. that satisfy customers' needs.
b. the form of packaging.
c. of the thing you want to sell.
d. to win over new customers.
e. customers have easy access to information.
f. to help finance the next generation product.
g. and your customers will take care of you.
h. analysis of feedback.
i. advertising in the press and media.
j. needs to be employed.

Reading for Language

1. True or false?
Sind diese Definitionen richtig oder falsch?

	True	False
Example: *Altruistic* behaviour is very selfish.	☐	☑

1. A *common aim* means that a plan is not worthwhile.
2. The *promotion* of a product means creating better quality.
3. *Feedback* is what you get when customers reply.
4. A *questionnaire* is someone who visits customers at home.
5. A *retailer* buys from the manufacturer and sells to the customer.
6. To *launch* a new product means to have dinner with customers.
7. Having a *competitive environment* means that selling can be difficult.
8. A *freebie* is another name for an alcoholic drink.
9. *Co-branding* means that more than one firm's name appears on the product.
10. A *cash cow* is another name for an unsuccessful product.

2. What does it mean?
Entscheiden Sie bitte, welche Bedeutung richtig ist.

Example:
Does *self-assertion* mean **a.** describing your life **b.** getting what you want?   **b**

1. Is a *dismissive verdict* **a.** a positive reaction **b.** a negative reaction?
2. Does the *distribution* of a product mean **a.** how it appears in newspapers **b.** how it is brought to the customer?
3. Does *constant liaison* mean **a.** good communication **b.** always meeting the same person?
4. Does a *sales rep* usually work **a.** outside the firm **b.** inside the firm?
5. Is a *marketing ploy* **a.** a mistake in strategy **b.** a plan to improve sales?
6. What is meant by *corporate identity*? **a.** knowing all the employees in a firm **b.** the appearance and image of a company
7. Is an *informercial* **a.** an informal advertisement **b.** advertising with lots of information?
8. Does the *phasing* of a campaign mean **a.** getting the timing right **b.** keeping the cost down?
9. When a measure is *implemented*, does it mean **a.** it needs support from elsewhere **b.** it is carried out?
10. Does a *one-stop-shop* mean **a.** customers never go back **b.** customers can find everything they need here?

3. Match them up
Welche Wörter passen zusammen?

Example: 1d

1. research
2. customer
3. focus
4. sales
5. soft
6. marketing
7. corporate
8. brand
9. cash
10. one-stop

a. mix
b. cow
c. shop
d. department
e. care
f. loyalty
g. sell
h. group
i. identity
j. rep

4. Translate
Übersetzen Sie bitte folgende Begriffe ins Deutsche.

Example:
expert knowledge = *Fachwissen*

1. customer-care ....
2. common aim ....
3. guideline ....
4. staff ....
5. competition ....
6. to satisfy ....
7. to implement ....
8. retailer ....
9. sales rep ....
10. to cater for ....

5. Crossword

Across
1 An "animal" earning money (7)
6 Replies from customers (8)
7 Who you are is your ... (8)
8 Advertising a product (9)

Down
2 Part of the market (7)
3 Something that costs nothing (7)
4 Everything to do with promoting and selling (9)
5 Examining something closely (8)

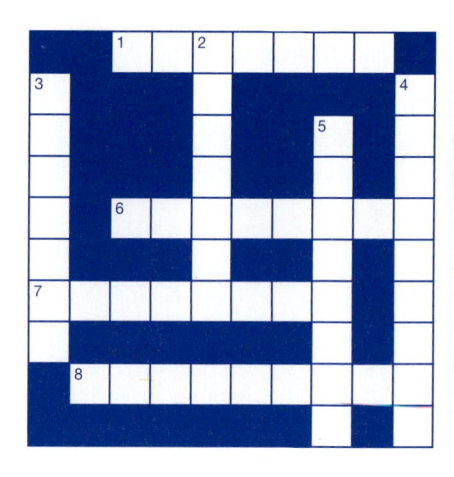

Reading for Understanding

1. Essential facts

Versuchen Sie bitte folgende Fragen zu beantworten.

Example:
What does market research involve?
a. asking customers what they think   **b.** advertising in the press? | a |

1. What does product development involve?
   a. distribution to retailers   **b.** testing the concept?
2. What does monitoring customer feedback involve?
   a. making a video of customer reactions   **b.** analysing what customers have said
3. What is the difference between hard and soft selling?
   a. hard selling means putting pressure on the customer
   b. a hard sell is what happens when a customer complains?
4. What is meant by the marketplace?
   a. the building where the retailer sells the product
   b. the people who are supposed to buy the product?
5. What is meant by marketing-mix?
   a. selling to several markets   **b.** the measures employed in promoting a product?
6. What do you think a piggy-back mailshot involves?
   a. advertising where costs are shared   **b.** an unusually expensive campaign?
7. What are the seven "p's"?
   a. a list of things a firm should never do
   b. important points to be decided when planning a product?
8. Advertising on the internet has meant
   a. firms can get to know customers better
   b. easier access to more information for customers?

9. Achieving brand loyalty means that customers
    a. will continue to buy from the same firm   b. decide to buy a new product?
10. When in principle marketing turns full circle, it means that
    a. feedback from one product proves useful in developing the next generation
    b. no one knows in which direction the campaign will go?

2. What does it really mean?
Würden Sie auf die folgenden Aussagen mit Ja oder Nein antworten?

Example:	Yes	No
Marketing is more than just advertising.	✓	☐

1. If you concentrate on development too much, you might forget the customer.
2. Firms nowadays need to guard against this happening.
2. Marketing executives don't really need to see the overall picture.
3. There are three basic elements: research, development, distribution.
4. It's important to find the right marketing-mix necessary for different products.
5. The list of "p" factors can help to decide the strategy.
6. Not many new ideas and techniques have emerged.
7. Instant information via the internet provides instant feedback.
8. All customers become well-known to firms as a result.
9. Loyal customers and longlasting success have become totally unimportant.
10. The distribution of one product should never influence the research on another.

3. What do you think?
Beantworten Sie folgende Fragen:

Example:
If you were a *marketing executive* would you
a. always put the product first?   b. always put the customer first?   *b*

1. Why do you think product developers might ignore customers?
    a. because they don't like them
    b. because they think they can judge quality better
2. Why do you think marketing needs to involve research, development and promotion?
    a. because it links the product with customers' wishes
    b. because it's the only way towards self-assertion?
3. What purpose do you think a focus group might fulfill?
    a. reach an objective view of the collected facts
    b. concentrate on the most important features?

4. Why do you think marketing staff should be in constant liaison with production staff?
   a. to speed up production **b.** to make sure the product follows customers' wishes?
5. Why do you think it becomes necessary to give customers "freebies"?
   a. because it's a cheap way of advertising
   b. to persuade them to come over to a new product?
6. Why do you think a product may have to be re-launched?
   a. because it has been totally unsuccessful so far
   b. because success has been moderate but not as expected?
7. Why do you think the "seven p's" were invented?
   a. because they help marketing people to remember what to do
   b. because marketing experts were looking for new words and phrases?
8. Why do you think *spam* has now become a common phenomenon?
   a. because it's a cheap and easy way of advertising to lots of people
   b. because electronic advertising convinces more people?
9. Why do think co-branding is sometimes a good option?
   a. because customers perfer two names to one
   b. because a new product can combine advantages?
10. Why do you think customers' brand loyalty is so valuable to marketing executives?
    a. because it makes them feel independent
    b. because it will provide reliable feedback for the next generation product?

Over to you

1. Plan a promotion campaign
Planen Sie Ihre eigene Werbekampagne.

Imagine you are the marketing manager of a firm selling a very desirable commodity (which you may choose yourself).
Using the seven "p's" described in the text, decide on your marketing-mix and write a short survey of your marketing plans to present to the Board of Directors.

2. Plan a talk
Planen Sie einen kurzen Vortrag zum Thema „Erfolgreiches Marketing."

Imagine you have to give a talk to your colleagues about the the principles of successful marketing. Make a list of the principles involved. Write headings and three sentences explaining each of them.

Unit 5

Contracts

Verträge mit Geschäftspartnern abzuschließen, gehört zum Alltag eines jeden Unternehmens. In einem üblicherweise schon recht komplexen Verfahren will man dabei bestimmte Dinge schriftlich festhalten – für den Fall des Falles. Im folgenden Text möchte eine amerikanische Software-Firma ein Programm von Joystix plc UK kaufen. Joystix bietet einen Lizenzvertrag an. Zu jeder Art Vertrag gehören einige Grundsätze – im Englischen wie im Deutschen. Auf diese Grundsätze und das dafür notwendige Vokabular konzentrieren sich dieser Text und die darauf folgenden Übungen.

Before you read
Versuchen Sie darüber nachzudenken, welche Grundsätze Sie klären müssten, wenn Sie irgendein für Sie wertvolles Produkt auf professioneller Basis an jemanden verkaufen wollen, der es vielleicht umändern will und dann weiterverkauft. Was müssten Sie absichern? Machen Sie eine Liste mit Stichwörtern. Die klassischen Standardfragen „wer, was, warum, wann, wo, wie?" werden Ihnen sicherlich eine Hilfe sein.

Agreement

made this day 14th July 2003
between

Super Software Inc.
Sunset Drive
Los Angeles, Ca.
U.S.A.   (hereinafter called the **Licensee**) of the one part

and

Joystix plc
King's Road
Manchester
England   (hereinafter called the **Licensor**) of the other part,

with reference to a computer software program created by the **Licensor** entitled **Playmix** (hereinafter called **the Work**).

It is hereby mutually agreed as follows:

1. Rights

Subject to the terms of this agreement, the Licensor hereby grants to the Licensee the exclusive licence to adapt the Work and produce and publish it in CD-ROM format in any language under their own imprint for sale throughout the world (hereinafter called the Licensed Edition). The Licensee undertakes to publish **the Licensed Edition** at their own expense. The Licensee shall not dispose of any subsidiary rights in the Licensed Edition without prior written permission from the Licensor.

2. Third Party Indemnity

The Licensee shall be responsible for obtaining, wherever necessary, permission for the use in the Licensed Edition of any copyright material controlled by third parties, for paying any fees required for such permissions and making appropriate acknowledgement in the Licensed Edition, thus indemnifying the Licensor against any claims made by such third parties.

3. Supply

To facilitate production of the Licensed Edition, the Licensor will supply the Licensee with all electronic data and files for the Work, together with an original manuscript as created by the original authors and presented to the original programmers and a copy of the necessary source codes for the original program.

4. Quality

The Licensee undertakes to ensure that the production quality of the Licensed Edition is of the highest standard and of no less quality than the original Work or other similar products published by the Licensee.

5. Acknowledgement

The names of the authors shall appear with due prominence on every copy of the Licensed Edition published together with the following copyright notice (c) 2003 Super Software Inc. Licensed from Joystix plc and based on the program Playmix (c) Joystix plc 2002.

6. User Licences and Support

The Licensee shall be responsible for including an end-user licence with every copy of the Licensed Edition.

7. Free Copies

Fifteen complimentary copies of the Licensed Edition shall be sent to the Licensor on publication.

8. Payment

The Licensee shall make the following payments to the Licensor in respect of the Licensed Edition:
A royalty of 10% (ten per cent) based on the sum received by the Licensee on all copies of the Licensed Edition sold by the Licensee.
For the purpose of this Agreement the term „sum received" shall mean the amount received by the Licensee on all copies of the Licensed Edition sold after deduction of any discounts, taxes, duties or costs incurred by the Licensee in respect of sales of the Licensed Edition.

9. Accounting

Accounts for the sale of the Licensed Edition shall be made annually by the Licensee to December 31st and presented together with all royalty payments due within three months of this date. Accounts shall include details of the number of copies of the Licensed Edition in stock at the beginning and at the end of the accounting period, the number of copies produced and the number of copies sold during that period.
Should payment be three months overdue, the licence shall lapse and all rights shall revert without further notice immediately to the Licensor.

10. Warranty

The Licensor hereby warrants to the Licensee that they have the right and power to make this agreement and that according to English law the Work will in no way whatever give rise to a violation of any existing copyright, or a breach of any existing agreement and that nothing in the Work is liable to give rise to a criminal prosecution or to a civil action for damages and the Licensor will indemnify the Licensee against any loss, injury or expense arising out of any breach or alleged breach of this warranty.

11. Termination

Subject to clauses 9, 12 and 13 of this agreement, the licence granted shall continue for a period of five years from the date of first publication of the Licensed Edition by the Licensee and thereafter shall be automatically renewed annually for a further year unless prior written notice is given by either party three months before the end of the year.

12. Breach

In the event of the Licensee being declared bankrupt or should they fail to comply with any of the conditions of this agreement and not rectify such failure within one month of having received notice from the Licensor to do so, then this agreement automatically becomes null and void and the licence granted to the Licensee shall revert to the Licensor without prejudice to any monies paid or due to be paid to the Licensor.

13. Notice of Change

Any and all notices with respect to any of the clauses of this agreement shall be made in writing in English and left at or sent by fax, e-mail or registered mail to the respective address of the Licensor or the Licensee given at the beginning of this agreement.

14. Governing Law

This agreement shall be governed by and interpreted and construed in all respects in accordance with the laws of England.

15. Miscellaneous

This agreement contains the full and complete understanding between the parties and supersedes all prior arrangements, whether oral or written, concerning the subject matter of this agreement, and may not be varied without prior written agreement between the parties.

The undersigned declare themselves in agreement with the above

Signed... Signed ....
on behalf of the Licensee   on behalf of he Licensor

Vocabulary

hereinafter *(adv. fml)*	im Folgenden	**of the other part** *(adv. fml)*	andererseits
licensee *(n.)*	Lizenznehmer		
of the one part *(adv. fml)*	einerseits	**mutually** *(adv.)*	gegenseitig, gemeinsam
licensor *(n.)*	Lizenzgeber	**entitled** *(p.p.)*	genannt

hereby *(adv. fml)*	hiermit		accounting *(n.)*	Buchführung, Abrechnung
rights *(n.)*	Rechte		annually *(adv.)*	jährlich
subject to *(prep.)*	abhängig von		in stock *(adv.)*	vorrätig
terms *(n.)*	Bedingungen		to lapse *(v.)*	verstreichen
to grant *(v.)*	gewähren, erlauben		to revert *(v.)*	zurückgehen
imprint *(n.)*	Markenzeichen, Firmennamen		warranty *(n.)*	Gewähr(leistung)
expense *(n.)*	Kosten		to give rise to *(v.)*	verursachen
to dispose of *(v.)*	verfügen über, verwerten		violation *(n.)*	Verletzung
			breach *(n.)*	Verstoß, Bruch
subsidiary rights *(n.)*	Nebenrechte		liable *(adj.)*	hier: möglicherweise imstande
prior *(adj.)*	vorherig			
permission *(n.)*	Erlaubnis		criminal prosecution *(n.)*	strafrechtliche Verfolgung
third party *(n.)*	Dritte(r)			
indemnity *(n.)*	Versicherung; Absicherung		civil action *(n.)*	zivilrechtlicher Prozess
responsible *(adj.)*	verantwortlich		damages *(n.)*	Schadensersatz
to obtain *(v.)*	erhalten, bekommen		termination *(n.)*	Abbruch, Beendigung
copyright *(n.)*	Urheberrecht		subject to *(prep.)*	abhängig von
fee *(n.)*	Gebühr, Vergütung		to grant *(v.)*	gewähren
to require *(v.)*	benötigen		thereafter *(adv.)*	danach
appropriate *(adj.)*	passend, entsprechend		prior *(adj.)*	vorherig
acknowledgement *(n.)*	Quellennachweis		bankrupt *(adj.)*	bankrott
to indemnify *(v.)*	absichern, versichern		to comply *(v.)*	einwilligen
claim *(n.)*	Anspruch		to rectify *(v.)*	berichtigen
supply *(n.)*	Lieferung		null and void *(adj.)*	null und nichtig
to facilitate *(v.)*	vereinfachen, erleichtern		without prejudice to *(adv.)*	ohne negative Auswirkung auf
source codes *(n.)*	Quell-Codes		monies *(n.)*	Gelder
with due prominence *(adv.)*	entsprechend hervorgehoben		clause *(n.)*	Klausel
			in writing *(adv.)*	in schriftlicher Form
end-user licence *(n.)*	Endverbraucherlizenz		governing law *(n.)*	maßgebendes Gesetz; Gerichtsstand
complimentary *(adj.)*	hier: kostenlos			
royalty *(n.)*	Honorar, Tantieme		to interpret *(v.)*	deuten
sum received *(n.)*	Erlös		to construe *(v.)*	ableiten
deduction *(n.)*	Abzug		to supersede *(v.)*	überholen
discount *(n.)*	Rabatt		undersigned *(n.)*	die Unterzeichnenden
duties *(n.)*	(Zoll-)Gebühren		on behalf of *(prep.)*	im Auftrag von
to incur *(v.)*	zuziehen, machen			

Reading for Gist

1. True or false?
Sind die folgenden Aussagen richtig oder falsch?

	True	False
Example: Super Software want to sell a licence.	☐	☑
1. A licence is the right to use a product.	☐	☐
2. The Licensor will supply the data.	☐	☐
3. The Licensee will finance the new product.	☐	☐
4. The Licensor pays a royalty to Super Software.	☐	☐
5. Payment will be made twice a year.	☐	☐
6. Joystix will terminate the agreement after five years.	☐	☐
7. There must be a copyright notice on the finished CD-ROM.	☐	☐
8. Joystix guarantees that the original product belongs to them.	☐	☐
9. All changes to the agreement must be made in writing.	☐	☐
10. Only one party needs to sign the agreement	☐	☐

2. Match them up
Welche dieser Satzteile passen zusammen?

Example: 1 i
The licensor grants the exclusive licence to adapt the work.

1. The licensor grants
2. The licensee indemnifies the licensor
3. The licensee ensures that the quality
4. The names of the authors shall
5. The royalty payment will be based
6. Accounts for sales
7. The licensor warrants that the work will not
8. The licence will be renewed
9. If the licensee becomes bankrupt,
10. The agreement may not be varied
11. The sum received means the money
12. The licence will be renewed automatically

a. give rise to any civil action for damages.
b. without prior written agreement.
c. the agreement becomes null and void.
d. on the sum received by the licensee.
e. automatically for a further year.
f. appear clearly on the Licensed Edition.
g. will be made annually to December 31st.
h. will not be less than the original work.
i. the exclusive licence to adapt the work.
j. against any claims from third parties.
k. unless written notice is given.
l. from sales after deductions.

| 1. .... | 2. .... | 3. .... | 4. .... | 5. .... | 6. .... |
| 7. .... | 8. .... | 9. .... | 10. .... | 11. .... | 12. .... |

Reading for Language

1. Odd one out
Welches Wort passt nicht in die jeweilige Gruppe?

1	2	3	4
a) licensee	a) rights	a) hereinafter	a) bankrupt
b) licensor	b) permission	b) thereafter	b) deduction
c) third party	c) indemnity	c) prior	c) discount
d) royalty	d) warranty	d) hereby	d) duties
e) end-user	e) source code	e) mutually	e) expense

2. Translate
Bitte übersetzen Sie folgende Begriffe ins Deutsche.

1 licensee ....

2 imprint ....

3 subsidiary rights ....

4 sum received ....

5 accounting ....

6 warranty ....

7 breach ....

8 damages ....

9 bankrupt ....

10 clause ....

3. Match the meaning
Welche Sätze haben die gleiche Bedeutung?

Example: 1c

1. The licensee shall not dispose of any subsidiary rights without prior permission..
2. The licensee will indemnify the licensor against any claims from third parties.
3. The licensee will make appropriate acknowledgement of any copyright material.

4. The licensor warrants to the licensee that there will be no violation of existing copyright.
5. The licence shall lapse and all rights revert without further notice to the licensor.
6. This agreement supersedes all prior arrangements.
7. Accounts shall include details of the number of copies in stock.
8. Any and all notices with respect to any clauses shall be made in writing in English.

a. Super Software will print the names of all the people whose material they use.
b. If either of the partners wishes to change anything, they must first ask in written form.
c. Super Software is not allowed to license the product further to anyone else.
d. Super Software must report every year how many copies of the product they have.
e. his contract is final.
f. Joystix promises that they have the right to give them the licence.
g. Super Software promises to pay if anyone should make any claim on Joystix.
h. Super Software will lose the licence and Joystix keeps all the rights.

1. .... 2. .... 3. .... 4. .... 5. .... 6. .... 7. .... 8. ....

4. The right verb
Bitte setzen Sie das richtige Verb in die Lücken ein.

Example:
This agreement shall be *interpreted* in accordance with the laws of England
a. obtained   **b.** interpreted

1. The licensor .... the licence to the licensee.
   a. grants   **b.** obtains

2. If third parties .... fees, the licensee will pay them.
   a. facilitate   **b.** require

3. Super Software will .... Joystix against any third party claims.
   a. incur   **b.** indemnify

4. If payment is overdue the licence shall ....
   a. lapse   **b.** appear

5. The agreement becomes null and void if the licensee fails to .... with the conditions.
   a. comply   **b.** rectify

5. Contract-speak
Welcher Ausdruck ist rein formeller Art und nur in solchen Dokumenten anzutreffen?

Example: 1 b
hereinafter

1	2	3	4	5
a) annually	a) entitled	a) of the other part	a) permission	a) in stock
b) hereinafter	b) discount	b) terms	b) appropriate	b) claim
c) responsible	c) warranty	c) supply	c) of the one part	c) to comply
d) expense	d) hereby	d) in writing	d) to interpret	d) to obtain
e) to require	e) to grant	e) to dispose of	e) fee	e) null and void

6. Crossword

Across
2 The money you have to pay. (7)
6 A company owned by another company. (10)
7 To make right again. (7)
8 Without any money. (8)

Down
1 Another word for conditions. (5)
3 What you have when someone allows you to do something. (10)
4 Ownership of a piece of writing or music. (9)
5 Another word for demand. (5)

7. What does it mean?
Versuchen Sie folgende Fragen zu beantworten.

Example: 2 b

1. What is a *warranty*?
   a. a guarantee ☐
   b. a police document ☐

2. What is a *royalty*?
   a. a member of the Queen's family ☐
   b. payment on sales ☐

3. What are *damages*?
   a. repairs ☐
   b. compensation ☐

4. What is a *third party*?
   a. someone else ☐
   b. another place ☐

5. What does *supersede* mean?
   a. to improve ☐
   b. to replace ☐

Reading for Understanding

1. What does it mean?
Welche Bedeutung passt am besten zu den folgenden Sätzen?

Example:
Does *mutually agreed* mean
a. both agree?   b. maybe we can agree? | *a* |

1. Does *subject to the terms* mean
   a. depending on the conditions being kept?
   b. at the end of the period of contract?
2. Does *the exclusive licence* mean
   a. an excellent choice?   b. no other person is involved?
3. Does *indemnifying against claims* mean
   a. taking on the responsibility?   b. refusing to do improvements?
4. Does *with due prominence* mean
   a. with the right qualified people?   b. in a suitably important place?
5. Does *end-user licence* mean
   a. permission for customer usage?   b. final guarantee?
6. Does *should payment be overdue* mean
   a. if you pay too much?   b. if you are too late in paying?
7. Does *give rise to any violation* mean
   a. ask for compensation?   b. cause harm or damage?
8. Does *without prejudice to any monies* mean
   a. the money can be forgotten?   b. any payments made are not affected?
9. Does *liable to give rise to* mean
   a. likely to cause?   b. with an obligation to request?
10. Does *without further notice* mean
    a. dependent on written confirmation?   b. effective immediately?

2. Key features of the contract
Ordnen Sie diese Begriffe den englischen Vertragsklauseln zu.

Example:
6b Zahlung – clause stating terms of payment

1. [ ] Gegenstand – 2. [ ] Parteien – 3. [ ] Rechteeinräumung – 4. [ ] Urhebernennung – 5. [ ] Garantien – 6. [ ] Zahlung – 7. [ ] Zahlungsmodus – 8. [ ] Kündigung – 9. [ ] Vertragsbruch – 10. [ ] Gerichtsstand

- **a.** Clause covering failure or fault
- **b.** Clause stating the terms of payment
- **c.** Clause stating the area of jurisdiction
- **d.** Clause naming the object of the agreement
- **e.** Clause describing how and when payment is to be made
- **f.** Clause determining what permission is for
- **g.** Clause saying who is making an agreement with whom
- **h.** Clause stating conditions for termination
- **i.** Clause giving guarantee on original product
- **j.** Clause making certain acknowledgement of copyright

3. Who is responsible?
Wer ist für was beim Vertragsabschluss zuständig? Der Lizenzgeber (a) oder der Lizenznehmer (b)?

Example:	a. Licensor	b. Licensee
Who provides the annual accounts of sales?	☐	☑
1. Who makes the agreement?	☐	☐
2. Who grants the rights?	☐	☐
3. Who indemnifies against third party claims?	☐	☐
4. Who supplies the data?	☐	☐
5. Who guarantees the quality of the final new product?	☐	☐
6. Who includes the end-user licence?	☐	☐
7. Who provides the free copies?	☐	☐
8. Who guarantees the quality of the original product?	☐	☐
9. Who determines the area of jurisdiction?	☐	☐
10. Who retains the rights if there is a breach of contract?	☐	☐

4. Perspectives

Beim Formulieren der Klauseln haben die beiden Vertragspartner oft unterschiedliche Interessen und Absichten. Welcher Partner hat bei welcher Klausel welches Interesse?
Hat bei den folgenden Punkten der Lizenzgeber oder der Lizenznehmer den Vorteil?

	a. Licensor	b. Licensee
Example: Acknowledgement of the original	☑	☐
1. Exclusive right to adapt the work	☐	☐
2. Responsibility for third parties	☐	☐
3. Annual accounting	☐	☐
4. Warranty for original	☐	☐
5. Licence lapse if payment overdue	☐	☐
6. Publish at own expense	☐	☐
7. Sale of subsidiary rights	☐	☐
8. Ensure quality of production	☐	☐
9. Supply of electronic data	☐	☐
10. Supply of free copies	☐	☐
11. Royalty paid after deductions	☐	☐
12. Automatic renewal of licence	☐	☐

Over to you

1. Imagine

Stellen Sie sich vor, Sie sind jetzt der Lizenznehmer. Sie haben den Vertrag sorgfältig gelesen. Schreiben Sie auf, bei welchen Klauseln Sie bessere Konditionen haben möchten.

Write a letter to the licensor and give reasons for the changes you ask for. For example: five free copies instead of fifteen; 5% royalty; terms of payment etc.

2. A summary

Schreiben Sie eine Kurzfassung des Agreements.

Write down who receives what from whom and who is required to fulfill what conditions.

Unit 6

Invoices

Eingegangene Rechnungen zu prüfen, bevor sie bezahlt werden, eigene Rechnungen korrekt aufzusetzen und pünktlich zu stellen gehört sicherlich zum Alltag eines jeden Unternehmens. Im Handelsverkehr mit dem In- und Ausland gibt es aber, bevor es zur Rechnungsstellung kommt, viele Faktoren, die zu berücksichtigen sind. Darunter nicht nur das grundsätzliche Überprüfen der Kreditwürdigkeit eines neuen Kunden oder Geschäftspartners und die ihm eingeräumten Konditionen, sondern auch Detailfragen bezüglich Art und Umfang der Frachtkostenübernahme, Zollerklärungen und Steuerangelegenheiten. Je nach kulturellem Hintergrund des Geschäftspartners können diese falsch verstanden, falsch interpretiert, falsch angewendet werden. Bei der Rechnungsstellung dann gibt es Missverständnisse. Um das grundsätzliche Kommunikationsproblem zu entschärfen, wurden die internationalen Regeln für die Auslegung handelsüblicher Vertragsformeln geschaffen. Im folgenden Text wird beschrieben, welche Prinzipien dahinter stecken.

Before you read
Denken Sie an die wichtigsten Elemente in jeder Rechnung. Was müsste logischerweise immer darin enthalten sein? Was muss der Kunde wissen? Worauf muss der Verkäufer achten? Machen Sie eine erste provisorische Liste.

6

Sales Invoice *Black & White plc*	Despatch to:	Invoice No.: Date:
		Customer No.:
		Terms of payment: Currency:
Tel. Fax Email Contact person: Extension:	Delivery terms:	Carrier/Route:

Product Code	Description	Quantity	Unit price	VAT 17%	Total net price
Total					Total net Discount VAT Gross amount payable

"Send me the bill!"

That money talks
I won't deny.
I heard it once:
It said "Goodbye"!

Everyone worries about money. No one more so than the manufacturer despatching his (or her) goods off to a comparatively unknown customer. "Will I ever get paid?" is the nagging question at the back of their minds. The bigger the order, the bigger the worry. Particularly if the customer is overseas. Balanced against this worry is the desire and the need to sell the goods – but it's no good waiting until the last minute and then entering into a long-distance game of poker. These things have to be sorted out in advance.

But it's here that the fun begins. Creditworthiness, references, terms of delivery, terms of payment, retention of ownership, method of shipment, insurance are all factors that need to be considered in detail but often remain unseen in the generalities of the yearly balance sheet. All this to make sure the deal goes through and the invoice gets paid.

What lies behind these details? At best a list of internationally agreed commercial expressions known as *Incoterms*, abbreviated to the following: EXW, FCA, FS, FOB; CFR, CIF; CPT, CIP, DAF, DES, DEQ, DDU,

DDP. These terms are the basic components of export contracts. Courts tend to rely on them. Thought up by the International Chamber of Commerce they are an essential ingredient of international trade. But for the most part they cover only the terms for delivery.

EXW means EX WORKS. EXW *Bristol*, therefore, means that the customer pays all costs and bears the risk of loss or damage to the goods from the moment they leave the factory in Bristol. FOB *Southampton* means FREE ON BOARD the ship at the port of shipment. The customer pays for transport from that moment. CIF *Rotterdam* means COST, INSURANCE; FREIGHT to the port of Rotterdam. The customer pays for transport and risks from that point in the journey onwards. The other terms determine just how much of the journey between factory and customer the respective partners in the deal are expected to pay for.

Before these terms of delivery can be agreed and included in the invoice, terms of credit and payment must also be agreed. Phrases like "goods remain the property of the supplier until payment has been made in full" and "payable within 30 days" are self-explanatory. A discount of 2% granted if payment is made within 3 days is a ploy intended to encourage swift transfer of funds and help the manufacturer's cash-flow. If a particularly large amount of money is involved and the customer is unknown, it is obviously prudent for any self-respecting purveyor of wares to find out how trustworthy the prospective customer is. A request for references and/or guarantees might be made, and a letter of credit from the customer's bank has a very reassuring effect. On a smaller scale the terms may well be COD or *cash on delivery*.

Whatever is to be agreed, it would seem only too logical to have this done before the goods leave the factory. The ensuing invoice can then be sent immediately and promptly dealt with. Communication is the key. Good communication will also serve to solve any snags and pitfalls that might occur despite conscientious preparation. Should the goods be late or faulty, in excess of or below the numbers ordered, responsibilities can be decided. The invoice is a mere formality – the air has been cleared beforehand. Nevertheless it should still include every point of reference from the customers name and order number to a description of the goods and the quantities involved – not forgetting the price, of course.

Incoterms *(International commercial terms)*

Kunde übernimmt:

EXW (Ex works) ... Kosten ab Fabrik/Lager in (Ortsname)
FCA (Free carrier) ... ab Übernahme durch Transportfirma in (Ortsname)
FAS (Free alongside ship) ... ab Hafen vor Verladung (Ortsname)
FOB (Free on board) ... ab Hafen (Güter bereits an Bord) (Ortsname)
CFR (Cost and freight) ... Kosten und Transport ab (Ortsname)
CIF (Cost, insurance and freight) ... Kosten, Versicherung und Transport ab (Ortsname)
CPT (Carriage paid to) ... Transportkosten ab (Ortsname)
CIP (Carriage and insurance paid to) ... Transportkosten und Versicherung ab (Ortsname)
DAF (Delivered at frontier) ... Kosten ab Landesgrenze (Ortsname)
DES (Delivered ex ship) ... Kosten ab Ankunft in Hafen (Ortsname)
DEQ (Delivered ex quay) ... Kosten nach Entladung in Hafen (Ortsname)
DDU (Delivered duty unpaid) ... Zahlung von Zollgebühren
DDP (Delivered duty paid) ... nicht Zahlung von Zollgebühren

(vgl. Glossar)

Vocabulary

invoice (n. fml.)	Rechnung	port of shipment (n.)	Verladungshafen
bill (n.) BE	hier: Rechnung	freight (n.)	Fracht
mere (adj.)	bloß	transport (n.)	Transport
formality (n.)	Formalität	to determine (v.)	bestimmer
to deny (v.)	abstreiten	respective (adj.)	jeweilig
manufacturer (n.)	Hersteller, Produktionsfirma	terms of credit (n.)	Kreditbedingungen
		property (n.)	Eigentum, Besitz
to despatch (v.)	versenden	supplier (n.)	Lieferant
comparatively (adv.)	vergleichsweise	payable (adj.)	zahlbar
nagging (adj./pr.p.)	quälend, keine Ruhe lassend	self-explanatory (adj.)	selbsterklärend
		discount (n.)	Skonto, Rabatt
overseas (adv.)	im Ausland, in Übersee	to grant (v.)	gewähren
long-distance (adj.)	über eine weite Strecke	ploy (n.)	Strategie, Trick
to sort out (v.)	in Ordnung bringen	to encourage (v.)	ermuntern, anregen
creditworthiness (n.)	Kreditwürdigkeit	swift (adj.)	rasch, schnell
reference (n.)	Referenz	transfer (n.)	Überweisung
terms of delivery (n.)	Lieferbedingungen	funds (n.)	Gelder
terms of payment (n.)	Zahlungsbedingungen	cash-flow (n.)	Cashflow, Bruttoertragslage
retention (n.)	Beibehaltung, Zurückhaltung		
		prudent (adj.)	klug, umsichtig
ownership (n.)	Besitz	purveyor (n. fml.)	Händler, Lieferant
shipment (n.)	Verschiffung	wares (n. fml.)	Waren
insurance (n.)	Versicherung	trustworthy (adj.)	vertrauenswürdig
generality (n.)	Allgemeinheit	prospective (adj.)	interessiert, in Frage kommend
yearly (adj.)	jährlich		
balance sheet (n.)	Finanzbericht	request (n.)	Bitte
to go through (v.)	durchgehen, gelingen	guarantee (n.)	Garantie
commercial (adj.)	kommerziell	letter of credit (n.)	Kreditbrief, Akkreditiv
Incoterms (n.)/ International commercial terms	Internationale Bezeichnungen für Transportbedingungen	reassuring (adj.)	beruhigend
		scale (n.)	Größenordnung
		ensuing (adj.)	daraus resultierend
to abbreviate (v.)	abkürzen	promptly (adv.)	prompt, umgehend
court (n.)	Gericht	to deal with (v.)	erledigen
essential (adj.)	wesentlich	key (n.)	Schlüssel
ingredient (n.)	Bestandteil	to solve (v.)	lösen
to cover (v.)	abdecken	snag (n.)	Haken, Schwierigkeit
to bear (v.)	tragen	pitfall (n.)	Falle, Fallstrick, Hauptschwierigkeit
risk (n.)	Risiko		
loss (n.)	Verlust	conscientious (adj.)	gewissenhaft
damage (n.)	Beschädigung	faulty (adj.)	fehlerhaft
goods (n.)	Güter, Waren	in excess of (prep.)	über

to clear the air (v.)	die Atmosphäre reinigen	unit price (n.)	Stückpreis, Einzelpreis
beforehand (adv.)	vorher	VAT (n.)	MwSt
extension (n.)	Durchwahl	(Value Added Tax)	Mehrwertsteuer
currency (n.)	Währung	total net price (n.)	Gesamtnettopreis
carrier (n.)	Transportfirma, Spediteur	gross amount payable (n.)	zu zahlende Gesamtsumme

Reading for Gist

1. True or false?
Sind diese Aussagen richtig oder falsch?

	True	False
Example: The terms "bill" and "invoice" refer to different things.	☐	☑
1. If the customer is unknown, manufacturers will worry about the invoice.	☐	☐
2. Before an invoice can be issued, only two things need to be made clear.	☐	☐
3. *Incoterms* are not recognized by courts.	☐	☐
4. *Incoterms* are internationally agreed terms of reference for transporting goods.	☐	☐
5. *Incoterms* determine who pays for what.	☐	☐
6. A letter of credit doesn't help very much.	☐	☐
7. The offer of a discount will motivate a customer to pay quickly.	☐	☐
8. An invoice needs to include every possible point of reference.	☐	☐
9. Terms of credit and delivery are best agreed after the invoice has been sent.	☐	☐
10. *Incoterms* were written by the International Chamber of Commerce.	☐	☐

2. Match them up
Welche Satzteile passen zusammen?

Example: 1 f
Everyone worries about money.

1. Everyone worries
2. The bigger the order
3. Details remain unseen
4. *Incoterms* are the basic components
5. The customer pays for transport and risks
6. Goods remain the property of the supplier
7. Granting a discount is a ploy
8. It would be prudent of a supplier

9. A letter of credit
10. On a smaller scale terms may be

a. from that point in the journey onwards.
b. until payment has been made in full.
c. to encourage swift payment.
d. to find out how trustworthy a customer is.
e. in the yearly balance sheet.
f. about money.
g. has a reassuring effect.
h. cash on delivery.
i. the bigger the worry.
j. of export contracts.

Reading for Language

1. Fill in the gaps
Ergänzen Sie bitte folgende Sätze mit dem passenden Wort aus dieser Liste.

insurance	guarantees	ingredient	abbreviations	conscientious	gross
	delivery	ownership	prudent	cash-flow	commerce

Example:
Incoterms were thought up by the International Chamber of <u>*Commerce*</u>.

1. *Incoterms* are an essential .... of international trade.

2. Terms of payment and .... need to be agreed in advance.

3. The supplier may retain .... until the goods are paid for.

4. *Incoterms* are nearly always used as ....

5. A swift transfer of funds will help the supplier's ....

6. A supplier may ask for references and .... if large amounts of money are involved.

7. Mistakes can be made despite .... preparation.

8. It is .... of a supplier to find out if a customer is trustworthy.

9. In case of accident or loss supplier and customer take out ....

10. At the end of the invoice the customer sees the .... amount payable.

2. What do they mean?
Welche Bedeutung haben die folgenden Ausdrücke?

Example:
Is a *pitfall*
  a. a kind of accident
  b. a case study? — **a**

1. Does *to despatch goods* mean
   a. to receive a delivery
   b. to send off an order?
2. Does *retention* mean
   a. keeping something
   b. giving something away?
3. Does *prudent* mean
   a. careful
   b. careless?
4. Does *conscientious* mean
   a. with a great deal of care and attention to detail
   b. knowing what you are doing is wrong?
5. Is a *prospective customer* someone who
   a. doesn't want to buy anything
   b. may want to buy something?
6. Is a *nagging question*
   a. something that continues to worry you
   b. an unimportant event?
7. Is a *letter of credit*
   a. another word for a reference from your employer
   b. a financial guarantee from your bank?
8. Is the word *funds*
   a. just another expression for money
   b. a special word for stocks and shares?
9. Does the word *property* mean
   a. something that is correct and legal
   b. something that belongs to someone?
10. Is a *carrier*
    a. a firm that only takes messages
    b. a transport firm?
11. Does the word *swift* mean
    a. fast
    b. slow
12. Does the word *purveyor* have the same meaning as
    a. purchaser
    b. seller

3. Match them up
Was bedeuten diese *Incoterms*? Ordnen Sie die Abkürzungen den richtigen Bedeutungen zu.

Example: 1 f

1. CIF
2. FAS
3. EXW
4. CIP
5. FOB
6. DES
7. DDP
8. DAF
9. FCA
10. CFR
11. DDU
12. CPT
13. DEQ

a. Ex works
b. Free carrier
c. Free alongside ship
d. Free on board
e. Cost and freight
f. Cost, insurance and freight
g. Carriage paid to …)
h. Carriage and insurance paid to …)
i. Delivered at frontier
j. Delivered ex ship
k. Delivered ex quay
l. Delivered duty unpaid
m. Delivered duty paid

4. Odd one out
Welches Wort passt nicht in die jweilige Wortgruppe? Unterstreichen Sie das jeweilige Wort.

1.
a. invoice
b. bill
c. discount
d. transfer
e. manufacturer

2.
a. freight
b. transport
c. goods
d. trustworthy
e. shipment

3.
a. loss
b. currency
c. snag
d. pitfall
e. risk

4.
a. gross amount
b. total net price
c. letter of credit
d. VAT
e. unit price

5. Crossword

Across
3 The dangers during transport (4)
5 The document asking for payment (7)
7 A document proving creditworthiness (9)
8 A kind of tax (3)
9 Goods being transported (7)

Down
1 International trade expression (8)
2 A special reduction in price (8)
4 Transport by sea (8)
6 An arrangement for later payment (6)

Reading for Understanding

1. Essential facts
Ordnen Sie die folgenden Begriffe den Wortgruppen zu.

a. Supplier	b. Payment	c. Customer	d. Transport
1. creditworthiness references letter of credit bank	2. incoterms method of shipment insurance freight	3. credit terms discount 30 days credit transfer	4. risk invoice manufacturer factory

1. .... 2. .... 3. .... 4. ....

2. Understanding the text
Versuchen Sie bitte folgende Fragen zu beantworten.

Example:
According to the text is a manufacturer likely to worry most about
    a. transport firms **b.** unknown customers?   *b*

1. What does the manufacturer have to balance against this worry
   a. the need to sell his product **b.** his wish for retention of ownership?
2. Checking a customer's creditworthiness is in the manufacturer's interest
   a. before despatching the goods **b.** while the goods are being shipped?
3. If there were ever a dispute, the use of Incoterms in the agreement would be
   a. helpful because courts rely on them **b.** unnecessary because they don't guarantee payment
4. *Incoterms* help business partners to state clearly and precisely
   a. who writes the invoice **b.** who is responsible for certain costs during transport?
5. If a supplier has to deal with a relatively unknown customer he might send the goods **a.** free of charge **b.** cash on delivery?
6. In principle, delivery terms EXW rather than FOB are
   a. more advantageous to the customer **b.** less of an advantage to the customer?
7. The offer of a discount is often
   a. only a friendly gesture **b.** designed to ensure payment is made quickly?
8. Which is cheaper for the supplier **a.** DDU **b.** DDP?
9. The total net price of the goods is **a.** the cost for all items less value added tax **b.** the cost including value added tax ?
10. On the invoice printed here where would the *incoterms* be included
    a. under "carrier/route" **b.** under "delivery terms"?

3. What do you think?
Woran müssten Lieferant und Kunde denken, wenn es um Lieferung und Rechnungsstellung geht? Wer von beiden hat in erster Linie folgende Gedanken?

	Supplier	Customer
Example: When will I get my money?	✓	☐
1. Can I trust them to deliver on time?	☐	☐
2. Can I trust him to pay on time?	☐	☐
3. Can I rely on good quality?	☐	☐
4. How favourable are the terms of credit?	☐	☐
5. What do I do if the goods arrive in faulty condition?	☐	☐
6. When does he want his money?	☐	☐
7. I insist on retention of ownerhip until the bill is paid.	☐	☐
8. I find this letter of credit from his bank very reassuring.	☐	☐
9. The discount they are offering of 5% is quite generous.	☐	☐
10. Do I have to pay VAT?	☐	☐

Over to you

1. Receiving an invoice
Setzen Sie nun wieder einmal Ihre Lesekompetenz in die Tat um und schreiben Sie eine Reklamation.

Imagine you have just received a bill for some new office furniture that you ordered from a firm in Britain.. Not only did the furniture arrive late but two items were missing and another was damaged. You agreed that all insurance and freight costs should be paid by the supplier CIF to your office address. Write to your supplier describing the goods and requesting immediate replacment.

2. Writing an invoice
Stellen Sie eine offizielle Rechnung aus. Machen Sie sich eine Fotokopie vom Rechnungsformular auf Seite 62 und ergänzen Sie sie nun mit den relevanten Daten, die Sie relativ frei erfinden dürfen.

Imagine you are the sales director of Black & White plc in Bristol, GB. You sell raincoats to a large chain of department stores in Germany. The latest delivery of 500 went out last week. Write the appropriate invoice.

Unit 7

Company Finance

Die Jahresversammlung der Aktionäre steht bevor oder eine Aufsichtsratssitzung oder die gefürchtete Prüfung vom Finanzamt! Ein Rechenschaftsbericht muss her, die Erfolgsbilanz muss nachgewiesen werden, die Aktivitäten des vergangenen Jahres müssen im Zusammenhang mit den Finanzen gesehen werden. Und hierfür bringt die jährliche Analyse mit harten Fakten immer eine klare Aussage, zeigt Tendenzen auf im Vergleich zum Vorjahr, gibt Aufschluss über Bereiche, wo im nächsten Jahr etwas getan werden muss. Dabei ist die Rechnung relativ simpel – auch wenn die Beschaffung der notwendigen Statistiken alles andere als leicht ist und das Ergebnis vielfältig interpretierbar. Um profitabel zu sein müssen die Einnahmen höher liegen als die Ausgaben! Nur sind das Bezeichnungen, die nicht immer im Vordergrund einer Berechnung stehen. Eine Vielzahl von Faktoren kann diese Berechnung beeinflussen.
Nun ist die Aufgabe der Prüfer genauso einfach: Ist der Betrieb gesund oder marode? Sind alle Posten berücksichtigt worden? Sind sie korrekt und logisch nachvollziehbar erfasst? Gibt es Widersprüche in der Statistik? Ist das Ergebnis glaubwürdig?
Sie wollen zunächst einmal prüfen, ob das Geschäftsjahr profitabel war, aber natürlich auch wie die Firma insgesamt dasteht mit allen Vermögenswerten und Verbindlichkeiten, die in einer Gewinn- und Verlustrechnung nicht ausdrücklich erwähnt werden.
Die beiden folgenden Beispielen zeigen – wie ein Jahresbericht zusammengestellt werden könnte. Ihre Aufgabe wird es sein, die Rolle des Prüfers zu übernehmen.

Before you read
Denken Sie kurz über das Management Ihrer eigenen Finanzen nach. Sind Sie „profitabel"? Oder bleibt bei Ihnen auch manchmal „viel Monat am Ende des Geldes" übrig? Welche Konsequenzen hätte ein solcher Zustand für eine Firma, die ständig Geld braucht für die Entwicklung neuer Projekte und daher auf die Unterstützung ihres Aufsichtsrates angewiesen ist? Machen Sie sich ein paar Notizen über das, was Sie in dem Fall für wichtig halten.

7

The Annual Audit

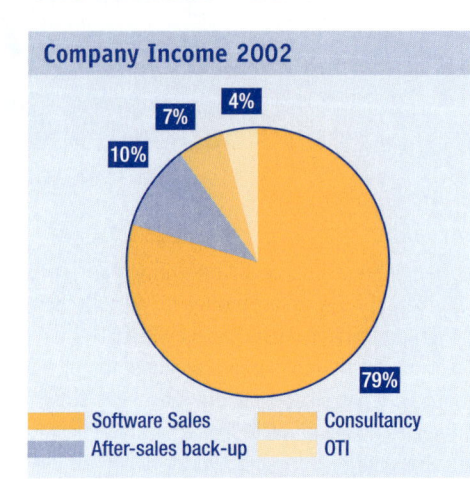

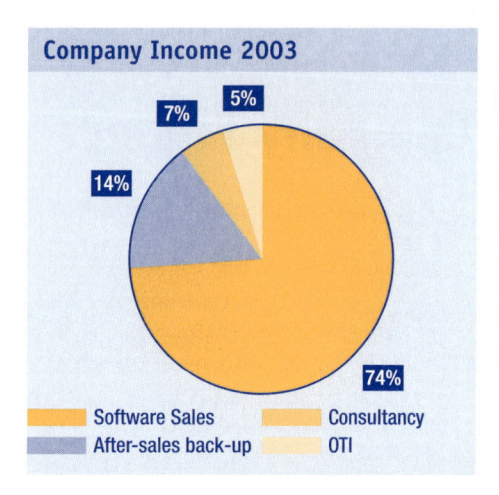

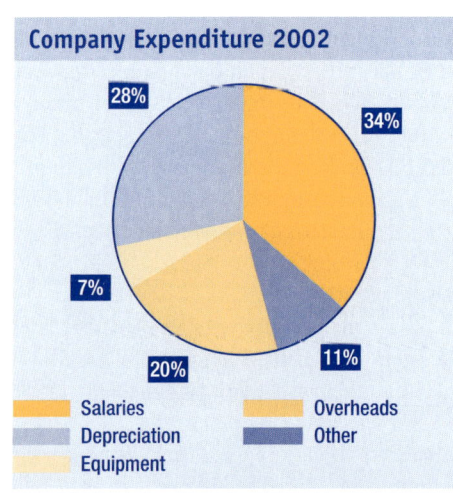

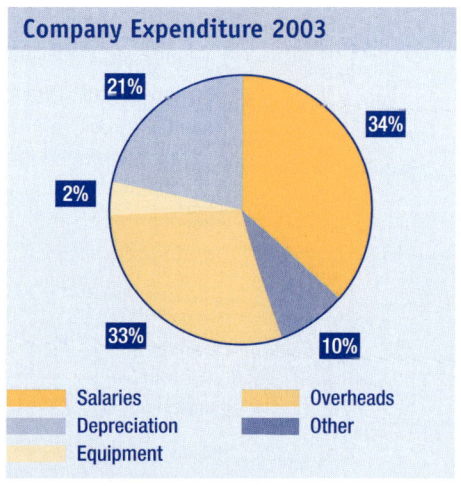

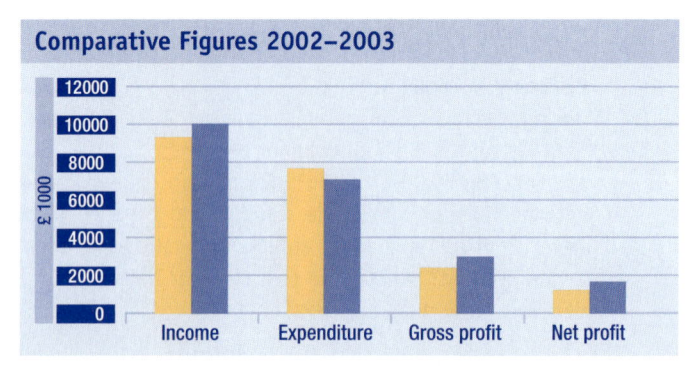

Company Income 2002

- 79% Software Sales
- 10% After-sales back-up
- 7% Consultancy
- 4% OTI

Company Income 2003

- 74% Software Sales
- 14% After-sales back-up
- 7% Consultancy
- 5% OTI

Company Expenditure 2002

- 34% Salaries
- 11% Overheads
- 28% Depreciation
- 20% Equipment
- 7% (Equipment)
- Other

(Salaries 34%, Overheads 11%, Depreciation 28%, Equipment 20%, Other 7%)

Company Expenditure 2003

- 34% Salaries
- 10% Overheads
- 21% Depreciation
- 33% Equipment
- 2% Other

Comparative Figures 2002–2003

(Bar chart, £ 1000s, showing Income, Expenditure, Gross profit, Net profit for 2002 and 2003)

72

Profit & Loss Account
for Joystix UK plc
for the year to December 31, 2003

Figures are in thousands of pounds sterling	2003	2002
Income		
Revenue from sales of computer software	7,285	7,490
Revenue from after-sales back-up	1,396	974
Revenue from consultancy service	728	716
Other trading income	487	385
Total annual turnover for the company	**9,896**	**9,565**
Expenditure		
Employees' salaries and other costs	2,570	2,380
Depreciation of fixed assets	788	766
New equipment	2,537	1,420
Maintenance and overheads	165	495
Other operational outlay	1,628	1,924
Total annual expenditure	**7,688**	**6,985**
Resulting operating profit	**2,208**	**2,580**
Net interest payable on bank loans	8	9
Profit before tax	2,200	2,571
Tax payable	440	514
Resulting annual profit after tax	**1,760**	**2,057**
Dividends to shareholders	528	476
Profit retained	1,232	1,581
Share earnings		
Profit divided by number of shares	30p	44p

Company Balance Sheet
for Joystix UK plc
for the year to December 31, 2003

Figures are in thousands of pounds sterling	2003	2002
Company's fixed assets:		
Starting capital	1,000	1,000
Property	500	480
Equipment	4,300	3,600
Investment sources	250	340
Total fixed assets	**6,050**	**5,420**
Company's current assets:		
Cash in hand	1,232	1,581
Stock	840	489
Monies owed to the company	598	195
Total current assets	**2,670**	**2,265**
Debts and monies payable by the company		
within one year	100	160
Interest and tax	448	523
Dividends	528	476
Total net current liabilities	**1,076**	**1,159**
Long-term debts	2,800	3,600
Total assets less total liabilities	**4,844**	**2,926**
Share capital	**1,000**	**785**
Total financial reserves	**5,844**	**3,711**

Vocabulary

annual *(adj.)*	jährlich	plc *(Public Limited Company) (n.)*	GmbH
audit *(n.)*	Buchprüfung		
Profit & Loss Account *(n.)*	Gewinn- und Verlustrechnung	sterling *(n.)*	britische Währung
		income *(n.)*	Einkommen, Einnahmen

revenue *(n.)*	Einkünfte, Einnahmen	**share** *(n.)*	Aktie
sales *(n.)*	Verkäufe	**earnings** *(n.)*	Ertrag, Verdienst
after-sales	Kundendienst	**to divide** *(v.)*	teilen
back-up *(n.)*		**balance sheet** *(n.)*	Bilanz, Bilanzaufstellung
consultancy service *(n.)*	Beratungsdienst	**starting capital** *(n.)*	Startkapital
other trading income *(n.)*	sonstige Einkünfte	**property** *(n.)*	hier: Immobilien
		equipment *(n.)*	hier: Inventar
turnover *(n.)*	Umsatz	**investment sources** *(n.)*	Kapitalanlagen
expenditure *(n.)*	Ausgaben		
employee *(n.)*	Arbeitnehmer(in), Angestellte(r)	**current assets** *(n.)*	Umlaufvermögen
		cash in hand *(n.)*	verfügbare Geldmittel
salary *(n.)*	Gehalt	**stock** *(n.)*	hier: Bestände
depreciation *(n.)*	Wertminderung	**monies** *(n.pl)*	Gelder, Beträge
fixed assets *(n.)*	festes Anlagevermögen	**to owe** *(v.)*	schulden
		monies owed to the company *(n.)*	Außenstände
equipment *(n.)*	Geräte, Einrichtung, Ausstattung	**debts** *(n.pl.)*	Schulden
maintenance *(n.)*	Instandhaltung	**monies payable by the company** *(n.)*	finanzielle Verpflichtungen, Verbindlichkeiten
operational outlay *(n.)*	Betriebskosten		
to result *(v.)*	sich ergeben	**current liabilities** *(n.)*	laufende Verbindlichkeiten
operating profit *(n.)*	Betriebsgewinn		
net *(adj.)*	Netto	**assets and liabilities** *(n)*	Aktiva und Passiva
interest *(n.)*	Zins		
payable *(adj.)*	zahlbar	**long-term debts** *(n)*	langfristige Verbindlichkeiten
bank loan *(n.)*	Bankdarlehen		
profit before tax *(n.)*	Gewinn vor Steuer	**share capital** *(n)*	Aktienkapital
dividend *(n.)*	Dividende	**financial reserves** *(n.*	Finanzreserven, Rücklagen, Gesamtvermögen
shareholder *(n.)*	Aktionär		
to retain *(v.)*	(ein)behalten		

Reading for Gist

1. Match them up
Welche der folgenden Posten gehört wohin? Zu den Einnahmen A) oder zu den Ausgaben B)?

	A) Income	B) Expenditure
Example: 1 B)	☐	✓
1. Costs for new equipment	☐	☐
2. Maintenance and overheads	☐	☐

3. Depreciation of assets ☐ ☐
4. Other trading income ☐ ☐
5. Revenue from sales ☐ ☐
6. Consultancy services ☐ ☐
7. Salaries ☐ ☐
8. Interest on bank loans ☐ ☐
9. Dividends ☐ ☐
10. Money from customer services ☐ ☐

2. Odd one out
Welche der folgenden Posten gehört *nicht* zur Gruppe? Bitte unterstreichen Sie das Wort.

1. *Assets*	2. *Liabilities*	3. *Income*	4. *Reserves*
a. property	a. stock	a. sales revenue	a. fixed assets
b. cash in hand	b. long-term debts	b. monies owed	b. profit
c. stock	c. tax	c. operational outlay	c. bank loan
d. debts	d. interest payments	d. other trading	d. share capital

3. True or false?
Welche der folgenden Aussagen treffen zu und welche nicht?

Example:	True	False
The annual audit takes place once a year.	✓	☐
1. The figure of 1,000 in the list is really one million pounds.	☐	☐
2. Income minus expenditure gives us the operational profit.	☐	☐
3. Employees salaries are part of the firm's trading income.	☐	☐
4. Long-term debts have to be paid within a year.	☐	☐
5. Maintenance and overheads are part of the firms fixed assets.	☐	☐
6. Share capital is what the firm pays out to shareholders.	☐	☐
7. The depreciation of fixed assets counts as expenditure.	☐	☐
8. The firm has several sources of revenue.	☐	☐
9. The firm made a profit in 2003.	☐	☐
10. The firm didn't make a profit in 2002.	☐	☐

Reading for Language

1. Match them up
Welche Wörter aus den zwei Listen passen zusammen?

Example: 1 g

1. fixed
2. computer
3. annual
4. trading
5. bank
6. share
7. starting
8. balance
9. cash
10. long-term

a. debts
b. sheet
c. loan
d. in hand
e. software
f. audit
g. assets
h. income
i. earnings
j. capital

2. The right meaning
Welche der zwei Bedeutungen ist richtig?

Example:
Is *revenue* another word for **a.** income? **b.** dividends?   `a`

1. Is *pounds sterling* just another way of expressing **a.** UK£? **b.** US dollars?
2. Does the term *liabilities* refer to **a.** monies the firm expects to receive? **b.** monies the firm is expected to pay out?
3. Is a *dividend* something the firm **a.** pays out to its shareholders? **b.** adds to its fixed assets?
4. What does *depreciation of assets* involve? **a.** money spent on new equipment **b.** loss in value of property
5. What does a *profit and loss account* contain? **a.** a list of what belongs to the firm **b.** a list of what the firm has earned and spent during the year
6. What does a *balance sheet* show? **a.** what the company is worth at the end of the year **b.** what the company's annual income is
7. What is meant by the term *turnover*? **a.** total income before any deductions are made **b.** the money gained when a firm is sold
8. Does the word *stock* mean **a.** products made by a firm but not yet sold? **b.** sales from products during the year?
9. What is *share capital*? **a.** the money given to shareholders by the firm **b.** the money paid into the firm by all the shareholders
10. What is meant by the term *investment sources*? **a.** money that will have to be paid to other customers **b.** money invested by the firm outside the business

3. Match them up
Versuchen Sie den folgenden Begriffen die richtigen Übersetzungen zuzuordnen.

Example: 1 h

1. profit & loss account
2. other trading income
3. profit before tax
4. turnover
5. operational outlay
6. liabilities
7. long-term debts
8. consultancy service
9. revenue
10. depreciation

a. Gewinn vor Steuer
b. Umsatz
c. Betriebskosten
d. Verbindlichkeiten
e. Beratungsdienst
f. Einkünfte
g. Wertminderung
h. Gewinn- und Verlustrechnung
i. langfristige Schulden
j. andere Einkünfte

4. Crossword

Across
1 Another word for valuable property (6)
4 The money you make on a deal (6)
6 Money the bank might give you (4)
8 Money you pay to the state (3)
9 All the money from sales (8)
10 The opposite of 4 across (4)

Down
2 Products that you haven't yet sold (5)
3 Money you pay out (6)
5 Money you pay on a bank loan. (8)
7 It happens once every year. (6)

Reading for Understanding

1. Essential facts
Welche der folgenden Aussagen stimmen und welche nicht?

	True	False
Example: All the firm's revenue in a year results in the annual turnover.	✓	☐
1. Without turnover there would be no profit.	☐	☐
2. Without profit there would be no dividend.	☐	☐
3. Turnover will vary but expenditure remains constant.	☐	☐

4. If you invest in new equipment, your expenditure will go down. ☐ ☐
5. Employees' salaries are usually a low expenditure item. ☐ ☐
6. Profit retained is the money that remains after tax has been paid. ☐ ☐
7. Share earnings are calculated by multiplying the profit by the
   number of shares. ☐ ☐
8. In general terms, fixed assets are money and current assets are property. ☐ ☐
9. Without liabilities a firm would be more profitable. ☐ ☐
10. A public limited company is owned by the managers. ☐ ☐

2. What does it really mean?
Versuchen Sie bitte folgende Fragen zu beantworten.

Example:
When a company is faced with an annual audit, does it mean that there's going to be **a.** a check on the company's performance? **b.** a public meeting to caculate taxes? | *a* |

1. When the shareholders are shown the company balance sheet, do they get to read **a.** a report on the managers' behaviour? **b.** a report of the financial status of the company?
2. When the manager says that the annual turnover was good, does he mean **a.** that the company has been sold again this year? **b.** that the money created from sales has increased?
3. What is meant by the depreciation of fixed assets? **a.** the theoretical loss in value of property and equipment **b.** the money paid for repairs to property and equipment
4. If your annual expenditure were to increase a lot, would you have **a.** saved a large amount on money unexpectedly? **b.** spent more money throughout the year than in the year before?
5. What might be the likely cause for a decrease in operational outlay? **a.** the company managed to work more efficiently **b.** employees became very lazy
6. If you discovered that this year your share earnings were higher than last year, would you **a.** be very pleased about the company's performance? **b.** be worried about the cost of new equipment?
7. If current liabilities were higher than the company's income would you conclude that **a.** the firm's property was losing value? **b.** the company had too many bank loans to repay?
8. Which current assets are usually the most useful to a company? **a.** remaining stock? **b.** cash in hand?
9. If share capital increases what has happened during the year? **a.** the number of shares bought by shareholders has increased **b.** the annual dividend was lower
10. If the cash in hand was much lower than the value of stock, would you assume **a.** that sales had been lower than expected? **b.** that the price of new equipment had risen?

3. What do you think?

Versuchen Sie nun die beiden Berichte zu interpretieren, indem Sie folgende Fragen beantworten.

Example:
Why do you think turnover increased despite lower revenue from the sale of software? **a.** Because maintenance costs were lower. **b.** Because more was earned from consultancy and customer care services. — *b*

1. Why do you think the value of equipment as fixed assets increased in 2003? **a.** Because the firm had invested quite heavily in new equipment. **b.** Because maintenance costs decreased.
2. Why do you think share capital increased in 2003? **a.** Because people bought more shares. **b.** Because long-term debts became less.
3. Why do you think the figure for "stock" as current assets was higher in 2003? **a.** Because production of software packages was higher but not all had been sold. **b.** Because there was less cash in hand.
4. Why were financial reserves higher in 2003? **a.** Because assets increased and liabilities decreased. **b.** Because there was a decrease in operating profit.
5. Why do you think long-term debts decreased in 2003? **a.** Because there was more money owed to the company. **b.** Because the firm was able to pay off more of the bank loans.
6. Why do you think the share earnings were lower in 2003? **a.** Because more shares were sold and profits were down. **b.** Because share capital decreased as well.

Over to you

1. Checking the figures

Lesen Sie die beiden Berichte noch einmal. Versuchen Sie nun folgende Fragen zu beantworten:

Having studied the reports carefully, please answer these questions:

1. Is the firm of Joystix profitable? Say why or why not.
2. Is their financial base a sound one? Say why or why not.
3. Does their source of income seem reliable? Say why or why not.
4. Where do you think they could save on expenditure next year?
5. What trends can you see?

2. Write a short report

Schreiben Sie einen kurzen, klar und einfach formulierten Bericht für die Aktionäre.

Having analysed the two sets of figures, write a short report in simple language for the shareholders meeting telling the shareholders what has happened during the past year and explaining the figures in the lists.

Stock Markets

Unit 8

Der Traum eines jeden kleinen oder großen „Unternehmers" – steigende Aktienkurse, satte Gewinne. Was sich hinter den Kulissen der Aktienbörsen abspielt, welche Gefahren und Risiken sich dort für den Spekulanten verbergen, wie das Zusammenspiel von Erfolg und Hoffnung, Empfehlung und Vertrauen, versprochener Dividende und Risikobereitschaft das Verhalten der Investoren lenkt und prägt, das sind alles Faktoren, die einerseits durch unsere Wirtschaft herbeigeführt werden, die aber andererseits auch die Wirtschaft insgesamt beeinflussen können. Um diese Wechselwirkung geht es im folgenden Text aus einer amerikanischen Zeitung.

In diesem Zeitungsartikel aus der Weltmetropole New York wird darüber berichtet, welche Faktoren für Ebbe und Flut in der Welt der Börsenmakler und Investoren verantwortlich sein könnten.

Before you read
Geheimquelle für schlaue Rechner oder Lottospiel für Besserverdienende? Wie stehen Sie zum Aktienkauf oder zum Vertrauen auf Wertpapiere, Festgelder oder Fonds? Schreiben Sie zunächst eine Liste von Plus- und Minuspunkten, die man bedenken müsste.

Wall Street Special

Bears Beat Bulls

More bad news from the stock markets and the reasons for it

from Peter Jones in New York

For two weeks now the bears have been running wild on Wall Street. Share prices have been dropping dramatically every morning before rallying by midday as the wave of selling diminished and the major market indexes Dow Jones, Nasdaq, Hang Seng tried to bounce back.

The reasons seem to be clear enough: not only has American consumer spending slowed down but news of insider-dealing and suspect accounting procedures have served to undermine confidence severely. News of another terrorist bomb has just served to compound the issue. The Dow Jones Industrial Average was 120 points down on the previous week, the Nasdaq managed a slight recovery but ended the week 4% lower and the Hang Seng dipped briefly below an all-time low before ending at 2% below the seasonal average. Hardest hit have been airline stocks but reports suggest that selling cell-phone services has become tough work, subscriber growth falling far short of projected targets.

The expert view seems to be that the three major pillars of the old bull market – technology, media and telecom – have been broken into smaller pieces and redistributed. It will depend on how old companies adjust and new companies manage what is still seen essentially as a growth market. However, it seems the lows are going to continue until the last remaining excesses have been removed from the market and the professionals have returned to being the "honest brokers" consumers and investors can trust.

Meanwhile in Europe on the Frankfurt, Paris and London stock exchanges, things post 9.11. don't look better. Dax and FTSE indexes show poor recovery trends and brokers are having great problems recommending stock in any branch of the travel industry too dependent on air travel. Gilt edge stocks and government bonds seem safe enough though.

An interesting trend is the British involvement on Frankfurt's Eurex futures

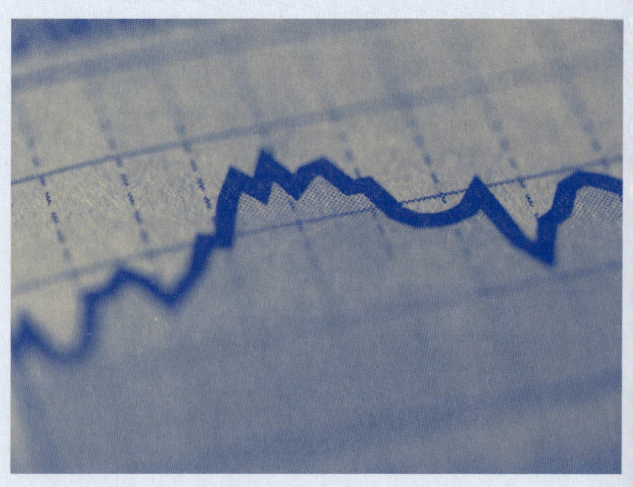

Wall Street Special

exchange. A report published this week shows that UK investors were resonsible for 40% of contracts compared with German investors' 28%. Five years ago Germany had 81% of business and Britain only 7%.

The introduction of screen-based trading at Eurex and other exchanges has made the geographical base less important. Following the move from floor-trading to remote trading from terminals most of the trades now originate in other countries.

Meanwhile back stateside the US has to face a crisis. Corporate scandals, alleged fraud and cover-ups, accusations of tax evasion, dodgy accounting, the invention of fictitious subscribers at cable TV companies, Wall Street analysts artificially supporting the price of shares they thought were worthless have all combined to undermine confidence in American business. And naturally enough speculation about business ethics leads to negative speculation on the stock markets – the bears beat the bulls.

Vocabulary

stock market *(n.)*	Aktienmarkt, Börse	to undermine *(v.)*	unterminieren
bears *(n.)*	Baisse (Ausdruck für fallende Aktienpreise, negative Entwicklung)	confidence *(n.)*	Vertrauen
		severely *(adj.)*	ernsthaft
		to compound *(v.)*	verstärken
bulls *(n.)*	Hausse (Ausdruck für steigende Aktienpreise, positive Entwicklung)	issue *(n.)*	Angelegenheit
		to dip *(v.)*	sinken, nach unten gehen
share prices *(n.)*	Aktienpreise	all-time *(adj.)*	historisch, Rekord-
to rally *(v.)*	sich erholen	seasonal *(adj.)*	saisonbedingt
to diminish *(v.)*	verringern, mindern	airline stocks *(n.)*	Aktien der Fluggesellschaften
Dow Jones *(n.)*	amerikanischer Preisindex	cell-phone *(n.)*	Mobiltelefon, Handy
		subscriber *(n.)*	Teilnehmer, Kunde
Nasdaq *(n.)*	amerikanischer Preisindex	growth *(n.)*	Wachstum
		target *(n.)*	Ziel
Hang Seng *(n.)*	Hong Kong Preisindex	pillar *(n.)*	Säule
to bounce back *(v.)*	zurückspringen	bull market *(n.)*	Konjunktur, postiver Trend
consumer spending *(n.)*	Verbraucherausgaben		
insider dealing *(n.)*	(illegale) Insider-Geschäfte	to redistribute *(v.)*	neu verteilen
		to adjust *(v.)*	justieren
suspect *(adj.)*	verdächtig	the lows *(n.)*	Tiefpunkte
accounting *(n.)*	Buchführung	excesses *(n.)*	Exzesse
procedure *(n.)*	Verfahren	honest *(adj.)*	ehrlich, redlich

broker (n.)	Kaufmann, (Börsen)Makler	screen-based (adj.)	bildschirmgesteuert, online
consumer (n.)	Verbraucher	floor-trading (n.)	Geschäfte direkt an der Börse selbst
stock exchange (n.)	Börse		
post (adj.)	nach	remote (adj.)	fern(gesteuert)
Dax (n.)	deutscher Preisindex	stateside (adv.)	in den Staaten (USA)
FTSE (n.)	britischer Preisindex	corporate scandal (n.)	Industrieskandal
index (n.)	Index, Verzeichnis	alleged (adj.)	angeblich
recovery (n.)	Erholung	fraud (n.)	Betrug
to recommend (v.)	empfehlen	cover-up (n.)	Vertuschung
branch (n.)	Branche	tax evasion (n.)	Steuerhinterziehung
gilt edge stocks (n.)	Regierungsfonds	dodgy (adj. infml.)	verdächtig, suspekt
government bonds (n.)	Regierungswertpapiere	fictitious (adj.)	erfunden, nicht wirklich
involvement (n.)	Beteiligung, Verwicklung		
		subscriber (n.)	Kunde, Teilnehmer
futures (n.)	Termingeschäfte, Futures	artificially (adv.)	künstlich
		worthless (adj.)	wertlos
Eurex (n.)	Frankfurter Online-Börse	confidence (n.)	Vertrauen
		speculation (n.)	Spekulation
investors (n.)	Investoren	ethics (n.)	Ethik

Reading for Gist

1. True or false?
Sind diese Aussagen richtig oder falsch?

Example:	True	False
"Bulls" and "bears" are special expressions used to describe market trends.	☑	☐

1. Share prices have been rising recently.
2. The Dow Jones index indicates market trends.
3. Several events have influenced the markets negatively.
4. Trends in Europe have been much better.
5. British investors have been using a German stock exchange.
6. A lot of trading is now done by computer online.
7. The American economy is facing a crisis.
8. Several scandals in industry have helped to calm investors´ nerves.
9. Some analysts in Wall Street have been supporting the wrong shares.
10. „Bears Beat Bulls" means that economic trends are positive.

2. Match them up
Welche der folgenden Aussagen passen zusammen?

Example: 10 a
There has been speculation about business ethics = People are worried that business is dishonest

1. The bears have been running wild.
2. Major market indexes have been trying to bounce back.
3. Consumer spending has slowed down.
4. Consumer confidence has been undermined.
5. The Hang Seng reached an all-time low.
6. Hardest hit have been airline stocks.
7. Screen-based trading has made the geographical base less important.
8. Alleged fraud and cover-ups have combined with other factors.
9. There have been accusations of tax evasion.
10. There has been speculation about business ethics.

a. People are worried that business is dishonest.
b. Shares in airline companies have fallen.
c. Accusations of cheating have accompanied other reasons.
d. There has been a drastic decline in market trends.
e. The share index in Hong Kong fell to a record low point.
f. Working online has made the distance between countries seem smaller.
g. Some of the most important share markets have tried to recover.
h. People are now being more careful with their money.
i. Some people are suspected of cheating on paying the government.
j. People have become very uncertain about the economy.

Reading for Language

1. Fill in the gap
Ergänzen Sie folgende Sätze mit dem richtigen Wort oder Ausdruck.

Example:
Share .... have been dropping dramatically.
a. costs   b. prices   *b*

1. Confidence has been undermined by ....
   a. consumer spending.   b. insider-dealing.
2. News of another bomb has served to .... the issue.
   a. diminish   b. compound

3. Subscriber growth in cell-phone services has fallen short of .... targets.
   a. projected
   b. previous

4. The major .... of the old market have been broken into smaller pieces.
   a. stocks
   b. pillars

5. .... are having problems recommending stock in the travel industry.
   a. Subscribers
   b. Brokers

6. The lows will continue until the .... have been removed from the market.
   a. excesses
   b. exchanges

7. There has been a distinct move to screen-based .... from terminals.
   a. speculation
   b. trading

8. Some cable TV companies invented .... customers.
   a. fictitious
   b. worthless

2. Odd one out
Welches Wort oder welcher Ausdruck passt nicht zu den anderen in der Gruppe?

1	2	3	4
a) broker	a) growth	a) Dax	a) future
b) customer	b) target	b) FTSE	b) low
c) investor	c) trading	c) Nasdaq	c) bull
d) subscriber	d) fraud	d) gilt edge	d) bear

1. .... 2. .... 3. .... 4. ....

3. The right meaning
Welche Bedeutung haben die folgenden Sätze?

Example:
Does *running wild* mean
a. out of control?
b. exciting?
a

1. Does *rallying* mean
   a. getting weaker?
   b. getting stonger?

2. Does *to compound the issue* mean
   a. to make things easier?
   b. to make things more difficult?

3. Does *alleged fraud* mean
   a. worthless shares?
   b. suspicion of stealing money?

4. Are *fictitious subscribers*
   a. imaginary people?
   b. real customers?

5. Is *a corporate scandal*
  a. an industrial crime?   **b.** a shocking event involving everyone?
6. Does *to invest in futures* mean
  a. to trust in government policy?   **b.** to invest in the promise of later business?
7. Are *gilt edge stocks*
  a. attractively designed documents?   **b.** bonds issued by the government?
8. Does the term *business ethics* refer to
  a. a moral code of behaviour in business?
  b. international politics?

4. Translate
Bitte übersetzen Sie folgende Ausdrücke ins Deutsche.

Example:
stock exchange – *Börse*

1. confidence   ....

2. growth   ....

3. cell-phone   ....

4. broker   ....

5. consumer   ....

6. suspect   ....

7. accounting   ....

8. to recommend   ....

9. honest   ....

10. tax evasion   ....

8

5. Crossword

Across
2 The money you pay to the government. (3)
5 Someone who buys and sells shares for you. (6)
6 Statistics showing market trends. (5)
7 A word for market confidence. (5)

Down
1 Positive thinking. (10)
2 Aim or goal. (6)
3 Without any value. (9)
4 Someone who wants to buy shares. (8)
7 A word for market pessimism. (5)

Reading for Understanding

1. Essential facts

Lesen Sie bitte die folgende Liste von Faktoren, die die ökonomische Situation charakterisieren. Ordnen Sie die Begriffe entweder den Ursachen oder den Auswirkungen zu.

Example:
There has been a general lack of confidence on the US market. ☑ **Ursache**   ☐ **Auswirkung**

	Ursache	Auswirkung
1. news of insider-dealing	☐	☐
2. suspect accounting procedures	☐	☐
3. selling cell-phone services more difficult	☐	☐
4. terrorist activities	☐	☐
5. no trust in airlines	☐	☐
6. corporate scandals	☐	☐
7. alleged fraud and cover ups	☐	☐
8. tax evasion	☐	☐
9. companies need to adjust	☐	☐
10. invention of fictitious subscribers	☐	☐
11. artificial support of worthless shares	☐	☐
12. negative speculation on the stock markets	☐	☐

2. Understanding the text
Welche Antwort ist richtig?

Example:
What is the difference between bulls and bears?
a. bulls indicates positive and bears negative market trends
b. bears are a sign of economic recovery, bulls a sign of recession → *a*

1. According to the text, are trends in Europe better than in America?
   a. no **b.** yes
2. What is the main reason for poor recovery trends in Europe?
   a. reports of insider-dealing
   b. the travel industry suffering due to the attack on the World Trade Center
3. What changes have been taking place in Europe?
   a. an improvement in business ethics
   b. the introduction od screen-based trading on stock exchanges
4. Who seem to be more eager to invest in Frankfurt?
   a. the Germans **b.** the British
5. What needs to be done in the US?
   a. excesses need to be removed from the market
   b. professionals need to be replaced
6. What do the experts think has happened to the old market?
   a. its major pillars have been broken up **b.** investors lost interest in it
7. When will US investors regain their trust?
   a. when subscriber growth rises **b.** when the honest bokers return
8. What do market indexes like the Dow Jones show?
   a. trends in the economic climate **b.** targets for customer spending
9. What is the name of the German price index?
   a. FTSE **b.** Dax
10. What is the difference between screen-based trading and floor-trading?
    a. Floor-trading is in the stock exchange building, screen-based can be anywhere
    b. The broker needs to stand up for floor-trading, he has to sit down for screen-based

3. What do you think?
Beantworten Sie diese Fragen:

Example:
Why do you think share prices dropped?
a. Because confidence has been undermined. ✓
b. Because more shares were sold. ☐

1. Why do you think confidence in the markets was undermined?
   a. Because consumer spending went up ☐
   b. Because of reports of dishonesty ☐

2. Why do you think airline stocks were hit hardest?
   a. Because of the attacl on the World Trade Center ☐
   b. Because of the rising price of airline fares ☐

3. Why do you think it will take time for the markets to recover?
   a. Because the Dow Jones Average is down. ☐
   b. Because consumers won't trust them until brokers prove their honesty. ☐

4. Why do you think the travel industry has been hit so badly?
   a. Because no one wants to fly after the 9.11. disaster. ☐
   b. Because cell phone sales have dropped. ☐

5. Why do you think the Eurex exchange has been successful?
   a. Because it makes trading easier between countries. ☐
   b. Because it is based in Frankfurt. ☐

Over to you

1. What should I invest in?
Stellen Sie sich vor, Sie haben 100.000 Euro als Investitionskapital. Sie rufen Ihre Bank oder Ihren Börsenmakler an und stellen eine Liste von Fragen.

What questions will you need to ask? Write a list of all the points you would like explained before you decide to invest your money.

2. Check the Internet
Rufen Sie Nasdaq (oder einen der anderen internationalen Preisindexe oder elektronischen Börsen) per Suchmaschine im Internet auf.

Using the information you find on the Internet write a short report describing the services that are offered.

Unit 9

Takeovers

Die Zeitungen sind immer voll davon: Eine neue Firmenehe wird geschlossen, ein Riese schluckt einen Zwerg, ein anscheinend marodes Unternehmen bittet um Hilfe ... mal ist es gewollt, mal hat man keine Wahl, mal keine Chance gegen die aggressive Expansionspolitik anderer. Hinter den Schlagzeilen verbergen sich wirtschaftliche Schicksale, moderne Romane der Firmengeschichte. Dass sich dahinter oft eine harte Wahrheit verborgen hält, eine alte Familienfirma vielleicht, die es nicht mehr geschafft hat zu modernisieren, falsche Managementstrategien, die das geplante Budget nicht einhalten ... oder Firmen, die sich in der Euphorie einer früheren Stunde übernommen haben, ... oder neue Märkte, die den Zugriff mit vereinten Kräften zum Vorteil beider Partner versprechen. All das sind Gründe für Veränderungen in der breiten Landschaft einer Ökonomie, die sich vom Unternehmertum ernähren muss. Allerdings muss man unbedingt zwischen Übernahme und Kooperation differenzieren. Ein *joint venture* ist kein *merger*, und ein *merger* ist kein *takeover* ...

Die Unterschiede und auch das, was sich dort im Hintergrund abspielen könnte, lesen Sie in den folgenden drei Kurztexten, die verschiedene Stadien im möglichen Verlauf einer Übernahme darstellen.

Before you read
Denken Sie kurz über die möglichen Gründe für eine Kooperation oder eine Übernahme zwischen zwei Firmen nach. Schreiben Sie eine kurze Liste dieser Gründe und der möglichen Vor- und Nachteile.

The Multi-Play File

HIGHLY CONFIDENTIAL

Memo
From: John Grisedale
To: Susanne Bradshaw
Date: 15th May 2003

Ref. Multi-Play

Susanne,
Confirming our telephone conversation of this morning. I'd like you to prepare a report on Multi-Play Software for our next Board Meeting at the end of June. As you know we are looking to expand our business in the youth market where Multi-Play have been strong in the past and I have it on good authority that they are looking for a buyer. And that several other firms are showing interest.
However, discretion is essential at this stage. It is important that we don't show our hand too early. The matter is highly confidential, as I am sure you will appreciate. No one at Multi-Play is to be contacted as yet.
Please let me have your report by June 10th so that we may discuss it before the meeting.

Thanks and good luck,

John

HIGHLY CONFIDENTIAL

Merger Proposal
Assessment report on *Multi-Play Software*

To: John Grisedale CEO
Joystix UK plc

From: Susanne Bradshaw, Finance Director

Date: June 9, 2003

As requested in your Memo dated 15th May 2003 here is my report on Multi-Play with a provisional assessment of what I see as the advantages and disadvantages of a possible merger and recommendations for further investigation before we commit ourselves.

The information I have managed to obtain comes from several sources.
- Multi-Play's own publicity material, prospectuses, catalogues etc.
- Their annual business and financial report.
- Their website homepage
- An independent confidential study from Andrews Business Consultants.

Multi-Play is a family firm founded 30 years ago by Managing Director Robin Kennedy, now in his seventies. The firm has been run for the past five years by his son Brian as CEO. Rumour has it that they no longer see eye to eye.
The firm has its head office in Manchester and ten branches throughout the north of England with a total staff of 420. Industrial relations have in general been good, but there is some unrest at the moment due to what is seen as an uncertain future.
Turnover last year was estimated at 60 million pounds. But profits were down for the fourth year in succession. Due to the relatively large number of staff and not knowing what assets are available, it is difficult to assess the firm´s real financial standing.

Reasons for possible merger
We would be acquiring
- a well-established, highly respected firm with branches in our vicinity and area of operation
- Their market outlets would supplement our own. Their range of products covers extra market niches we have not yet been able to reach. Some product does, however, overlap.
- a good clientele, a skilled workforce, a system of good communications
- By combining these with our own we could reach short-term expansion with minimal investment and loss of time and resources.
- The firm does not seem to be in particular or acute financial difficulty

Reasons against
- We must expect opposition from the unions if staff cuts are involved.
- Growth prospects on their present line of products is limited.
- Being a family firm their management style differs considerably from ours.
- We should foresee problems in reaching understanding with the present CEO.

My recommendation would be as follows:
I feel it is rather too early to commit ourselves.
- We should have an in-depth feasibility study prepared.
- We should then set up a meeting here to discuss the possibility amongst ourselves.
- We should not neglect to look into merger possibilities with other firms.
- We should then, if still interested, set up a meeting with Multi-Play to discuss possibilities and finances
- We would need a consultant PR specialist to advise should the outcome be positive

Susanne Bradshaw

The Daily Trumpet

Takeover Rumours Confirmed

The board of Multi-Play Software, the well-known Manchester-based family firm will meet on Monday next to consider an expected takeover bid from Joystix, their Manchester-based rivals for the future market in tailor-made management software for small businesses.

According to sources as yet undisclosed, Joystix is preparing a bid in the region of 20 million pounds for a majority holding. The MP board is expected to approve the bid with an announcement made to that effect later in the week.

If the deal goes ahead, it will mark the end of an era and effectively of a traditional family business, but the start of new opportunities for both firms under combined management. For Joystix this is the latest acquisition in what is now a fairly long line of similar mergers and takeovers initiated by Joystix's forward-looking CEO, John Grisedale. Share prices are expected to rise as a result of what experts see as a very positive development for both companies. The future now looks even brighter, even though the assimilation of workforces may cause some disruption on the union front if job losses are involved. „We have made our offer, but whatever happens now, we will continue to create new valuable synergies in our company to cater for new targets in an expanding market with international outlets," said John Grisedale. Next week promises to give him the added resources he has been looking for.

Vocabulary

confidential *(adj.)*	vertraulich
to confirm *(v.)*	bestätigen
to prepare *(v.)*	vorbereiten
board meeting *(n.)*	Direktorenkonferenz
to expand *(v.)*	expandieren
youth market *(n.)*	Jugendmarkt
to have it on good authority	aus verlässlicher Quelle wissen
discretion *(n.)*	Diskretion
stage *(n.)*	hier: Stadium
to show one's hand *(v.)*	seine Karten zeigen, auf den Tisch legen
matter *(n.)*	Angelegenheit
to appreciate *(v.)*	hier: verstehen
merger *(n.)*	Zusammenfluss, Fusion
proposal *(n.)*	Vorschlag, Angebot
assessment *(n.)*	Einschätzung
CEO *(n.* Abkürzung Chief Executive Officer)	Firmenleiter
finance director *(n.)*	Finanzdirektor
provisional *(adj.)*	vorläufig
advantage *(n.)*	Vorteil
disadvantage *(n.)*	Nachteil
recommendation *(n.)*	Empfehlung
investigation *(n.)*	Untersuchung
to commit oneself *(v.)*	sich festlegen

to manage to (v.)	jmd gelingen, es schaffen	well-established (adj.)	gut etabliert
to obtain (v.)	bekommen	highly respected (adj.)	hoch geschätzt
source (n.)	Quelle	vicinity (n.)	Nähe
publicity material (n.)	Werbematerialien	area of operation (n.)	Absatzgebiet, Tätigkeitsbereich
prospectus (n.)	Prospekt		
annual (adj.)	jährlich	market outlet (n.)	Marktbereich
independent (adj.)	unabhängig	to supplement (v.)	ergänzen
study (n.)	Studie	range (n.)	Angebot
consultant (n.)	Fachberater, Beratungsdienst	market niche (n.)	Marktnische
to found (v.)	gründen	to overlap (v.)	überlappen
managing director (n.)	Generaldirektor	clientele (n.)	Klientel
		skilled (adj.)	mit Fachausbildung
in his seventies	in den Siebzigern, schon über siebzig	workforce (n.)	Mitarbeiterstab
		short-term (adj.)	kurzfristig
to run (v.)	hier: leiten	expansion (n.)	Vergrößerung, Ausdehnung, Expansion
rumour (n.)	Gerücht		
rumour has it (v.)	man munkelt	investment (n.)	Investition
no longer (adv.)	nicht mehr	loss (n.)	Verlust
to see eye to eye (v.)	sich verstehen	resources (n.)	Ressourcen
head office (n.)	Zentralbüro, Zentrale	particular (adj.)	besondere
branch (n.)	Niederlassung	acute (adj.)	akut
staff (n.)	Mitarbeiter und Mitarbeiterinnen	to expect (v.)	erwarten
		opposition (n.)	Opposition
industrial relations (n.)	Betriebsverhältnisse	unions (n.)	Gewerkschaften
		staff cuts (n.)	Kündigungen, Entlassungen
unrest (n.)	Unruhe		
due to (prep.)	aufgrund, wegen	growth prospects (n.)	Wachstumserwartungen
future (n.)	Zukunft		
turnover (n.)	Umsatz	present (adj.)	gegenwärtig
to estimate (v.)	schätzen	to differ (v.)	sich unterscheiden
profits (n.)	Gewinn	considerably (adv.)	beträchtlich
be down (adv.)	hier: niedriger ausfallen	to foresee (v.)	voraussehen
		to reach (v.)	erreichen
in succession (adv.)	hintereinander	as follows (adv.)	wie folgt
assets (n.)	Vermögen, Finanzreserven	to commit oneself (v.)	sich festlegen
available (adj.)	verfügbar	in-depth (adj.)	gründlich
to assess (v.)	(ein)schätzen	feasibility study (n.)	Machbarkeitsstudie
standing (n.)	Ruf, Reputation	to set up (v.)	arrangieren
to acquire (v.)	acquirieren, erwerben	to neglect to (v.)	etwas nicht tun, unterlassen, vergessen

9

to look into *(v.)*	untersuchen	to mark *(v.)*	markieren, zeichnen
consultant *(n.)*	Fachberater, Beratungsdienst	opportunity *(n.)*	Gelegenheit
		acquisition *(n.)*	Kauf, Übernahme
PR *(n.)*	Öffentlichkeitsarbeit	fairly *(adv.)*	hier: ziemlich
outcome *(n.)*	Ergebnis	to initiate *(v.)*	einleiten
takeover *(n.)*	Übernahme	forward-looking *(adj.)*	vorwärts schauend, progressiv denkend
Manchester-based *(adj.)*	mit Sitz in Manchester	share *(n.)*	Aktie
takeover bid *(n.)*	Kaufversuch	assimilation *(n.)*	Assimilierung, Integration
rival *(n.)*	Rivale		
tailor-made *(adj.)*	maßgeschneidert	workforce *(n.)*	Mitarbeiter(stab)
undisclosed *(adj.)*	geheim	disruption *(n.)*	Störung
in the region of *(prep.)*	ungefähr, nahezu	on the union front *(adv.)*	auf Seiten der Gewerkschaften
majority holding *(n.)*	Mehrheitsanteil	job losses *(n.)*	Arbeitsplatzverluste, Entlassungen
to approve *(v.)*	bewilligen		
announcement *(n.)*	Pressemeldung	synergy *(n.)*	Synergie
to that effect *(adv.)*	entsprechend	target *(n.)*	Ziel
deal *(n.)*	Geschäft, Handel	outlet *(n.)*	Absatzmöglichkeit
to go ahead *(v.)*	durchgehen, gelingen	added *(adj.)*	zusätzlich

Reading for Gist

1. Match them up
Welche Satzteile passen zueinander?

Example: 1 h

1. I have it on good authority
2. Discretion is essential
3. The information obtained
4. Multi-Play is a family firm
5. Turnover last year
6. Profits were down
7. Their market outlets
8. We could reach short-term expansion
9. We must expect opposition
10. It is rather too early

a. founded 30 years ago.
b. was estimated at 60 million pounds.
c. from the unions.
d. would supplement our own.
e. with minimal investment.
f. to commit ourselves.
g. comes from several sources.
h. that they are looking for a buyer.
i. for the fourth year in succession.
j. at this stage.

Reading for Language

1. What does it mean?
Welche Bedeutung passt am besten?

Example:
Does *highly confidential* mean **a.** we're all very sure of ourselves? **b.** it should be kept secret? | *b* |

1. Does *showing our hand* mean **a.** asking for time to think? **b.** revealing our plans?
2. Does *not seeing eye to eye* mean **a.** preparing separate reports? **b.** not agreeing with one another?
3. If *industrial relations* are good, does it mean **a.** that there is unrest in the factory? **b.** that employer and employees agree?
4. If a product is *tailor-made* for a market, does it mean **a.** it fits requirements exactly? **b.** it required a specialist designer?
5. If a new *synergy* is created, does it mean **a.** that combined management produces positive results? **b.** that resources are lost?

Reading for Understanding

1. Essential facts
Welche dieser Aussagen stimmen und welche nicht?

	True	False
Example: John Grisedale wants to keep his plans a secret at first.	✓	☐
1. Susanne Bradshaw produces a generally unfavourable report.	☐	☐
2. Even though turnover seems high, Multi-Play's profits are decreasing.	☐	☐
3. Susanne Bradshaw recommends immediate takeover discussions.	☐	☐
4. If Joystix obtain a majority holding, they will effectively control Multi-Play.	☐	☐
5. John Grisedale later makes a statement to the press about the merger.	☐	☐

2. What does it really mean?
Versuchen Sie nun folgende Fragen zu beantworten.

Example:
Does "Here is my provisional assessment" mean **a.** My report will need additions later? **b.** My report is final? | *a* |

1. Does "their market outlets would supplement our own" mean **a.** the markets can be combined? **b.** the markets are identical?

2. Does having "an in-depth feasibility study prepared" mean **a.** having further talks with the Multi-Play board? **b.** organizing a more detailed examination of the possibilities and consequences?
3. What is a "consultant PR specialist"? **a.** an expert in dealing with the press and public opinion **b.** an advisor on industrial relations
4. If the MP board is "expected to approve the bid", does this mean **a.** there will be opposition to the merger? **b.** everyone has finally agreed?
5. If there is "an assimilation of workforces", does this mean **a.** that staff from both firms will be re-integrated into the the new structure? **b.** that all staff will remain in their present jobs?

3. What do you think?
Wie interpretieren Sie die Aussagen im Text?

Example:
Why do you think John Grisedale wants to keep things confidential at first?
a. because other firms might find out and make a better offer first **b.** because he's not sure of what he's doing

a

1. Why does Susanne Bradshaw recommend further investigation? **a.** because Multi-Play is too highly respected in the market **b.** because she hasn´t been able to find out the firm's real financial standing
2. Why do you think John Grisedale is interested in Multi-Play? **a.** because it's a family firm **b.** because he wants to expand his business
3. What does John Grisedale tell the press? **a.** that a merger is necessary because of markets getting smaller **b.** that together the two firms will be stronger than before
4. Why do you think the MP board will approve the bid? **a.** because it will secure their future **b.** because they are afraid of the unions
5. Why do you think experts view the merger as a very positive development? **a.** because they no longer see eye to eye with family businesses **b.** because under combined management the firm will be able to cater for wider markets

Over to you

PR Report
Beweisen Sie nun, dass Sie alles richtig gelesen und die Situation verstanden haben. Schreiben Sie einen kurzen Bericht für die Presse.

Imagine you represent the firm of Public Relations Consultants called in by Joystix to handle the subsequent press releases. Write a short report for the press from the Joystix' point of view outlining the events and the advantages for all concerned, being careful not to damage Joystix' image.

Unit 10

Trade Fairs

Zur Marketingstrategie eines jeden Produktherstellers gehört sicherlich der öffentliche Auftritt und die öffentliche Ausstellung seiner Waren. Eine Handelsmesse mit ihrem zentralen Standort und ihren vielseitig nutzbaren räumlichen Einrichtungen bietet Firmen die Gelegenheit, nicht nur die eigenen Produkte auszustellen, sondern auch die der Konkurrenz anzuschauen, in relativ kurzer Zeit viele persönliche Kontakte zu knüpfen sowie schnell und effizient wichtige Punkte direkt zu besprechen und Geschäfte unmittelbar abzuschließen. „Sehen und gesehen werden" lautet die Devise, um die eigene Präsenz im Markt zu sichern. Eine Messe bietet natürlich auch andere Möglichkeiten für eine erweiterte Werbepolitik. Veranstaltungen, die im Rahmen einer Messe in den Konferenzräumen organisiert werden und zu denen besondere Gäste eingeladen werden, können sehr effektive Werbemaßnahmen sein. Wie eine Aktienbörse kann eine Messe ein lebenswichtiger Umschlagplatz für die Verbreitung von Branchenkenntnissen sein.
Welche Vorteile die Teilnahme an einer Messe bietet und woran die teilnehmende Firma rechtzeitig vorher denken muss, zeigen Ihnen die folgenden drei kurzen Texte.

Before you read
Welche Vorteile bietet Ihrer Meinung nach die Teilnahme an einer Messe? Schreiben Sie eine kurze Liste der wichtigsten Punkte.

P & T Mediacraft

Memo
Date: 10. 9. 03
From: CEO Jonathan Phillips
To: Marketing Department
Ref: ProBest Trade Fair

Having just received the enclosed messages advertising next year's ProBest Trade Fair at the South and West Exhibition Centre in Bristol in April, I would like to remind everyone how important our participation is going to be and that preparation must be thorough and begun early. I share the belief not only that we need to see and be seen at such venues with a view to gathering information and making new contacts, but that this time around we will be meeting our business partners to make important decisions affecting our future. It is important therefore that our presence be felt, our exhibition stand impressive and our products on display attractive and convincing.

I would like a meeting in my office next Tuesday 11am to discuss the preliminaries and answer the following questions:
– choice of products
– timetabling
– prices
– presentation
– stand construction
– general logistics

JP

(Encl. S&WEC brochure and print–out of ProBest website)

Official brochure

The South & West Exhibition Centre – Bristol

Participation in international trade fairs is an efficient way for producers to showcase their products to export markets. The advantages include audience concentration, face-to-face communication and the opportunity to meet and get to know new business partners. Compared with other methods of selling and promotion, advertising through direct mail, sales literature, the general press and specialist journals or television commercials, trade fair participation offers a far less expensive but equally effective and targeted platform.

6 reasons why your firm absolutely needs to attend trade fairs at the S&WEC
- **Information**: the opportunity to present key issues and obtain in-depth knowledge of current and future developments
- **Contacts**: make new business contacts and strengthen existing ones
- **Decison-makers**: meet leading companies and their spokesmen and -women
- **Short distances**: one of the most modern exhibition centres in the world enables you to include any number of appointments into a short space of time
- **Special events**: the opportunity to offer and/or attend special presentations, discussions and forums in any of our conference rooms
- **Facilities**: 5 spacious and air-conditioned exhibition halls, 20 separate conference rooms of variable size, 5 restaurants, 3 cafeterias, 6 snackbars. The centre is also within easy reach of the city, main railway station and airport. All in all the ideal venue to make participation enjoyable and successful.

Contact our service manager.
All further information is available on our website with its download service
www.exhib.sandwec-bris.htm

Pro Best

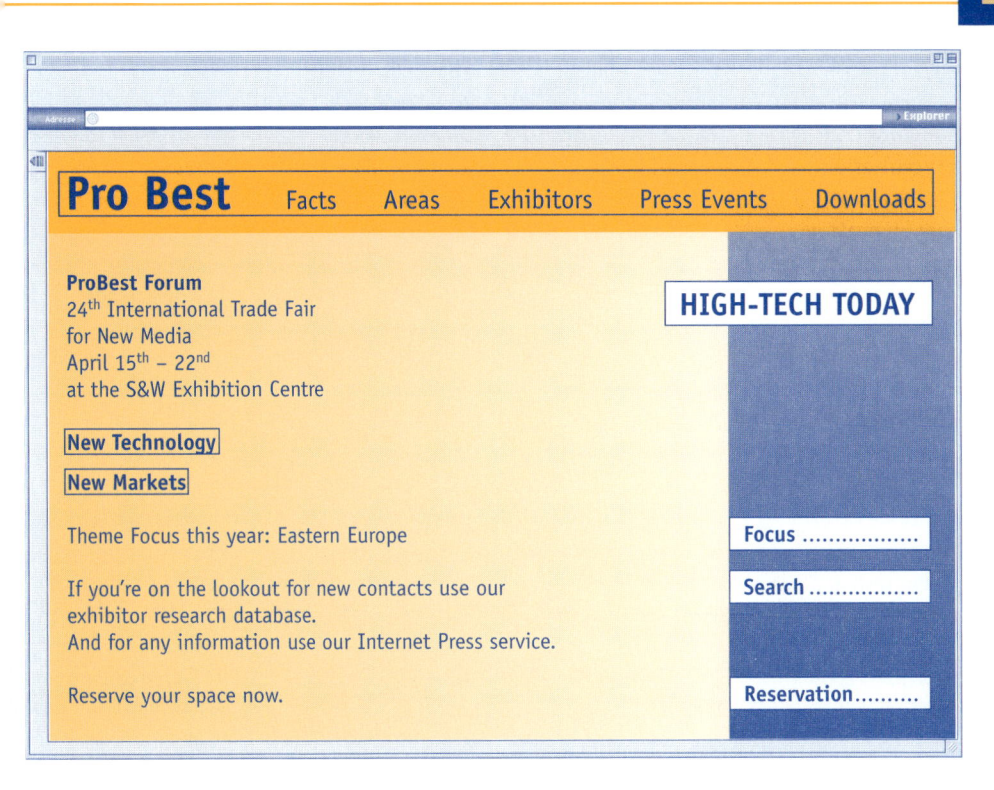

Facts · Areas · Exhibitors · Press Events · Downloads

ProBest Forum
24th International Trade Fair
for New Media
April 15th – 22nd
at the S&W Exhibition Centre

New Technology
New Markets

Theme Focus this year: Eastern Europe

If you're on the lookout for new contacts use our exhibitor research database.
And for any information use our Internet Press service.

Reserve your space now.

HIGH-TECH TODAY

Focus ....
Search ....
Reservation ....

Vocabulary

trade fair (n.)	Messe	**this time around** (adv.)	diesmal
CEO (Abbrev.) Chief Executive Officer	Firmenleiter, Generaldirektor	**to affect** (v.)	beeinflussen
		presence (n.)	Anwesenheit
enclosed (adj.)	beigefügt	**felt** (p.p. of feel)	gespürt
to advertise (v.)	Werbung machen für, ankündigen	**exhibition stand** (n.)	Messestand
		impressive (adj.)	imponierend
exhibition centre (n.)	Messe(zentrum)	**on display** (adv.)	ausgestellt
to remind (v.)	erinnern	**convincing** (adj.)	überzeugend
participation (n.)	Teilnahme	**preliminaries** (n.)	Vorbereitungsarbeiten
preparation (n.)	Vorbereitung	**choice** (n.)	Wahl
thorough (adj.)	gründlich	**timetabling** (n.)	Zeitplanung
to share (v.)	teilen	**stand construction** (n.)	Standaufbau
belief (n.)	Glaube	**brochure** (n.)	Broschüre
venue (n.)	Treffpunkt	**print-out** (n.)	Ausdruck
with a view to (prep.)	mit der Absicht um	**efficient** (adj.)	effizient
to gather (v.)	sammeln	**to showcase** (v.)	ausstellen

10

advantage (n.)	Vorteil	spokesman (n.)	Sprecher
to include (v.)	mit einschließen	to enable (v.)	es jmd. ermöglichen
audience (n.)	Konzentration der	appointment (n.)	(Besprechungs-)Termin
concentration	Aufmerksamkeit	space of time (n.)	Zeitraum
face-to-face (n.)	persönliche Kontakte	conference room (n.)	Konferenzraum
communication	direktes Anschreiben	facilities (n.)	Einrichtungen
direct mail (n.)	per Post	spacious (adj.)	geräumig
specialist journal (n.)	Fachzeitschrift	air-conditioned (adj.)	mit Klimaanlage
television	Fernsehwerbung	exhibition hall (n.)	Messehalle
commercials (n.)		separate (adj.)	getrennt
targeted (adj.)	gezielt	snackbar (n.)	Imbissstube
platform (n.)	Plattform, Basis	within easy	leicht erreichbar
to attend (v.)	besuchen, teilnehmen an	reach (adv.)	
		available (adj.)	erhältlich
key issues (n.)	die wichtigsten Fragen	theme focus (n.)	thematischer Schwerpunkt
to obtain (v.)	erhalten, bekommen		
in-depth (adj.)	eingehend, gründlich	to be on the lookout for (v.)	Ausschau halten nach
current (adj.)	aktuell		
to strengthen (v.)	verstärken	exhibitor (n.)	Aussteller
decision-maker (n.)	Entscheidungsträger	space (n.)	hier: Ausstellungs- oder Standfläche
leading (adj.)	führend		

Reading for Gist

1. Match them up
Welche Satzteile passen zusammen?

Example: 1 h

1. I would like to remind everyone
2. We need to see
3. We will be meeting our business partners
4. I would like a meeting
5. The advantages of participation in a trade fair
6. Here are six reasons why
7. You can meet leading companies and
8. You have the opportunity to offer
9. The centre is within
10. All further information is

a. include audience concentration.
b. to discuss the preliminaries.
c. special presentations.
d. your firm needs to attand trade fairs.
e. reach of the city.
f. and be seen.
g. available on our website.
h. how important our participation is going to be.
i. their spokesmen and -women.
j. to make important decisions.

2. True or false?
Sind die folgenden Aussagen richtig oder falsch?

Example:	True	False
Jonathan Phillips writes a memo to the marketing department of his firm.	✓	☐

	True	False
1. The CEO of Mediacraft reminds his staff that trade fairs are unimportant.	☐	☐
2. Jonathan Phillips wants to discuss arrangements with his staff in good time.	☐	☐
3. Bristol has a large exhibition centre.	☐	☐
4. The advantages of participating in a trade fair include direct mail advertising.	☐	☐
5. The short distances between stands at an exhibition make discussions difficult.	☐	☐
6. An exhibition centres doesn't usually have many facilities.	☐	☐
7. At a trade fair you can hold a special event in one of the conference rooms.	☐	☐
8. Trade fair participation is usually much more expensive that other methods of advertsing.	☐	☐
9. Restaurants and conference rooms make a trade fair an ideal venue for meetings.	☐	☐
10. You can find more information about trade fairs on the internet.	☐	☐

Reading for Language

1. Match them up
Welche Wörter passen zusammen, um Begriffe aus den Texten zu bilden?

Example: 1 d

1. trade
2. exhibition
3. key
4. decision
5. special
6. conference
7. theme
8. research

a. events
b. focus
c. database
d. fair
e. rooms
f. issue
g. maker
h. centre

2. True or false?
Sind diese Aussagen richtig oder falsch?

Example:	True	False
Venue is another word for the time and place where something happens.	✓	☐

	True	False
1. If a product is *convincing*, people will buy it.	☐	☐

2. *Preliminaries* is an expression used to describe events that come later. ☐ ☐
3. A *key issue* is another way of expressing an important matter. ☐ ☐
4. To *showcase* a product is another way of saying it's put on display. ☐ ☐
5. *Audience concentration* means that the public has to think very hard about the product. ☐ ☐
6. *Facilities* are the rooms and equipment provided in a building. ☐ ☐
7. An *exhibitor* is someone who participates in an exhibition. ☐ ☐
8. An *appointment* is another word for discussion. ☐ ☐
9. If preparation is *thorough*, then the organisation is usually bad. ☐ ☐
10. If business contacts are *strengthened*, they become more effective. ☐ ☐

3. Translation
Übersetzen Sie bitte folgende Wörter und Ausdrücke ins Deutsche.

Example:
The enclosed messages   *Die beigefügten Nachrichten.* ....

1. Exhibition Centre   ....
2. timetabling   ....
3. face-to-face communication   ....
4. theme focus   ....
5. key issues   ....

4. Crossword

Across
2 What you need at an exhibition to show your products (5)
5 A place where firms meet to show their products and gather information (9)
6 An advertisement on television (10)
7 Place and time for a meeting (5)
8 A self-service restaurant (9)

Down
1 People you meet and get to know (8)
3 A big meeting to discuss things (10)
4 A kind of magazine (7)

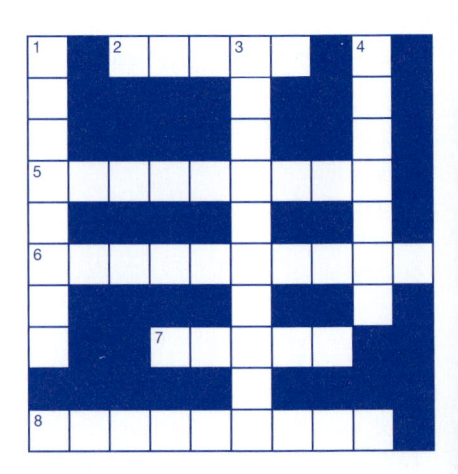

Reading for Understanding

1. Essential facts
Versuchen Sie folgende Fragen zu beantworten.

Example:
What does participation in a trade fair involve? **a.** Sending out sales literature by direct mail. **b.** Setting up a display stand in a large hall — *b*

1. Which is more important to Jonathan Phillips **a.** that Mediacraft's exhibition stand be impressive **b.** a decision on whether to participate
2. What does the Mediacraft CEO want to discuss with his staff? **a.** which exhibition to visit **b.** preparations for the ProBest Fair
3. Why is audience concentration achieved more easily at a trade fair? **a.** because the stands are attractive **b.** because visitors have everything they need in one place
4. Why is it easier to make contacts at at trade fair? **a.** because you can attend special events **b.** because you can meet people face-to-face
5. What does the trade fair internet research service offer? **a.** an alternative to taking part in the exhibition **b.** information on all exhibitors to make contact easier

2. What does it really mean?
Versuchen Sie bitte folgende Fragen zu beantworten.

Example:
What is Jonathan Phillips' belief? **a.** that it is essential for success to maintain a strong market presence **b.** that participation in the ProBest Trade Fair needs thorough discussion before a decision can be made — *a*

1. At the meeting called by the CEO, what will the marketing staff at Mediacraft need to discuss? **a.** the content of the trade fair centre's website **b.** the measures needed to ensure successful participation
2. What does the term *general logistics* involve? **a.** how to persuade customers to think about the right products **b.** how to organize people and events so that everything works according to plan
3. What main advantages does a trade fair have over advertising by TV commercials? **a.** It's much cheaper and more direct. **b.** Customers and business partners remain anonymous.
4. What main advantage does a trade fair venue have as far as appointments are concerned? **a.** You can get something to eat during the meeting. **b.** You can fit in several meetings with people from different places in a short space of time.

5. What advantage does the Trade Fair website offer possible exhibitors? **a.** They can reserve space at the exhibition for their stand. **b.** They can advertise their products there.

3. What do you think?
Versuchen Sie nun auch noch diese Fragen zu beantworten.

> *Example:*
> Why do you think trade fairs were invented? **a.** to make advertising opportunities cheaper **b.** to encourage business by making things more dynamic and efficient — *b*

1. What do you think is the most important reason for taking part? **a.** to save money on advertising elsewhere **b.** to maintain a market presence in view of the competition
2. What do you think is the main advantage a trade fair has to offer compared with other forms of advertising? **a.** There's a chance to meet old friends. **b.** A whole list of factors can be concentrated into a short space of time.
3. Why do you think it's important for an exhibition centre to have very good facilities? **a.** to attract more participants and thus generate more business **b.** to help exhibitors construct more attractive stands
4. What do you think is the quickest way to find more details and information about facilities and exhibitors? **a.** Contact the exhibition centre service manager **b.** Call up the trade fair website database

Over to you

1. Research
Welche Messen und Ausstellungen sind für dieses bzw. nächstes Jahr in Deutschland geplant?

Look up the exhibitions and trade fairs planned for next year in Germany on the internet. Look at the various exhibition centres and write a short report for your colleagues outlining what facilities are available at the various sites and what sources of information are available for your particular line of work.

2. Recommendation
Sie halten die Teilnahme an einer der Messen für unbedingt notwendig. Schreiben Sie eine Empfehlung für Ihren Chef oder Ihre Kollegen und Kolleginnen.

Imagine you have to convince your boss that participation in a coming trade fair is essential for the success of your firm in the future. Write a memo outlining the advantages as you see them and explain what needs to be done to ensure participation is a success.

Unit 11

International Business Relations

Auf der internationalen Bühne werden heutzutage von allen *business executives* wahre schaupielerische Leistungen erwartet, wenn es um die effektive Kommunikation mit dem Geschäftspartner geht. Der Schauspieler muss den richtigen Zugang zum Publikum finden, wenn er gut ankommen will. Er muss kommunizieren. Die hierfür notwendigen Fertigkeiten erwirbt er während seiner Ausbildung. Der *business executive* braucht ähnliche kommunikative Fähigkeiten, wenn er seinem Publikum gegenübersteht – umso mehr wenn das Publikum im Ausland ist. Wie sonst sollte er eine Produktpräsentation im weit entfernten Südafrika oder Schanghai vor dem dort zuständigen Verkaufspersonal erfolgreich durchführen, die frisch eingeflogene Delegation aus Lagos willkommen heißen, den Vorsitz bei der morgigen Besprechung mit den Kollegen aus New York übernehmen oder sogar den neuen Broschüretext für die Marketingkampagne in Spanien genehmigen?

Interkulturelle Kompetenz ist die Voraussetzung für gute Zusammenarbeit. Was das nun ist und welche Hürden man bei einer Begegnung der interkulturellen Art zu überwinden hat, erfahren Sie im folgenden Text.

Before you read
Denken Sie über Ihre bisherigen Erfahrungen mit ausländischen Kollegen, Mitarbeitern und Kontaktpersonen nach. Welche positiven und welche negativen Erfahrungen haben Sie gemacht? Was wäre besser gewesen, wenn …? Machen Sie eine kurze Liste nach den Kriterien „wichtig" und „weniger wichtig".

Cultural Barriers
A Game of Loops and Ladders?

"East is East and West is West and never the twain shall meet" is a famous quotation from a poem by Rudyard Kipling written towards the end of the 19th century. Now that globalisation and the idea of the global village in this new 21st century have become the latest phenomena, then surely Kipling's division can no longer hold true. Or can it?

Judging from reports from business people, consultants and trainers with experience in Europe and the Far East, particularly China, it seems that cultural differences still tend to be divisive when it comes to completing business deals or co-operating on project development. The same is also true when Europeans and Americans do business together. Different cultures and traditions, manners, behaviour patterns, idiomatic speech, expected role models or stereotypes and prejudices can often make real communication difficult despite the fact that everyone speaks the lingua franca, English..

There may well be different approaches to management concepts, a different and maybe unusual organizational structure to the firm you're dealing with. Hierarchies may be clearly defined and obvious, or more subtle lines may be drawn. And then there is the question of style at meetings and negotiations. Formal or informal? Open and brash or careful and diplomatic? How do we interpret the signs and signals we pick up? On our own terms or on the terms we think the others have adopted. How do we know? How do they know? How do we know that they know?

When a Chinese businessman says "yes", for example, it does not necessarily mean that he agrees with you, but only that he has understood what you said. When working towards the clinching of a deal Europeans often have the impression that the Chinese are forever reconsidering decisions made at a previous meeting. This is because they see decision-making not as a linear progression like the rungs of a ladder with stages that can be ticked off on a list, but as a series of "loops". It can be quite infuriating for Westerners to find that – in western terms – they haven't made any progress, whereas in fact behind the scenes the Chinese delegation has been working extremely hard within their own cultural context of "loops" to prepare the way for the final decision to be made – just as the westerners have been doing on their "ladder".

Such differences are not limited to East and West. The American style is certainly not always compatible with the European approach – although it must be said that this is a generalisation since both Americans with European experience and Europeans in frequent contact with Americans have long since learnt to accommodate and even adopt the others' idiosyncrasies. But if faced with irritation or a blank face then it is still worthwhile considering traditional images as a possible explanation. Americans tend to be seen as overtly friendly but superficially so, whereas Europeans are perceived of as reserved and dour. The soft American exterior with a hard center, the European hard exterior with little or no access to the private person – at least not for quite a long time and then only if real friendship develops.

The basic message seems to be for all business contacts: What works internally may not work with foreign partners – misinterpretations rather than misunderstandings are the most likely result. Criticism may be taken literally as a final verdict instead of the constructive advice it was intended to be. Praise or compliments coming unexpectedly may be construed as insincere or as a device to conceal some hidden motive. On the other hand it also pays to be careful: are these misunderstandings due to the different "culture" or are they misunderstandings of another nature much nearer to home that could occur anywhere with anyone?

Successful trade in the global village will mean recognizing and accepting differences, learning to understand and adapt, making compromises, meeting the others half-way – realising that not to do so would mean missing valuable opportunities. And if this works in a business environment then it might also work politically – at least there might be better general understanding even if that is not necessarily synonymous with actual agreement! At least one can then agree to differ and move on.

Vocabulary

barrier *(n.)*	Hürde, Barriere, Sperre	**globalisation** *(n.)*	Globalisierung, das Zusammenwachsen der Erde
loop *(n.)*	Schleife		
ladder *(n.)*	Leiter		
the twain *(n.)*	*arch*. die zwei, die beiden	**division** *(n.)*	Trennung
		to hold true *(v.)*	wahr sein

to judge *(v.)*	(be)urteilen	rung *(n.)*	Sprosse
consultant *(n.)*	Berater	stage *(n.)*	Stufe
Far East *(n.)*	Fernost	to tick off *(v.)*	als erledigt abhaken
particularly *(adv.)*	insbesondere	infuriating *(adj.)*	äußerst ärgerlich
to tend *(v.)*	neigen	in western terms *(adv.)*	nach westlichen Verhältnissen
divisive *(adj.)*	verfremdend	whereas *(conj.)*	während
project development *(n.)*	Projektentwicklung	behind the scenes *(adv.)*	hinter den Kulissen
manners *(n.)*	Sitten, Manieren	delegation *(n.)*	Delegation, Mannschaft
behaviour patterns *(n.)*	Verhaltensmuster		
speech *(n.)*	Sprache	limited to *(adj.)*	begrenzt auf
role model *(n.)*	Vorbild	compatible *(adj.)*	kompatibel, verträglich
prejudice *(n.)*	Vorurteil		
approach *(n.)*	Betrachtungsweise, Ansatz	generalisation *(n.)*	Verallgemeinerung
		experience *(n.)*	Erfahrung
to deal with *(v.)*	zu tun haben mit	frequent *(adj.)*	häufig
hierarchy *(n.)*	Hierarchie, Firmenstruktur, Rangordnung	long since *(adv.)*	schon längst
		to accommodate *(v.)*	akzeptieren
		idiosyncrasies *(n.pl.)*	Eigenheiten, Eigentümlichkeiten
to define *(v.)*	definieren		
obvious *(adj.)*	deutlich	to face *(v.)*	konfrontieren
subtle *(adj.)*	subtil	irritation *(n.)*	Verärgerung
style *(n.)*	Stil	blank *(adj.)*	leer, ausdruckslos
negotiations *(n.)*	Verhandlungen	worthwhile *(adj.)*	lohnend, wertvoll
formal *(adj.)*	formell	image *(n.)*	Vorstellung
informal *(adj.)*	informell	explanation *(n.)*	Erklärung
brash *(adj.)*	rau, unkultiviert, frech	to tend *(v.)*	neigen
		overtly *(adv.)*	nach außen hin, vordergründig
careful *(adj.)*	vorsichtig		
to interpret *(v.)*	interpretieren	superficially *(adv.)*	oberflächlich
sign *(n.)*	Zeichen	to perceive *(v.)*	wahrnehmen
to pick up *(n.)*	empfangen	reserved *(adj.)*	reserviert
terms *(n.)*	Bedingungen	dour *(adj.)*	mürrisch, verdrießlich
to adopt *(v.)*	annehmen	exterior *(n.)*	Außenseite, Äußeres
necessarily *(adv.)*	notwendigerweise	hard center *(n.)*	harter Kern
to clinch a deal *(v.)*	ein Geschäft abschließen	access *(n.)*	Zugang
		friendship *(n.)*	Freundschaft
forever *(adv.)*	immer und ewig	basic *(adj.)*	grundsätzlich
to reconsider *(v.)*	erneut überlegen	to work *(v.)*	funktionieren
decision *(n.)*	Entscheidung	internally *(adv.)*	intern
previous *(adj.)*	früher, vorherig	foreign *(adj.)*	ausländisch
linear *(adj.)*	gradlinig	misinterpretation *(n.)*	Fehldeutung

misunderstanding (n.)	Missverständnis	to occur (v.)	vorkommen
result (n.)	Ergebnis	to adapt (v.)	(sich) anpassen
criticism (n.)	Kritik	to meet half way (v.)	auf halbem Wege treffen, entgegenkommen
literally (adv.)	wörtlich		
verdict (n.)	Urteil		
instead of (prep.)	anstatt	to miss (v.)	verpassen
advice (n.)	Rat(schlag)	valuable (adj.)	wertvoll
to intend (v.)	beabsichtigen	opportunity (n.)	Gelegenheit, Chance
praise (n.)	Lob	environment (n.)	Umgebung, Umfeld
unexpectedly (adv.)	unerwartet	synonymous (adj.)	gleichbedeutend, synonym
to construe (v.)	interpretieren, deuten		
insincere (adj.)	unaufrichtig	actual (adj.)	tatsächlich
device (n.)	Vorwand, Trick	agreement (n.)	Übereinkunft, Einverständnis
to conceal (v.)	verdecken		
hidden (adj.)	geheim gehalten	to agree to differ (v.)	sich einigen, dass man unterschiedlicher Meinung ist
on the other hand (adv.)	andererseits		
it pays (v.)	es macht sich bezahlt	to move on (v.)	weitergehen
nearer to home (adv.)	näher liegend, vordergründiger		

Reading for Gist

1. Match them up
Setzen Sie bitte die richtigen Satzhälften zusammen.

Example: 1 d

1. Globalisation has become
2. Cultural differences
3. Real communication can be difficult
4. There may well be different approaches
5. Europeans often have the impression
6. The American style is not always
7. What works internally
8. Compliments coming unexpectedly
9. Successful trade in the global village
10. If this works in a business environment

a. it might also work politically.
b. that the Chinese are forever reconsidering decisions.
c. may not work with foreign partners.
d. a new phenomenon.
e. will mean accepting differences.
f. still tend to be divisive.
g. despite the fact that everyone speaks English.
h. compatible with the European approach.
i. to management concepts.
j. may be construed as insincere.

2. True or false?
Sind diese Aussagen richtig oder falsch?

Example:	True	False
Rudyard Kipling wrote "East is East and West is West ……".	☑	☐

	True	False
1. It is no longer true that cultural differences cause problems in business.	☐	☐
2. Different cultures and traditions can make real communication difficult.	☐	☐
3. Approaches to management are all usually the same in different countries.	☐	☐
4. Decision-making in China does not follow a linear progression.	☐	☐
5. European and American styles are always compatible.	☐	☐
6. Americans tend to be seen as friendly on the outside.	☐	☐
7. Criticism can be taken too literally.	☐	☐
8. Praise is always used to conceal a hidden motive.	☐	☐
9. Misunderstandings occur only when cultures are different.	☐	☐
10. Success in business deals means making compromises.	☐	☐

3. Headlines
Welche Überschrift passt am besten?

1. Paragraph 1
   a. BUSINESS NOW IMPOSSIBLE b. NOT ALWAYS EASY
2. Paragraph 2
   a. SO WHAT'S DIFFERENT? b. HOW DO WE MANAGE?
3. Paragraph 3
   a. IN CHINA YES MEANS NO b. LOOP OR LADDER?
4. Paragraph 4
   a. BEWARE OF MISUNDERSTANDING b. WE'LL NEVER UNDERSTAND
5. Paragraph 5
   a. FORGET THE REST b. TRADE AND POLITICS MAY GO TOGETHER

1. ………… 2. ………… 3. ………… 4. ………… 5. …………

Reading for Language

1. True or false?
Sind diese Aussagen richtig oder falsch?

Example:	True	False
Globalisation means that the world we live in is getting larger.	☑	☐

1. Different behaviour patterns can make communication difficult. ☐ ☐
2. Hierarchies are always obvious. ☐ ☐
3. Clinching a deal in China can be a problem for Europeans. ☐ ☐
4. Idiosyncrasies is another word for foolish actions. ☐ ☐
5. Brash behaviour is the opposite of being diplomatic. ☐ ☐
6. Overtly means the same as superficially. ☐ ☐
7. If you take something literally, you may not have understood it fully. ☐ ☐
8. A hidden motive is a kind of secret thought. ☐ ☐
9. If you meet someone half-way, you refuse to compromise. ☐ ☐
10. Understanding someone is not the same as agreeing with them. ☐ ☐

2. Match them up
Setzen Sie die richtigen Wortkombinationen zusammen.

Example: 1 h

1. To hold	a. pattern
2. Far	b. development
3. project	c. model
4. behaviour	d. a deal
5. idiomatic	e. verdict
6. role	f. the scenes
7. clinching	g. half-way
8. behind	h. true
9. final	i. speech
10. to meet	j. East

3. What does it mean?
Welche Antwort ist hier richtig?

Example:
If something *tends to be divisive*, does it mean
   a. that it creates a basis for agreement   **b.** pushes people further apart?   `b`

1. Is *manners* a word used to describe
      a. accepted and polite behaviour   **b.** strange ways of doing things? ☐
2. *Subtle* refers to something that is
      a. clear and well-defined   **b.** less obvious at first sight? ☐
3. If someone appears *dour*, they
      a. seem happy and friendly   **b.** don't smile or look cheerful? ☐
4. Giving a final *verdict* means the same as
      a. telling the truth   **b.** informing someone of your opinion? ☐

5. Being *insincere* means
   a. saying something you believe
   b. saying something you don't believe?
6. When you *conceal* something, you
   a. lose it
   b. hide it?
7. To *perceive* something means
   a. to see and understand something
   b. to accept something as normal?
8. *In a business environment* is another way of saying
   a. if business interests are protected
   b. in a business situation?

4. Odd one out
Welches Wort passt nicht in die jeweilige Gruppe? Bitte unterstreichen Sie das Wort.

1.	2.	3.	4.	5.
a. globalisation	a. businessman	a. culture	a. environment	a. necessarily
b. global village	b. consultant	b. quotation	b. criticism	b. superficially
c. Europe	c. trainer	c. manners	c. verdict	c. internally
d. the Far East	d. partner	d. behaviour	d. opinion	d. half-way
e. stereotype	e. opportunity	e. tradition	e. message	e. overtly

5. Crossword
Across
1 Another word for language (6)
5 Another word for difference (8)
6 To do with the whole world (6)
7 Not diplomatic (5)
8 Conditions (5)

Down
2 Compliments (6)
3 A kind of advisor (10)
4 In a straight line (6)

Reading for Understanding

1. Essential facts
Suchen Sie fünf Begriffe, die nicht in die folgende Liste passen.

Example: 3 English as lingua franca

Possible culture barriers

1. Cultural differences ☐
2. Different traditions ☐
3. English as lingua franca ☐
4. Strange manners ☐
5. Unfamiliar behaviour patterns ☐
6. The globalisation of world business ☐
7. Examples of idiomatic speech ☐
8. Expected role models ☐
9. Misleading stereotypes ☐
10. Making too many compromises ☐
11. Prejudices ☐
12. Differences in hierarchies ☐
13. Conflicting personal styles ☐
14. The distance between America and Europe ☐
15. Misunderstanding criticism and praise ☐
16. Not wanting to work with foreign business partners ☐

2. Understanding the text
Versuchen Sie folgende Fragen zu beantworten.

Example:
What did people believe before globalisation started? **a.** That East and West could never really understand each other. **b.** That everyone in the world was equal. | **b** |

1. What do experts in the world of business believe? **a.** That financial factors are the main casuse for misunderstandings. **b.** Differences in culture still cause problems during negotiations.
2. What kind of cultural differences are more likely to cause problems? **a.** language and clothes **b.** manners and behaviour
3. How is the style in which meetings are conducted likely to differ? **a.** in the degree of formality **b.** in the choice of language to be used
4. Why do Europeans often misunderstand the Chinese? **a.** Because they have the impression that decisions are being constantly changed. **b.** Because Chinese manners are more formal.
5. Why are the American and European styles not always compatible? **a.** Because they don't share the same language. **b.** Because American friendliness and European reserve are misunderstood.
6. What is the basic message for business people negotiating abroad? **a.** What works at home won't always work abroad. **b.** What you do at home will always be thought of as insincere.
7. What might happen if you criticize something abroad? **a.** Your business partner will immediately understand. **b.** Your business partner may feel insulted.
8. What might happen if you praise something? **a.** You may be considered insincere. **b.** You will be taken seriously at once.

3. What do you think?

Lesen Sie den Text noch einmal durch. Dann versuchen Sie folgende Fragen zu beantworten.

> *Example:*
> Why do you think East and West never really met in the 19th century? **a.** Because the means of communication were not as good as today. **b.** Because there was no need for them to do so.
>
> | *a* |

1. Why do you think idiomatic speech might be a factor? **a.** Because your business partner won't understand a word you say. **b.** Because what you say in one language may mean something completely different in another.
2. Why do you think stereotypes and prejudices might make communication difficult? **a.** Because people wouldn't talk to each other at all. **b.** Because business partners would be influenced by the wrong images in their minds.
3. Why might different hierarchies be a problem? **a.** Because bosses might feel insulted if they were suddenly ignored. **b.** Because only the bosses would feel comfortable.
4. Why do you think it will help to consider traditional images before dealing with other nationalities? **a.** Because they are always superficial and untrue. **b.** Because they may help to explain certain aspects of behaviour better.
5. Why do you think misunderstandings may occur even though both partners are aware of intercultural differences? **a.** Because both parties may just think differently about the business terms. **b.** Because different cultures are impossible to understand.
6. Why do you think most businesses will do their best to try and understand cultural barriers? **a.** Because they primary aim is to help maintain political stability. **b.** Because they need the business opportunities to maintain growth.

Over to you

1. Diplomatic service

Testen Sie nun Ihre neu gewonnene Lesekompetenz. Stellen Sie sich vor, Sie würden gebeten, ein Treffen zwischen einem/einer amerikanischen und einem/einer chinesischen Geschäftsmann/-frau zu organisieren.
Before the meeting write a short note to each of them warning them in general terms of reasons for possible misunderstandings.

2. Reminder

Machen Sie sich eine Liste von wichtigen Punkten.
In preparation for the meeting write a list of "Dos and Don'ts" that you yourself need to remember when dealing with your two business partners.

Unit 12

Multinationals

Wer ist denn wirklich verantwortlich für die ganzen Umweltschäden, die Naturkatastrophen und Energiekrisen, die unsere moderne Welt bedrohen? Sind das die Hersteller aller Geräte und Substanzen mit schädigender Wirkung? Oder die Benutzer dieser Geräte und Substanzen – Autofahrer, Landwirte …? Oder sind es die Großunternehmer, die skrupellos ihre Geschäfte auf Kosten des kleinen Mannes betreiben? Oder doch eher die Behörden und Staatsregierungen, die immer das Falsche regulieren, zu viele Vorschriften hier, zu wenig Kontrollen da? Nach den neuesten Skandalen mit großen Firmen zeigt man nun auf die internationalen Giganten, die *multinationals* als Quelle des Bösen, Kapitalismus in seiner schlimmsten Form. Als selbstbewusster und verantwortungsvoller Manager können Sie nun auch selbst Stellung nehmen, Schwarzmalerei mit der Politik der weißen Weste vergleichen. Folgender Text könnte Ihnen helfen, Ihre Arbeit in einem neuen Licht zu sehen. Zumindest soll er dazu beitragen, eine objektive Meinung zu bilden und zu weiteren Recherchen anzuregen.

Before you read
Was halten Sie von dem Spruch „Small is beautiful"? Warum wurde er Ihrer Meinung nach erfunden? Machen Sie eine kurze Liste der Vor- und Nachteile bei großen und kleinen Firmen. Welche davon treffen für Ihre eigene Firma zu? Was könnten Sie gegen die Nachteile unternehmen?

Globalisation – a modern scourge?

Peter Ballington

As the world gets smaller and the population larger, the rich get richer and the poor get poorer. True? If it is, then multinational companies are to blame – or so the participants at the Earth Summit would have us believe – for hindering the governments of the world in their task of protecting the environment, relieving poverty and improving the health of the population. Big business in the form of corporate industry is seen as the devil in disguise pushing democracy aside in pursuit of bigger and bigger profits on an international scale with no responsibility to any one government or custodial body. Thinking globally – once the rallying-cry of hard-pressed business managers - has now maybe become something of a stigma.

On closer analysis, however, there are several other factors involved which may expose this line of thought as naive and mistaken. First of all, multinational companies are far more open to criticism than small less significant business enterprises simply because they are so large and omnipresent. They take up a larger space in the public eye. Secondly, to condemn big business would be to condemn capitalism out of hand and to ignore the benefits it has brought since its development at the beginning of the 18th century. Living-standards and general well-being have improved beyond recognition as a result. In the 800 years between 1000 and 1820 per capita incomes in western Europe rose by 0.15% a year on average. Since then they have risen by 1.5% a year – ten times faster. Thirdly, in a kind of self-fulfilling prophecy the suspicion that big is bad and small is beautiful tends to become a creed and big business the scapegoat for all negative developments. Fourthly, it seems that not only is the good that big business does underestimated, but their actual power is also overestimated. Latest studies conclude that most multinational companies do not in fact have a global strategy and that only a very few like Nestlé and Unilever can really call themselves globally significant. Fifthly, over 15% of multinationals are losing money and are having to redefine their policies and scale down their enterprise. And finally, it is simply not true that multinationals are independent of governments. They rely on them to provide legal and financial measures of support. Proof of this came after the September 11 tragedy. Far from being independent, the multinational airlines clamoured for governmental help.

So maybe multinationals and big business are not so bad after all? At least we cannot lay the blame for all the world's problems at their door. The problems are too complicated for that. On the other hand, it would be equally naive to believe that big business did not seek out every loophole in the global structure and use it to its own economic advantage. Business is business after all.

It is the task of governments then, not only to provide support, but also to regulate and in a global sense to reach international agreement among themselves on issues like human rights, duties and tariffs, evironmental controls, taxes, loans and subsidies. But without a global consensus on the political level, multinational businesses may well continue to get all the blame for global problems whether wholly justified or not.

Vocabulary

globalisation (n.)	Globalisierung
scourge (n.)	Geißel
population (n.)	Bevölkerung
to blame (v.)	jmd die Schuld geben
participants (n.pl.)	Teilnehmer
Earth Summit (n.)	Gipfeltreffen zum Thema Umwelt
to have sb believe (v.)	jmd im Glauben lassen
to hinder (v.)	(ver)hindern
task (n.)	Aufgabe
environment (n.)	Umwelt
to relieve (v.)	erleichtern
poverty (n.)	Armut
to improve (v.)	verbessern
health (n.)	Gesundheit
corporate industry (n.)	Welt der Industrieunternehmen
devil (n.)	Teufel
disguise (n.)	Verkleidung
to push aside (v.)	zur Seite schieben
democracy (n.)	Demokratie
in pursuit of	auf der Jagd nach
scale (n.)	Größenordnung
responsibility (n.)	Verantwortung
custodial body (n.)	Aufsichtsbehörde

rallying-cry (n.)	Sammelruf	to conclude (v.)	folgern, zur Schlussfolgerung kommen
hard-pressed (adj.)	stressgeplagt	in fact (adv.)	in Wirklichkeit
stigma (n.)	Stigma, negatives Merkmal	to redefine (v.)	neu definieren
analysis (n.)	Analyse	policy (n.)	Strategie, (Haus)politik
several (adj.)	mehrere		
to involve (v.)	involvieren, mitbeteiligen	to scale down (v.)	verkleinern, reduzieren
to expose (v.)	enthüllen	independent (adj.)	unabhängig
mistaken (adj.)	verfehlt, fehlerhaft	government (n.)	Regierung
criticism (n.)	Kritik	to rely on (v.)	sich verlassen auf
significant (adj.)	bedeutsam	to provide (v.)	für etwas sorgen, liefern, zur Verfügung stellen
enterprise (n.)	Unternehmen		
omnipresent (adj.)	allgegenwärtig		
space (n.)	Raum, Platz	legal (adj.)	juristisch
public eye (n.)	Öffentlichkeit	measure (n.)	Maßnahme
to condemn (v.)	verdammen, verurteilen	proof (n.)	Beweis
		tragedy (n.)	Tragödie
capitalism (n.)	Kapitalismus	to clamour (v.)	lauthals bitten
out of hand (adv.)	voreilig	to lay the blame (v.)	die Schuld geben
to ignore (v.)	ignorieren	complicated (adj.)	kompliziert
benefits (n.pl.)	Vorteile	loophole (n.)	Lücke, Schlupfloch, Winkel
development (n.)	Entwicklung		
century (n.)	Jahrhundert	economic (adj.)	wirtschaftlich
living standards (n.pl.)	Lebensstandard	advantage (n.)	Vorteil
well-being (n.)	Wohlbefinden	to regulate (v.)	kontrollieren, regulieren, verwalten
to improve (v.)	(sich) verbessern		
beyond recognition	so, dass man es kaum wiedererkennt	sense (n.)	Sinn
		to reach agreement (v.)	sich einigen
per capita income (n.)	pro Kopf, individuell Einkommen	issue (n.)	Angelegenheit
on average (adv.)	im Durchschnitt	human rights (n.)	Menschenrechte
self-fulfilling prophecy (n.)	eine Vorhersage, die das Vorhergesagte selbst auslöst	duties (n.)	Zollgebühren
		tariff (n.)	hier: Zoll
		tax (n.)	Steuer
suspicion (n.)	Verdacht	loan (n.)	Darlehen
creed (n.)	Credo, Glaube	subsidy (n.)	Subvention
scapegoat (n.)	Sündenbock	consensus (n.)	Konsens
to underestimate (v.)	unterschätzen	level (n.)	Ebene
actual (adj.)	tatsächlich, wirklich	wholly (adv.)	gänzlich
to overestimate (v.)	überschätzen	justified (adj.)	gerechtfertigt

Reading for Gist

1. Headlines
Welche Überschrift passt am besten zum jeweiligen Absatz im Text?

1. **Paragraph 1**
   a. EARTH SUMMIT BLUES **b.** ARE MULTIS ANTI-DEMOCRATIC? **c.** GLOBAL HEALTH SCARE

2. **Paragraph 2**
   a. GLOBAL STRATEGY EXPOSED **b.** A CASE FOR CAPITALISM **c.** MULTIS MISUNDERSTOOD

3. **Paragraph 3**
   a. MULTIS BLAMELESS? **b.** ECONOMIC LOOPHOLES **c.** ADVANTAGE MULTIS

4. **Paragraph 4**
   a. MONEY TALKS LOUDEST **b.** POLITICIANS HAVE GLOBAL TASK **c.** BLAME THE MULTIS

1.	2.	3.	4. ....

2. True or false?
Sind die Aussagen in den folgenden Sätzen richtig oder falsch?

	True	False
Example: The participants at the Earth Summit meeting blame the multinational companies for the world's economic problems.	✓	☐
1. Big Business is seen as a custodial body.	☐	☐
2. Business managers may not want to think globally any more.	☐	☐
3. No-one notices what happens in big multinational companies.	☐	☐
4. Since big business started, living standards in Europe have improved.	☐	☐
5. Many people believe that small is beautiful.	☐	☐
6. There are not many companies that are really multinational.	☐	☐
7. Multinational companies are never dependent on governments.	☐	☐
8. Multinationals cannot be blamed for every problem.	☐	☐
9. Governments need to look at issues like human rights.	☐	☐
10. On a political level there is a global consensus.	☐	☐
11. Governments need to reach international agreement.	☐	☐
12. Big Business is not to blame at all.	☐	☐

3. Match them up
Welche Satzteile passen zusammen?

Example: 1 e

1. As the world gets smaller
2. Big business is seen
3. Thinking globally
4. Multinational companies are
5. To condemn big business would be
6. Living-standards have improved
7. The suspicion that big is bad
8. Some multinationals are having
9. Maybe multinationals are not
10. It is the task of governments

a. so bad after all?
b. to condemn capitalism out of hand.
c. to reach international agreement.
d. tends to become a creed.
e. the population gets larger.
f. as the devil in disguise.
g. may have become a stigma.
h. beyond recognition.
i. far more open to criticism.
j. to scale down their enterprise.

Reading for Language

1. Match them up
Welche Begriffe lassen sich aus diesen Wörtern bilden?

Example: 1 f

1. Earth
2. custodial
3. rallying-
4. hard-
5. living
6. well
7. self-fulfilling
8. human
9. per capita
10. public

a. eye
b. standards
c. rights
d. prophecy
e. income
f. Summit
g. body
h. being
i. cry
j. pressed

2. True or false?
Welche dieser Aussagen trifft zu, welche nicht?

	True	False
Example: *To hinder* means to help someone.	☐	☑
1. *To relieve poverty* means to help people who have little money.	☐	☐
2. *Corporate industry* refers to all the small firms that provide services.	☐	☐

3. *Per capita income* is the money each person earns individually. ☐ ☐
4. If you have a *suspicion*, you have positive thoughts about someone. ☐ ☐
5. If you are made the *scapegoat*, everyone blames you for what went wrong. ☐ ☐
6. *Creed* is just another name for big business. ☐ ☐
7. If something has a *loophole* in it, then it is perfect and faultless. ☐ ☐
8. *Duties and tariffs* are special taxes paid on goods and transactions. ☐ ☐
9. If you feel *justified* in what you've done, you think you were right. ☐ ☐
10. If something is done *out of hand*, it has not been thought about properly. ☐ ☐

3. Odd one out
Welches Wort passt nicht in die jeweilige Gruppe? Bitte unterstreichen Sie das Wort.

Example: 1 d

1.
a. big business
b. corporate industry
c. multinational company
d. public eye

2.
a. living-standards
b. scapegoat
c. well-being
d. per capita income

3.
a. tariff
b. taxes
c. duties
d. tragedy

4.
a. to blame
b. to underestimate
c. to overestimate
d. to conclude

5.
a. government
b. democracy
c. capitalism
d. stigma

6.
a. benefit
b. strategy
c. plan
d. enterprise

4. Translation
Bitte übersetzen Sie folgende Begriffe ins Deutsche.

Example:
Enterprise - *Unternehmen*

1. participant ....
2. on average ....
3. actual power ....
4. proof ....
5. human rights ....
6. loan ....
7. airline ....

8. health ....
9. suspicion ....
10. creed ....

5. Crossword

Across
1 Your state of well-being (6)
5 Another word for business (10)
7 A hundred years (7)
8 Saying what is wrong with something (9)

Down
2 A company that flies aeroplanes (7)
3 Another word for belief (5)
4 Rule of the people (9)
6 Top of a mountain (6)

Reading for Understanding

1. Essential facts

Im folgenden Text sind fünf der zehn mit Ziffern gekennzeichneten Fakten falsch dargestellt. Welche sind das?

With the process of globalisation increasing, rich people are being asked to condemn big business (1). Multinational companies are seen to be looking for bigger profits in international markets (2) and supporting democratic principles (3). But this is not true and public opinion is mistaken(4). Because they are so large it is impossible for them to keep everything they do a secret (5), but nevertheless they are responsible for keeping per capita incomes low (6) and actually enjoy being held responsible for negative developments in the world (7). Despite the fact that 15% of multinationals are losing money (8), they can all remain independent of governments (9) while looking for ways to turn globalisation to their own advantage (10).

| A. .... | B. .... | C. .... | D. .... | E. .... |

2. What does it really mean?

Versuchen Sie nun folgende Fragen zu beantworten.

Example:
What kind of public image do multinational companies seem to have?
a. positive   b. negative   *b*

1. What are multinationals being blamed for?
   a. supporting governments   b. standing in governments' way
2. What used to be the favourite slogan of business managers?
   a. Think globally.   b. Think locally.
3. Why is this negative view on multinationals probably wrong?
   a. Because they continue to be successful.
   b. Because several other factors need to be considered.
4. How long have big business and capitalism existed?
   a. since the beginning of the 20th century
   b. since the beginning of the 18th century
5. How much faster did people's earnings increase in the last two hundred years compared with the eight hundred years before that?
   a. ten times faster   b. fifteen times faster
6. Why do multinationals tend to be made the scapegoat for lots of the world's difficulties?
   a. Because they can afford to take the blame.
   b. Because people don't trust big organisations.
7. What kind of proof do we have that multinationals need government support?
   a. Multinational airlines asked for help after the tragedy of September 11.
   b. Nestlé and Unilever remain globally significant.
8. What would it be too naive to believe about multinationals?
   a. That they only have the interests of governments at heart.
   b. That they only seek economic advantages.
9. Whose responsibility should it be to agree on issues like human rights?
   a. the multinational companies'   b. international governments'
10. What are the likely consequences of not having a global consensus on the political level?
    a. The multinationals will continue to get richer.
    b. The multinationals will continue to get the blame.

3. What do you think?

Wie stehen Sie zu den *Multinationals*? Versuchen Sie anhand des Textes folgende Fragen zu beantworten.

> *Example:*
> Why do you think the large airline companies had to ask for government help following the tragedy of September 11 in New York?
> **a.** Because the financial losses that followed were so large.
> **b.** Because they wanted to prove their independence. | a |

1. Why do you think ordinary people tend to mistrust very large businesses?
   a. Because these companies seem very rich and ordinary people are relatively poor.
   b. Because the world is getting smaller and people are now better informed.
2. Why do you think mutinational companies came under suspicion at the Earth Summit?
   a. Because they are now responsible to governments.
   b. Because people think they ignore democracy in favour of bigger profits.
3. Why do you think living standards and incomes have risen more quickly in the last two hundred years?
   a. Because business managers have been hard-pressed.
   b. Because business has generated economic success on a large scale.
4. Why do you think only very few big companies are globally significant?
   a. Because of the great difficulties in creating a truly effective global strategy.
   b. Because they are still independent of government controls.
5. Why do you think governments might do better to agree on global regulations for multinational companies?
   a. To remove any loopholes and remove suspicion.
   b. To justify new taxes and tariffs.

Over to you

Giving an interview

Stellen Sie nun Ihre Lesekompetenz auf die Probe. Bereiten Sie sich auf ein Fersehinterview vor.

Imagine you are an internationally experienced business manager about to be interviewed by your local TV station on the topic of multinational companies and their influence on politics and the world economy. Prepare a short statement outlining your views and make a list of the most important facts you discovered in this text to help you when replying to any questions you might be asked.

Unit 13

New Technologies

Wer von uns hat sich nicht irgendwann mit wachsender Ungeduld entweder vor dem Geldautomaten oder dem Bankschalter anstellen müssen? Abgesehen von dieser Geduldsprobe hat es natürlich auch Zeit gekostet, die Bank überhaupt aufzusuchen, vorher den Weg dorthin zurückzulegen, womöglich einen Parkplatz zu suchen und sicherzustellen, dass man auch wirklich alle Papiere bei sich hat. Oder wenn es um die Beantragung eines Kredits geht, oder um ein kurzes Beratungsgespräch, wie lange hat man dennoch warten müssen?

Aber auch am Arbeitsplatz weiß jede Buchhaltung von einer scheinbar unendlichen Flut von Überweisungsformularen, Computerausdrucken und in Papierform abzuheftenden Belegen.

Neue Technologien wie Online-Banking versprechen, nicht nur solche Warterei aus dem Alltagsgeschäft der Banken zu entfernen und dabei für zufriedenere Kunden zu sorgen, sondern auch den Zahlungsverkehr bei Firmen zu beschleunigen und dessen Verwaltung zu erleichtern. Eine Reihe von Vorteilen wird angeboten, die für den zeitgeplagten Berufstätigen – ob Kleinunternehmer, Angestellter, Manager, Hausfrau oder -mann – zunächst verlockend klingt.

In den folgenden zwei Texten werden die Vor- und Nachteile der neuen Technologie für den Normalverbraucher erläutert. Und was für den kleinen Mann gilt, trifft prinzipiell auch für größere Firmen zu. E-Business oder E-Commerce sind weitere Systeme, die erst durch neue Computertechnologien möglich geworden sind, die aber auch die gleichen inhärenten Vor- und Nachteile haben.

Before you read

Welche Dienstleistungen bietet Ihnen Ihre jetzige Bank? Auf welche Art und Weise erledigen Sie Ihre allfälligen Bankgeschäfte? Wie erhalten Sie Information über Ihren Kontostand? Wie kommunizieren Sie mit dem Bankpersonal? Wie organisieren Sie einen Darlehensantrag oder den Kauf von Aktien oder Wertpapieren?

Erstellen Sie eine kurze Übersicht und überlegen Sie dann, wieviel Zeit die Erledigung einzelner Posten normalerweise in Anspruch nimmt und welche dieser Posten vielleicht für Sie bequemer durch eine direkte Computerverbindung zu Ihrer Bank erledigt werden könnten.

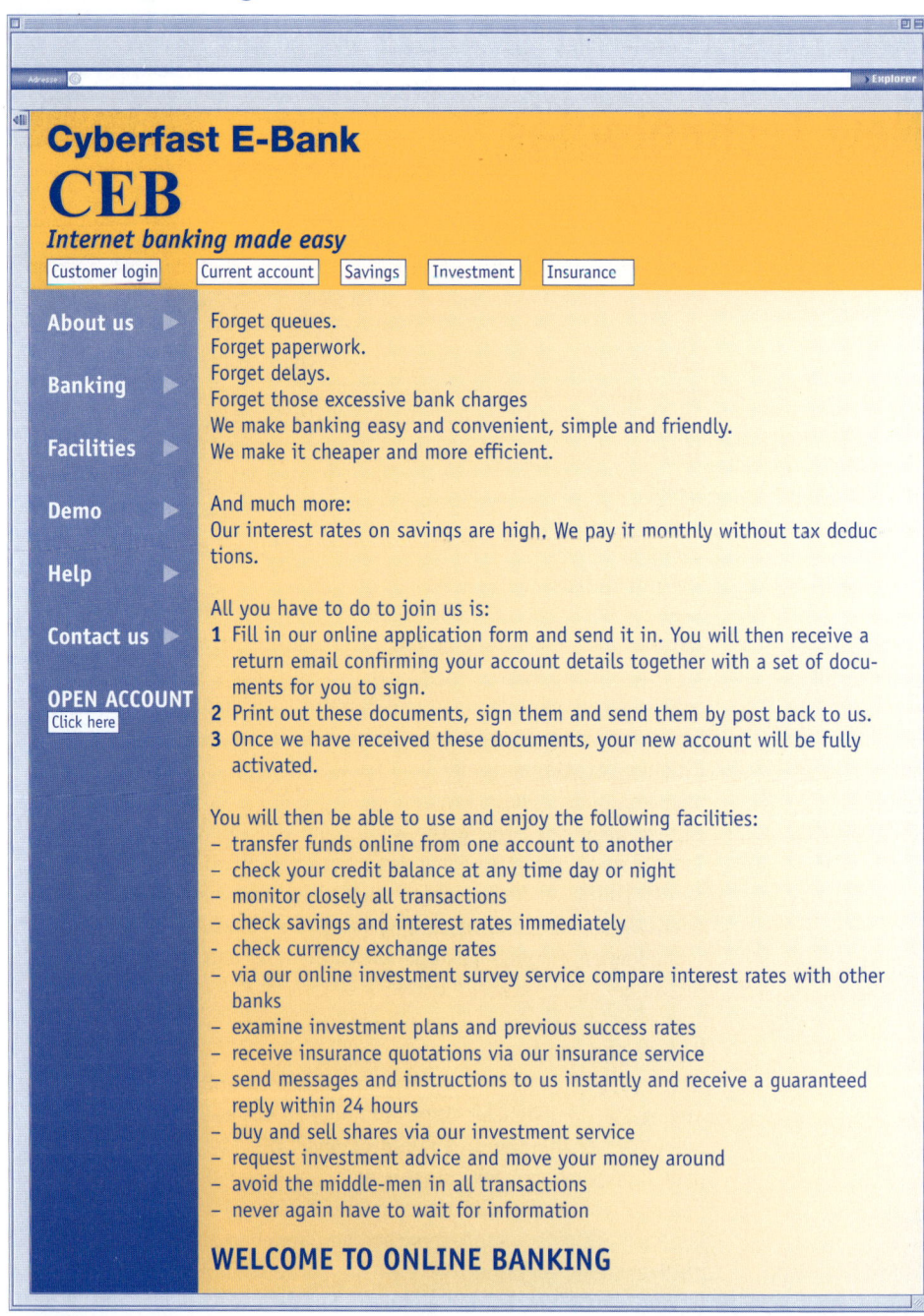

Online Banking

Cyberfast E-Bank
CEB
Internet banking made easy

| Customer login | Current account | Savings | Investment | Insurance |

About us ▶

Banking ▶

Facilities ▶

Demo ▶

Help ▶

Contact us ▶

OPEN ACCOUNT
Click here

Forget queues.
Forget paperwork.
Forget delays.
Forget those excessive bank charges
We make banking easy and convenient, simple and friendly.
We make it cheaper and more efficient.

And much more:
Our interest rates on savings are high. We pay it monthly without tax deductions.

All you have to do to join us is:
1 Fill in our online application form and send it in. You will then receive a return email confirming your account details together with a set of documents for you to sign.
2 Print out these documents, sign them and send them by post back to us.
3 Once we have received these documents, your new account will be fully activated.

You will then be able to use and enjoy the following facilities:
- transfer funds online from one account to another
- check your credit balance at any time day or night
- monitor closely all transactions
- check savings and interest rates immediately
- check currency exchange rates
- via our online investment survey service compare interest rates with other banks
- examine investment plans and previous success rates
- receive insurance quotations via our insurance service
- send messages and instructions to us instantly and receive a guaranteed reply within 24 hours
- buy and sell shares via our investment service
- request investment advice and move your money around
- avoid the middle-men in all transactions
- never again have to wait for information

WELCOME TO ONLINE BANKING

The Financial News

Online Banking

Online Banking – Jewel or Janus?

by our technical correspondent Michael Greene

As technology provides us with more and more sophisticated means of manipulating our environment in general and our means of communication in particular, the wonders of the internet promise to make many a dream come true by letting us get *online* at any time and gain instant access to an Aladdin's cave of worldwide wonders. One of these jewels might well prove to be internet finance, e-business, e-commerce or for the man in the street – online banking. No more walking to the local branch in town and waiting in a queue for the cash dispenser machine or the human bank clerk behind the counter. Manage your money easily, quickly, efficiently in the comfort of your own home at any time you wish. A new wonder of the modern age.

Or is it?

There's an old and popular phrase in business: "There's no such thing as a free lunch". Is there maybe a hidden price to pay for such convenience? A recent survey has shown that several factors have to be considered on the downside. Numerous customers complain of technical problems and false promises – things just don't happen as quickly and efficiently as they were led to believe they would. Users of Apple Macintosh machines find that systems are not always compatible. There is still some paperwork to be done, particularly when cheques have to be processed.

Apart from these annoyances, the main fear seems to be one of security, fear of theft either by bank staff or by hackers getting into the system, and fear of unauthorised people gaining access to private information. The data protection act is no guarantee of security against wrongdoers or felons.

On an international level there can be both legal and cultural problems. Local jurisdiction may make it impossible for foreign customers to get support for any claims. Websites may be misunderstood in different settings. The use of colour can be critical: red and black mean different

things to Europeans than they do to Asians. Icons may also be the source of misinterpretation. In short: there was never a better case for the old Latin watchwords CAVEAT EMPTOR – let the buyer beware! The advice of the experts is as follows:
– Beware of clones. Trust only banks with proven records and genuine names.
– Beware of emails with extraordinary investment offers with very high interest rates.
– Beware of bogus stock exchange reports from obscure sources
– Beware of bases. Be sure you know what country the bank or financial company is based in and what the legal situation is.

It seems that the Australians have long since recognized the two faces of this Janus and statistics show that more than 50% of bank customers now use the online facility compared with only 10% in Europe. In the United States banks are continuously updating methods of maintaining security. They advise customers to change their passwords regularly and banks to use the latest anti-virus software. In addition to the well-established PIN system (personal identification numbers), small electronic devices called PIDs (personal identification devices) are being introduced. Customers can use them anywhere just like a car key to access their account.

There is no doubt that online banking is here to stay, but it will not remove the need for a very watchful eye. Money will never manage itself.

Vocabulary

customer *(n.)*	Kunde, Kundin	**funds** *(n.)*	Gelder
current account *(n.)*	Girokonto, Kontokorrent	**credit balance** *(n.)*	Kontostand, (Haben-) Saldo
savings *(n.)*	hier: Sparkonten	**to monitor** *(v.)*	beobachten, verfolgen
investment *(n.)*	Anlagen, Investment	**transaction** *(n.)*	Transaktion,
insurance *(n.)*	Versicherung(swesen)	**currency** *(n.)*	Währung
queue *(n.)*	Schlange	**exchange rate** *(n.)*	Wechselkurs
facilities *(n.)*	hier: Dienstleistungen	**survey** *(n.)*	hier: Übersicht
delay *(n.)*	Verzögerung, Wartezeit	**success rate** *(n.)*	Erfolgsquote
excessive *(adj.)*	übermäßig	**insurance quotation** *(n.)*	Versicherungsangebot
bank charges *(n.)*	Bankgebühren		
convenient *(adj.)*	praktisch, zweckmäßig	**share** *(n.)*	Aktie
account *(n.)*	Konto	**advice** *(n.)*	Rat, Beratung
interest rate *(n.)*	Zinssatz	**to avoid** *(v.)*	vermeiden
tax deduction *(n.)*	Steuerabzug	**middle-men** *(n.)*	Mittelsmänner, Zwischenhändler, Vermittler
application form *(n.)*	Anmeldeformular		
to confirm *(v.)*	bestätigen		
account details *(n.)*	Einzelheiten, Angaben zum Konto	**jewel** *(n.)*	Juwel
		Janus *(n.)*	Janus (altgriechischer Gott mit zwei Gesichtern)
set *(n.)*	Satz		

sophisticated *(adj.)*	sophistiziert, klug	unauthorised *(adj.)*	nicht autorisiert, unberechtigt
to manipulate *(v.)*	manipulieren	to gain access *(v.)*	sich Zugang verschaffen
environment *(n.)*	Umwelt		
means *(n.)*	Mittel		
in particular *(adv.)*	insbesondere	data protection act *(n.)*	Datenschutzgesetz
Aladdin's cave *(n.)*	die Höhle des Aladdin, märchenhafte Schätze	wrongdoer *(n.)*	Missetäter
		felon *(n.)*	(Schwer-)Verbrecher
commerce *(n.)*	Kommerz, Geschäfte	level *(n.)*	Ebene, Niveau
local branch *(n.)*	nächste Zweigstelle, Niederlassung	legal *(adj.)*	juristisch
		local *(adj.)*	lokal, örtlich
cash dispenser *(n.)*	Geldautomat	jurisdiction *(n.)*	Rechtssprechung, Rechtssystem
bank clerk *(n.)*	Bankangestellte(r)		
counter *(n.)*	Schalter	to misunderstand *(v.)*	missverstehen
comfort *(n.)*	Komfort, Bequemlichkeit, Behaglichkeit	source *(n.)*	Quelle
		misinterpretation *(n.)*	Fehldeutung
There's no such thing.	So etwas gibt es nicht.	case *(n.)*	Fall
lunch *(n.)*	Mittagessen	watchword *(n.)*	Parole
hidden *(adj.)*	verdeckt, verborgen	to beware *(v.)*	sich in Acht nehmen
convenience *(n.)*	hier: Annehmlichkeit	clone *(n.)*	Klon
recent *(adj.)*	jüngste(r,s), neueste (r,s)	to trust *(v.)*	vertrauen
		proven *(adj.)*	hier: erfolgreich
survey *(n.)*	hier: Untersuchung, Umfrage	record *(n.)*	hier: Vorgeschichte
		genuine *(adj.)*	echt, genuin
to consider *(v.)*	in Betracht ziehen	extraordinary *(adj.)*	außerordentlich
downside *(n.)*	die negative Seite	bogus *(adj.)*	falsch, erfunden
numerous *(adj.)*	viele, zahlreiche	stock exchange *(n.)*	Börse
to complain *(v.)*	sich beschweren	obscure *(adj.)*	unbekannt, unklar
false *(adj.)*	falsch	base *(n.)*	Standort
promise *(n.)*	Versprechen	to recognize *(v.)*	erkennen
to be led to believe *(v.)*	jdn man glauben lassen	continuously *(adv.)*	kontinuierlich, fortlaufend
paperwork *(n)*	Schreibarbeit, „Papierkrieg"	to update *(v.)*	auf den neuesten Stand bringen
cheque *(n. BE)*	Scheck	to maintain *(v.)*	aufrechterhalten
to process *(v.)*	bearbeiten	password *(n.)*	Passwort
annoyance *(n.)*	Ärgernis	regularly *(adv.)*	regelmäßig
fear *(n.)*	Angst, Befürchtung	latest *(adj.)*	neueste(r,s)
security *(n.)*	Sicherheit	well-established *(adj.)*	gut etabliert, bewährt
theft *(n.)*	Diebstahl	device *(n.)*	Gerät
bank staff *(n.)*	Mitarbeiter der Bank	to remove *(v.)*	entfernen
hacker *(n.)*	Hacker	watchful *(adj.)*	aufmerksam, wachsam

Reading for Gist

1. Match them up
Welche dieser Satzhälften passen zusammen?

Example: 1 g

1. Our interest rates
2. You will be able to use
3. The wonders of the internet
4. There's no such thing
5. Numerous customers complain
6. There is still some paperwork to do
7. The main fear seems to be
8. On an international level
9. Trust only banks
10. U.S. banks advise their customers

a. as a free lunch.
b. of technical problems.
c. one of security.
d. the following facilities.
e. there can be legal and cultural problems.
f. to change their passwords regularly.
g. on savings are high.
h. with proven records.
i. when cheques have to be processed.
j. promise to make dreams come true.

2. Headlines
Welche Überschrift passt am besten zu welchem Absatz im Zeitungsartikel?

1. **Paragraph 1**
   a. ALADDIN AND HIS MAGIC COMPUTER b. JEWEL IN THE ENVIRONMENT
   c. ONLINE MAKES DREAMS COME TRUE d. MANIPULATING MONEY

2. **Paragraph 2**
   a. AT YOUR CONVENIENCE b. CHECK YOUR OWN CHEQUES c. APPLE COMPLAINS
   d. NO FREE LUNCH

3. **Paragraph 3**
   a. SAFETY FIRST MAIN WORRY b. HACKERS WELCOME c. BANK STAFF FEAR
   d. SYSTEM GUARANTEE

4. **Paragraph 4**
   a. INTERNATIONAL CHAOS b. LET THE BUYER BEWARE c. DANGEROUS COLOURS
   d. BEWARE OF EXPERTS

5. **Paragraph 5**
   a. JANUS SHOWS THE WAY b. KEEP YOUR PIN c. PASSWORD PROBLEMS
   d. AUS AND US WELL AHEAD

1. .... 2. .... 3. .... 4. .... 5. ....

3. True or false?
Sind diese Aussagen richtig oder falsch?

Example:	True	False
With an online account you can check your bank balance from home.	☑	☐

1. With an online account you cannot make money transfers. ☐ ☐
2. Operating an online account takes far longer than going to a cash dispenser. ☐ ☐
3. Some customers with online accounts have been disappointed. ☐ ☐
4. People are usually worried about hackers stealing their money. ☐ ☐
5. Different countries may use websites in different ways. ☐ ☐
6. It is dangerous to trust unusual offers sent by email. ☐ ☐
7. All stock exchange reports are definitely reliable. ☐ ☐
8. In Australia comparatively few customers have online accounts. ☐ ☐
9. Banks in the United States are very careless about security matters. ☐ ☐
10. New kinds of security device have been invented. ☐ ☐

Reading for Language

1. Match them up
Welche Definitionen passen zu den folgenden Begriffen?

Example: 1 e

1. bank charges
2. interest rates
3. credit balance
4. currency exchange rate
5. application form
6. tax deduction
7. current account
8. savings
9. cash dispenser
10. bank clerk

a. member of staff in a bank
b. the money the government takes
c. your normal bank account for everyday
d. what you write to open a bank account
e. what you pay for banking services
f. a machine that gives you money
g. the money left in your account
h. how much foreign money is worth
i. how much you earn a year on savings
j. money put aside to earn interest

2. Odd one out
Welches Wort passt nicht in die jeweilige Gruppe? Bitte unterstreichen Sie das Wort.

1.	2.	3.	4.	5.
a. queues	a. funds	a. e-commerce	a. genuine	a. survey
b. delays	b. application forms	b. e-business	b. bogus	b. quotation
c. annoyances	c. set of documents	c. insurance	c. trust	c. advice
d. comfort	d. return emails	d. online banking	d. proven	d. cheque

3. What does it mean?
Welche Bedeutung passt am besten zu den folgenden Wörtern und Begriffen?

Example:
A *current account* contains the money in your bank **a.** that you use every day? **b.** that you use to pay for your electricity? | a

1. If your bank has a *local branch*, **a.** is it a large building in the centre of the city? **b.** a smaller building very near where you live?
2. If something is described as *convenient* **a.** is it easy to find and use? **b.** is it part of a more complicated process?
3. What is a *free lunch*? **a.** cheap advertising **b.** a meal at midday that someone buys for you
4. If something has a *downside*, does it **a.** have disadvantages? **b.** belong to the centre of a city?
5. If a bank has a *proven record*, does it mean **a.** it has always been the best bank? **b.** it's reliable because past results were always good?
6. Is an *obscure source* of information **a.** somewhere you know very well? **b.** a place that you are not very sure of?
7. Does *maintaining security* mean **a.** keeping things safe? **b.** repairing machines?
8. Does a *bogus report* contain **a.** information that is true and reliable? **b.** false information?
9. Is a *wrongdoer* **a.** someone who is always making mistakes? **b.** someone who commits a crime or an offence?
10. If something is an *annoyance*, is it **a.** a pleasant experience? **b.** something you don't like or agree with?

4. Crossword

Across
1 What you have when things are safe (8)
7 Money you don't want to use yet (7)
8 Money that you have in your account (6)
9 Money you don't have in your account (5)

Down
2 A risk you take to earn more money (10)
3 Where your money is kept in a bank (7)
4 A special word you need for your account (8)
5 A special tool (6)
6 The short form of Personal Identity Number (3)

Reading for Understanding

1. Essential facts
Welche der folgenden Aussagen über den Textinhalt stimmen und welche nicht?

Example:	True	False
The online system promises to make banking less efficient.	☐	☑

	True	False
1. All you have to do to join an online bank is to sign a set of documents sent to you by email and send them back by post.	☐	☐
2. Online banks offer customers a wide range of different facilities.	☐	☐
3. Online banking would not be possible without the internet.	☐	☐
4. With some customers the online connection fails to work efficiently.	☐	☐
5. People are afraid of bank staff working online.	☐	☐
6. Foreign websites could prove to be a source of misunderstanding.	☐	☐
7. The internet makes legal problems simple and convenient.	☐	☐
8. There are no disadvantages involved with the new technology.	☐	☐
9. Australian customers can rely on the sytem being 100% secure.	☐	☐
10. In the United States customers have a new method of identification.	☐	☐

2. What does it really mean?
Welche der folgenden Eigenschaften sind Vorteile und welche sind Nachteile?

Example:	Advantage	Disadvantage
Less paperwork	☑	☐

	Advantage	Disadvantage
1. No more queueing	☐	☐
2. Technical problems	☐	☐
3. Lack of security	☐	☐
4. Legal problems abroad	☐	☐
5. Lower bank charges	☐	☐
6. False financial reports	☐	☐
7. Cultural misunderstandings	☐	☐
8. Fast transfer of funds	☐	☐
9. False promises	☐	☐
10. No need to walk	☐	☐

3. What do you think?
Was halten Sie von den neuen technologischen Errungenschaften?

Example:
Why do you think banks offer online services at all? **a.** to attract more customers while employing fewer bank staff **b.** to protect the environment with less paperwork — *a*

1. Why do you think customers are attracted to online banking? **a.** Because it promises to be easier than having to visit a bank. **b.** Because they can trust the bank more.
2. Why do you think online banks can offer higher interest rates on savings? **a.** Because they have more money from foreign business. **b.** Because they don't need to employ so many staff.
3. Why do you think present online customers might not be satisfied? **a.** Because technical problems are very frustrating. **b.** Because currency exchange rates change a lot.
4. Why do you think some customers might not like online banking at all? **a.** Because they prefer talking to real people face to face in the bank. **b.** Because they don't know how to open an account.
5. Why do you suppose potential customers may be afraid of security problems? **a.** Because they might lose all their money. **b.** Because hackers might annoy them.
6. Why do you think the data protection act is no guarantee of security? **a.** Because banks continuously update their software. **b.** Because criminals will usually find a way despite the law.
7. Why do you think online bank customers might meet with legal difficulties when dealing with foreign partners in other countries? **a.** Because the law in foreign countries might be different and not suppport them. **b.** Because the currency is different.
8. Why do you think the use of colour might be a problem in communication, especially in banking? **a.** Because red is used for minus figures in Europe but not in Asia. **b.** Because websites abroad don't use colour.

Over to you

Private business
Wie attraktiv ist Online-Banking für Sie?

Numerous banks already offer Telebanking or Online Banking services. Choose from the following two alternative tasks the one that corresponds with your own circumstances.
a) You already have an online account. Would you recommend it to your friends? Write a short report describing the advantages and disadvantages of the system.
b) You don't yet have an online account. Use a search engine on your computer to find offers of online banking on the internet. Compare the services offered and write a short report saying why you would or wouldn't like to use an online bank.

Unit 14

Environmental Issues

Ozonloch über der Antarktis, Staubwolke über Asien, Magnetfeldverschiebung, Ausweitung der Sahelzone in Afrika, El Niño im pazifischen Raum, Erdrutsche in den Bergen, Meldungen von Hochwasser – unsere Erde zeigt Krankheitssymptome: Was macht die Industrie oder die Geschäftswelt dagegen? Allgemeiner Konsens ist, dass alle ökologischen Probleme wie in dem Märchen des Zauberlehrlings das Ergebnis unvorsichtiger und risikoreicher Projekte und profitgierigen Unternehmertums sind. Hybris und Ignoranz der Menschheit führen unweigerlich zu Umweltkatastrophen.

Aber viele haben diese Probleme erkannt und unternehmen auch Gegenmaßnahmen. Schließlich hat die *business world* nicht nur eine hohe Verantwortung, sondern auch die notwendigen Mittel, konkrete Schritte zu unternehmen.

In diesem Text geht es um eine Gegenmaßnahme besonderer Art und um die Anregung an alle *business manager*, die Konsequenzen ihrer Handlungen auch im Hinblick auf die Umwelt zu bedenken. Positiv gesehen könnten auch diese Maßnahmen profitabel sein, da sie ja im Dienste der Menschheit und im Interesse vieler Betroffener geschehen.

Before you read
Welche Arten von Umweltschäden kennen Sie?
Machen Sie eine Liste der fünf Ihrer Meinung nach wohl gefährlichsten. Schreiben Sie dazu jeweils eine mögliche Gegenmaßnahme, die Sie für sinnvoll und durchführbar halten.

Quenching Greeks' Thirst
Water supply problems on the island of Milos

by Daphne James

On the beautiful island of Milos there is a normal population of 7,000. During the holiday period in summer this increases to over 700,000. As a result the island is suffering from an acute water shortage. The groundwater table has receded to unreachable depths and sea water has now begun to pollute it. To provide drinking water for the island it has become necessary to transport over 300,000 tons of mineral water in bottles and 240,000 tons of water in tankers to Milos every year. The cost of doing this is gradually becoming prohibitive. The tourist industry has resulted in environmental damage, the pursuit of pleasure has brought pain to the land.

But all is not yet lost. There is a scheme afoot which promises not only to help the island but to create an example of positive thinking and a pragmatic approach to environmental problems with the aid of environmentally-friendly new technology. In cooperation with the Greek government and aided by EC funding, the German insurance group Gerling has launched a partly private, partly public partnership under the name of the Milos Project. By tapping into the geothermal energy available on the island they plan to run a desalination plant to produce drinking water from the sea. It will be the first project of its kind to choose a solution like this and has won support from the European Community due to its innovative nature. The process is simple: geothermal fluids from the earth's crust with a temperature of over 200 degrees Fahrenheit are pumped up to provide the energy required for the desalination of the seawater and to generate electricity. Once the heat has been used the fluids are injected back underground. The electricity they have helped generate is sufficient to pump and re-inject the fluids and thus keep running costs to a minimum.

The result will be not only a plentiful fresh water supply for the island at an estimated cost of $ 1.8/cubic meter compared with the previously huge sum of $ 356/cubic meter, but also the possibility of providing irrigation for local agriculture. In time, the groundwater table will recover and the system could then continue to provide a long-term sustainable energy source for the island.

The Gerling group are working on several similar projects elsewhere. They see them as a means of developing new insurance markets by meeting the needs of local communities while providing long-term environmentally-sound solutions. Their investment should therefore be of mutual benefit to all concerned and the scheme show that a positive, practical and profitable solution to some of the world's environmental problems can be achieved with the aid of old and new technologies combined in innovative ways. Just because technology has created environmental problems it does not follow that technology is evil. We must not throw out the baby with the bathwater. Indeed, the bathwater can be saved and the baby, too, as the Milos Project proves.

This is just one of the ways forward. The harnessing of solar power is another. In Germany and Japan there have been government subsidies for solar installations. Japan has installed 450 megawatts of solar power in private homes and businesses. Germany has achieved 150 megawatts against a mere 2 megawatts in Britain. There are planned increases in all three countries by 2005. Denmark on the other hand has invested in wind power and now generates 20% of its electricity that way.

However, in each case this has not been possible without substantial financial committment on the part of the governments. As the Earth Summit in Johannesburg in August of 2002 showed, private initiatives alone to utilise new technologies will not be enough. It needs a combined effort at the highest level with strict regulations to ensure our environmental future. The U.S. could learn a thing or two from these European initiatives.

Vocabulary

to quench *(v.)*	stillen	pursuit *(n.)*	Streben, Jagd (nach)
Greek *(n.)*	Grieche, Griechin	pleasure *(n.)*	Vergnügen
thirst *(n.)*	Durst	pain *(n.)*	Schmerz
population *(n.)*	Bevölkerung	scheme *(n.)*	Plan, Vorhaben
to increase *(v.)*	wachsen	afoot *(adv.)*	in der Mache
to suffer *(v.)*	leiden	positive thinking *(n.)*	positives Denken
acute *(adj.)*	akut	pragmatic *(adj.)*	pragmatisch
shortage *(n.)*	Knappheit	approach *(n.)*	Ansatz
groundwater table *(n.)*	Grundwasserspiegel	environmental *(adj.)* environmentally-friendly *(adj.)*	Umwelt- umweltfreundlich
to recede *(v.)*	zurückgehen		
unreachable *(adj.)*	unerreichbar	cooperation *(n.)*	Zuammenarbeit, Kooperation
depth *(n.)*	Tiefe		
to pollute *(v.)*	verunreinigen	to aid *(v.)*	helfen, unterstützen
prohibitive *(adj.)*	untragbar	funding *(n.)*	Finanzierung
to result in *(v.)*	hinauslaufen auf	insurance *(n.)*	Versicherung
environmental damage *(n.)*	Umweltschäden	to launch *(v.)*	starten
		public *(adj.)*	öffentlich

partnership *(n.)*	Partnerschaft	to meet the needs	Bedürfnisse befriedigen
to tap into *(v.)*	anzapfen		
geothermal *(adj.)*	geothermal	community *(n.)*	Gemeinschaft
energy *(n.)*	Energie	sound *(adj.)*	gesund
available *(adj.)*	vorhanden, zugänglich	mutual *(adj.)*	gemeinsam, gegenseitig
to run *(v.)*	hier: betreiben, unterhalten	benefit *(n.)*	Vorteil
desalination plant *(n.)*	Entsalzungsanlage	all concerned *(n.)*	alle Beteiligten
		profitable *(adj.)*	rentabel, lohnend
drinking water *(n.)*	Trinkwasser	to achieve *(v.)*	erreichen
of its kind	dieser Art	with the aid of	mit der Hilfe von
support *(n.)*	Unterstützung	to follow *(v.)*	hier: daraus folgen
innovative *(adj.)*	innovativ	evil *(adj.)*	böse
fluids *(n.)*	Flüssigkeiten	to throw out the baby with the bathwater	das Kind mit dem Bade(wasser) ausschütten
earth's crust *(n.)*	Erdkruste		
to provide *(v.)*	liefern		
to generate *(v.)*	erzeugen	indeed *(adv.)*	in der Tat
to inject *(v.)*	einspritzen	to save *(v.)*	retten
underground *(adv.)*	unterirdisch	forward *(adv.)*	nach vorn
sufficient *(adj.)*	ausreichend	harnessing *(n.)*	Nutzen, nutzbar Machen
running costs *(n.)*	Unterhaltskosten		
plentiful *(adj.)*	ergiebig	solar power *(n.)*	Sonnenkraft, -energie
supply *(n.)*	Vorrat		
to estimate *(v.)*	schätzen	subsidy *(n.)*	Subvention
to compare *(v.)*	vergleichen	solar installations *(n.)*	Sonnenkraftwerke
previously *(adv.)*	vorherig	mere *(adj.)*	bloß
huge *(adj.)*	riesig	increase *(n.)*	Zuwachs
possibility *(n.)*	Möglichkeit	wind power *(n.)*	Windkraft, -energie
irrigation *(n.)*	Bewässerung	substantial *(adj.)*	erheblich, sunstantiell
agriculture *(n.)*	Landwirtschaft	commitment *(n.)*	Verpflichtung, Engagement
to recover *(v.)*	sich erholen		
to continue *(v.)*	fortfahren, fortsetzen	to utilise *(v.)*	nutzen
		combined *(adj.)*	kombiniert
long-term *(adj.)*	Langzeit-	effort *(n.)*	Anstrengung
sustainable *(adj.)*	haltbar	level *(n.)*	Niveau, Ebene
energy source *(n.)*	Energiequelle	regulations *(n.)*	Verordnungen, Vorschriften
elsewhere *(adv.)*	anderswo		
means *(n.)*	Mittel	to ensure *(v.)*	sicher stellen

Reading for Gist

1. True or false?
Sind diese Aussagen richtig oder falsch?

	True	False
Example: The normal population of Milos is over 700,000.	☐	☑
1. There is an acute shortage of drinking water on the island.	☐	☐
2. The population now exports water in bottles.	☐	☐
3. The cost of supplying water is now minimal.	☐	☐
4. The large number of tourists has caused damage to the environment.	☐	☐
5. Help has been promised from Germany.	☐	☐
6. A factory will be built to pump water into the sea.	☐	☐
7. The earth will provide the necessary energy.	☐	☐
8. Agriculture will also be able to profit from the scheme.	☐	☐
9. New technologies always create environmental problems.	☐	☐
10. Different energy sources are being tested in Europe.	☐	☐

2. Match them up
Welche Satzteile gehören zusammen?

Example: 1 e

1. During the holiday season
2. The groundwater table has receded
3. The tourist industry has resulted
4. By tapping into the geothermal energy
5. The project has won EC support
6. Once the heat has been used
7. The system could then continue to provide
8. The investment should therefore be
9. The harnessing of solar power
10. It needs a combined effort at the highest level

a. of mutual benefit to all concerned.
b. due to its innovative nature.
c. to ensure our environmental future.
d. is another way forward.
e. the population increases.
f. they plan to run a desalination plant.
g. to unreachable depths.
h. a long-term energy source.
i. the fluids are injected back underground.
j. in environmental damage.

3. Headlines
Wählen Sie die beste Schlagzeile für den jeweiligen Absatz

1. **Paragraph 1**
   a. WATER FOR ALL ON MILOS **b.** MILOS GROWS **c.** PLEASURE BRINGS PAIN TO PEOPLE OF MILOS
2. **Paragraph 2**
   a. PLAN TO SAVE GREEK WATER **b.** FRESH WATER IN DANGER **c.** GERMANS INSURE WATER SUPPLY
3. **Paragraph 3**
   a. AGRICULTURE RUINED **b.** DRAMATIC FALL IN PRICE OF SUPPLY **c.** WATER DRUNK IN CUBIC METRES
4. **Paragraph 4**
   a. INSURANCE CLAIMS RISE **b.** BABY AND BATHWATER SAVED **c.** TECHNOLOGY ON TRIAL
5. **Paragraph 5**
   a. FREE SUNSHINE IN JAPAN **b.** WIND POWER JUST HOT AIR **c.** NEW ENERGY SOURCES EXPLORED
6. **Paragraph 6**
   a. GOVT. AID A MUST **b.** EARTH SUMMIT FAILS **c.** THE FUTURE IS PRIVATE

1.	2.	3.	4.	5.	6. ....

Reading for Language

1. Choose the right word
Wählen Sie das richtige Wort zur Ergänzung folgender Sätze.

Example:
The normal *population* of Milos is 7,000. | **a** |
a. population   **b.** tourist industry   **c.** environment

1. The cost of transporting drinking water has become ....
   a. sufficient   **b.** unreachable   **c.** prohibitive
2. The island of Milos has suffered .... damage.
   a. sustainable   **b** environmental   **c.** necessary
3. New technology needs to be environmentally ....
   a. evil   **b.** acute   **c.** friendly
4. The new scheme will bring a .... supply of fresh water.
   a. private   **b.** plentiful   **c.** mutual
5. The plant will provide a .... energy source.
   a. sustainable   **b.** solar   **c.** similar

2. Match them up
Welche Wörter lassen sich miteinander kombinieren?

Example: 1 f

1. groundwater
2. positive
3. geothermal
4. insurance
5. desalination
6. earth's
7. mutual
8. solar
9. private
10. combined

a. plant
b. power
c. crust
d. initiative
e. fluids
f. table
g. effort
h. group
i. thinking
j. benefit

3. True or false?
Sind diese Aussagen richtig oder falsch?

Example:	True	False
A *scheme* is another name for a plan.	✓	☐

	True	False
1. *Geothermal fluids* are hot.	☐	☐
2. *Irrigation* is essential for agriculture.	☐	☐
3. A *desalination plant* puts salt into water.	☐	☐
4. A *solar installation* is another expression for sun-lamp.	☐	☐
5. *Environmentally sound* means the environment will not be damaged.	☐	☐
6. A *sustainable* energy source will only last for a very short time.	☐	☐
7. Something that is of *mutual* benefit to all means that it may not be realistic.	☐	☐
8. If a government shows *commitment* to a scheme, then it will agree to support it.	☐	☐
9. *Agriculture* is another word for farming.	☐	☐
10. A *sound* solution to a problem is one that will probably succeed.	☐	☐

4. Odd one out
Welches Wort passt nicht in die jeweilige Gruppe. Bitte unterstreichen Sie das Wort.

Example: 1 d

1.
a. energy
b. power
c. megawatt
d. damage

2.
a. geothermal
b. solar
c. acute
d. wind

3.
a. depth
b. partnership
c. scheme
d. plan

4.
a. long-term
b. mutual
c. sustainable
d. plentiful

5.
a. insurance
b. agriculture
c. irrigation
d. desalination

6.
a. to inject
b. to suffer
c. to install
d. to generate

7.
a. cost
b. funding
c. regulation
d. running costs

8.
a. commitment
b. shortage
c. initiative
d. effort

5. Crossword

Across
1 Another word for power (6)
5 When there is not much left (8)
6 When things get broken (6)
8 To make something dirty or poisonous (7)

Down
2 Coming hot out of the earth's crust (10)
3 Land surrounded by sea (6)
4 To do with the sun (5)
7 Another word for factory (5)

Reading for Understanding

1. Essential facts
Welche der folgenden Aussagen sind richtig und welche falsch?

	True	False
Example: The Greek island of Milos is short of water.	✓	☐

1. The groundwater table is now too low. ☐ ☐
2. The sea is being polluted as a result. ☐ ☐
3. Thousands of tons of mineral water have caused environmental damage. ☐ ☐
4. Help is being offered by means of a new scheme. ☐ ☐
5. Heat from below the earth will be used to generate electricity. ☐ ☐
6. The electricity will run a geothermal plant. ☐ ☐
7. Costs will be reduced by an enormous amount. ☐ ☐
8. It follows from this that new technologies are dangerous. ☐ ☐
9. Several countries are already using alternative energy sources. ☐ ☐
10. Our future depends totally upon private companies. ☐ ☐

2. What does it mean?

Versuchen Sie folgende Fragen zu beantworten.

Example:
Why do the people of Milos have to import their drinking water?
 a. to create geothermal energy   b. Because there's a water shortage.   `b`

1. Why has the pursuit of pleasure brought pain to the land?
    a. Because there are too many tourists who use all the water.
    b. Because mineral water is not good for agriculture.
2. What help will the Gerling group receive?
    a. insurance from the tourists   b. money from the European Community
3. What energy is already available on the island?
    a. solar power installations   b. heat sources form the earth's crust
4. Why will the system be a long-term sustainable energy source?
    a. Because the costs will be lower.
    b. Because the supply of seawater and geothermal fluids is so big.
5. How does the Gerling group hope to make the project profitable for themselves?
    a. by selling the drinking water   b. by developing new insurance markets
6. What is the principle behind these innovative schemes?
    a. combining old and new technologies for the mutual benefit of all
    b. using private enterprise
7. What have governments done in Europe to solve the energy problem?
    a. examined new technologies more closely
    b. provided subsidies for building solar and wind installations
8. What will be needed to ensure the environmetal future?
    a. a combined effort from private, public and government sources
    b. regular Earth Summit meetings

3. What do you think?
Wie interpretieren Sie die Aussagen im Text? Versuchen Sie nun auch folgende Fragen zu beantworten.

> *Example:*
> Why do you think the problem of water shortage occurred in the first place?
>   **a.** Because people were more interested in attracting tourists in order to earn money.
>   **b.** Because the sea had begun to pollute the groundwater.   `a`

1. Why do you think the cost of importing drinking water became prohibitive?
    a. Because of the damage to the environment.
    b. Because of the increasing need for more water for more tourists.
2. Why do you think the Milos Project could be important outside the island?
    a. Because it serves as an example to others.
    b. Because the tourist industry is important.
3. Why does the Milos Project work well on Milos?
    a. Because the weather is generally hot.
    b. Because Milos is an island with easy access to seawater.
4. Why do you think Japan has invested more in solar energy and Denmark more in wind power?
    a. Because they are the sources of energy most readily available there.
    b. Because they developed different technologies.
5. Why do you think governments might agree to provide substantial funding to similar schemes in future?
    a. Because it will help them to avoid more environmental problems in the future.
    b. Because they want to avoid supporting private business.

Over to You

1. Project proposal
Stellen Sie sich vor, Sie wurden beauftragt, die europäische Regierung um Unterstützung für das neue WINDSOL-Projekt zu bitten.
The WINDSOL project is a scheme to provide a sustainable energy supply for your local community using wind and solar power. Write a description of the project and a request for financial help to your local member of parliament. Think of how local firms might benefit.
List the advantages for the community and the environment compared with the present situation and compare it with schemes in other countries. Make a list of requirements and of the necessary regulations you think need to apply.

2. Search the net
Suchen Sie andere „Umwelt-Projekte".
Use the internet to find out about further environmentally friendly energy projects, some of which may have been in place for some time: the Dinorwic Pumping Station in North Wales, for example. Write a short report and make a list of the different technologies involved.

Unit 15

Taxation

Lohnsteuer, Einkommenssteuer, Vermögenssteuer, Erbschaftssteuer, Quellensteuer, Mehrwertsteuer, Umsatzsteuer, Kfz-Steuer, Luxussteuer – eine schier unendliche Liste. Für fast alles, was wir in der modernen Welt unternehmen, müssen wir anscheinend irgendeine Art Steuer zahlen, entweder direkt ans Finanzamt oder indirekt über unsere Einkäufe und täglichen Ausgaben. Aber es war nicht immer so und muss auch deshalb nicht immer so sein ... oder doch? Der Staat braucht Geld zur Finanzierung unseres Lebensstandards und der Stabilität. Der Steuerzahler leistet seinen Obolus nach inzwischen bewährten und akzeptierten Methoden und Systemen.

Durch die rasante Entwicklung der digitalen Technologie eröffnen sich viele neue Wege Geschäfte zu machen – so viele, dass die bisherigen Methoden bald verschwinden und durch Online-Techniken ersetzt werden. E-Mail, Online-Dienste über das Internet sind bereits etabliert und selbstverständlich. Aber, wie der folgende Text aus den USA zeigt, gibt es bei dieser Revolution nicht nur Änderungen in unserem Verhalten, die den status quo außer Kraft setzen könnten, sondern dann auch die Befürchtung, dass andere Systeme diesen Neuerungen angepasst werden müssen – insbesondere das Steuersystem als Finanzquelle für lokale und nationale Bedürfnisse. Allerdings ist das gar nicht so einfach, denn vieles bei *e-commerce* ist anders als bei herkömmlichen Methoden. Man sollte deshalb über Steuersysteme grundsätzlich nachdenken, bevor man voreilige Entscheidungen trifft. Hierzu hilft manchmal auch ein wenig Geschichte!

Before you read

Warum müssen wir eigentlich Steuern zahlen? Welche Arten von Steuern zahlen wir und warum? Welche Arten von Steuern kennen Sie aus eigener Erfahrung? Bevor Sie diesen etwas längeren Text lesen, versuchen Sie **a.** alle Ihnen bekannten Steuerarten aufzulisten und **b.** aus Ihrer letzten Lohn- oder Einkommenssteuererklärung eine Liste der wichtigsten Punkte zu schreiben, die dieser Art Steuererklärung zugrunde liegen.

Taxing Cyberspace

Re-thinking the principles of the U.S. tax system

from our New York correspondent

"Governments of the Industrial World, you weary giants of flesh and steel, I come from Cyberspace, the new home of Mind. On behalf of the future, I ask you of the past to leave us alone. You are not welcome among us. You have no sovereignty where we gather."
Songwriter John Perry Barlow, February 1996

A brief history of taxation

Since ancient times taxation has been a means of creating revenue for various purposes. The Egyptian pharaohs imposed taxes on such everyday commodities as cooking oil in order to help finance their lifestyle. The Athenians of ancient Greece raised a special tax in times of war and refunded it from the spoils they gained. They also imposed a poll tax on all foreigners. It was the Romans, however, who first created taxation systems with various grades and levels. Caesar Augustus decentralized the process by giving responsibility to individual cities within the Empire. He created an inheritance tax of 5 percent on all inheritances to provide a retirement fund for members of the miltary. He also introduced a sales tax of 4 percent on the sale of slaves and 1 percent on everything else.

Throughout the Middle Ages in Europe taxes were levied on land and property in almost every kind of regime. In Britain, legendary characters like Robin Hood fought the Sheriff of Nottingham, who imposed oppressive taxes on the poor. But it was in Britain that in the 14th century the idea of progressive taxation was born. Both poll tax and income tax were based on the individual's income and wealth – the rich paying more and the poor less.

In the 17th century, however, no less a figure than Oliver Cromwell introduced excise taxes on commodities like meat and grain – a regressive tax that placed an even heavier burden on the poor.

And let us not forget, it was the imposition of unjust taxation by the British King George III on the thirteen colonies that led to the American Revolution. It was in circumstances of war, too, that Abraham Lincoln introduced a progressive tax on income some one hundred years later – 3 percent on incomes over 600 dollars and 5 percent on incomes over 10.000 dollars!

Despite several changes after the war, even this was eventually declared unconstitutional.

Modern times

Since then it seems taxation has known no bounds, in the present-day State of New York alone we are confronted by the following:

Property Transfer Tax: involving Estate-Tax, Real Estate Transfer Tax

Sales & Use Tax: levied on transportation, services, food and hotels

Personal Income Tax: with its complicated system of personal status, tax brackets and credits

Excise Taxes: levied on tobacco products, alcoholic beverages, motor fuel, bets on horse racing and the proceeds from boxing and wrestling

Business Taxes: including Corporation Franchise Tax, Unrelated Business Income Tax, Corporation and Utility Tax, Petroleum Business Tax, Bank Tax, Insurance Tax....

The list seems endless.

The advent of the digital age

Past history and its established methods is now confronted by a new phenomenon: computers, the internet and electronic commerce. 36% of American families now have home computers. The number of U.S. websites is increasing by one per minute. In the world there are now upwards of 180 million computers, 645 million telephones and 1.2 billion televisions in over 160 countries.

However, commercialisation of the electronic revolution is still in its infancy, despite the fact that everyone recognizes the new technology's tremendous commercial potential. Digital technology combines what hitherto have been three separate areas – data, voice and video transmissions – into one new powerful combination that can provide instant access to software, video on demand, cable TV, music albums, books, newspapers and magazines, information data bases, education and job training, home banking, health care services, electronic bill payment, customer services, online stock trading, bulletin boards and chat rooms and, of course, last but certainly not least, email.

A taxing task

This enormous new commercial potential also has far-reaching consequences for the tax system. The income tax laws of individual U.S. states now have to apply to earnings from electronic commerce, but given the complex intangible and interstate nature of business via the internet, it becomes difficult to define a base for calculations. What kind of tax applies to e-commerce? Income tax, sales tax, services tax, property tax? Which statutes in which state apply? Whose jurisdiction is it? The state where the company is based ? Or where business is transacted? Or where the customer lives?

Then there is the federal aspect. Taxes in the U.S. are not just an issue of single state legislation. Federal and international tax rules may also apply and have to be adjusted. The US federal government does not impose sales taxes or taxes on transactions. There is, however, a 3 percent federal excise tax on amounts paid for "communication services" – which means telephone services – but what does this cover? How broad or narrow a field in this new digital context?

Internationally, the U.S., unlike most other countries, does not impose VAT or a national sales tax. So if there is a transaction via the internet between America and another country, does VAT apply? Which tax authority has jurisdiction? Will the American customer be faced with additional costs at the European rate of up to 20 percent VAT? Taxpayers anywhere may be subject to double taxation. And more down to earth: even if the product is defined, the location of the vendor, the base for taxation determined, the identity of the customer clear, where does the taxpayer obtain his or her all-important copy of the invoice marked "paid" in a paperless world?

An opportunity too good to miss

This lack of clarity only serves to strengthen what are already strong anti-tax feelings among the electorate. Politicians are well aware of this and of not wishing to discourage or impede business with inopportune new methods of taxation. The legislature is wary simply because the future is so hard to predict.

What is clear to all concerned, however, seems to be this: e-business will create enormous new sources of income and very attractive growth rates in industry and commerce both within and outside the United States. If the community as a whole is to benefit from this, the states must change and adapt their taxation methods or lose sources of revenue. To do this they need to determine:
– whether it is the vendor that has "nexus" with the taxing jurisdiction and is therefore responsible for filing tax returns
– whether a sales or use tax applies
– whether the sale is sourced or sited to a particular jurisdiction for income tax purposes.

The complexity of e-commerce, state tax rules and federal legislation means that the taxation of cyberspace will never be simple. But if an acceptable solution for all concerned is to be found, then states and businesses will have to work together.

Vocabulary

to tax (v.)	besteuern, mit einer Steuer belegen	**on behalf of** (prep.)	im Namen von
cyberspace (n.)	virtueller Raum, wo sich elektronische Information befindet	**sovereignty** (n.)	Hoheitsrechte
		to gather (v.)	zusammenkommen
		in ancient times (adj.)	in der Antike
giant (n.)	Riese	**revenue** (n.)	Einkünfte
flesh (n.)	Fleisch	**to impose** (v.)	hier: erheben, mit ... belegen
steel (n.)	Stahl		
mind (n.)	hier: Geist	**commodity** (n.)	Ware, Erzeugnis

150

cooking oil *(n.)*	Speiseöl
to raise *(v.)*	hier: erheben
to refund *(v.)*	zurückerstatten
spoils *(n.)*	Kriegsbeute
to gain *(v.)*	gewinnen
poll tax *(n.)*	etwa: Personen- oder Kopfsteuer
Roman *(n.)*	Römer
to create *(v.)*	kreieren
grade *(n.)*	Stufe
level *(n.)*	Ebene
process *(n.)*	Verfahren
responsibility *(n.)*	Verantwortung, Zuständigkeit
Empire *(n.)*	Reich
inheritance tax *(n.)*	Erbschaftssteuer
to provide *(v.)*	schaffen, zur Verfügung stellen
retirement fund *(n.)*	Pensionskasse
member *(n.)*	Mitglied
military *(n.)*	Militär
to introduce *(v.)*	einführen
sales tax *(n.)* AE	Verkaufssteuer
slave *(n.)*	Sklave
everything else *(pn.)*	alles andere
throughout *(prep.)*	während, den, die das …hindurch
Middle Ages *(n.)*	Mittelalter
to levy *(v.)*	erheben, einziehen
property *(n.)*	Besitz, Eigentum
legendary *(adj.)*	legendär
to fight *(v.)*	kämpfen
oppressive *(adj.)*	erdrückend, repressiv
the poor *(n.)*	die Armen
century *(n.)*	Jahrhundert
progressive taxation *(n.)*	progressives (gestaffeltes) Steuersystem
income tax *(n.)*	Einkommenssteuer
to be based on *(v.)*	basieren auf
individual *(n.)*	Einzelne(r)
income *(n.)*	Einkommen
wealth *(n.)*	Vermögen
excise tax *(n.)*	Verbrauchssteuer
meat *(n.)*	Fleisch
grain *(n.)*	Getreide
regressive *(adj.)*	regressiv, rückläufig
to place *(v.)*	hier: legen
even *(adv.)*	hier: noch
burden *(n.)*	Last, Belastung
imposition *(n.)*	Erhebung, Auferlegung
unjust *(adj.)*	ungerecht
circumstances *(n.)*	Umstände
despite *(prep.)*	trotz
eventually *(adv.)*	schließlich
to declare *(v.)*	erklären
unconstitutional *(adj.)*	verfassungswidrig
to know no bounds *(v.)*	keine Grenzen kennen
present-day *(adj.)*	heutig
Property Transfer Tax *(n.)* AE	etwa: Immobilienverkaufssteuer, Grunderwerbssteuer
Estate Tax *(n.)* AE	Erbschaftssteuer
Real Estate Transfer Tax *(n.)* AE	etwa: Grunderwerbssteuer
Sales & Use Tax *(n.)* AE	etwa: Verkaufs- und Verbrauchssteuer
transportation services *(n.)*	öffentliche Verkehrsmittel
food *(n.)*	hier: Nahrungsmittel
Personal Income Tax *(n.)* AE	persönliche Einkommensteuer
tax bracket *(n.)*	Steuergruppe
credits *(n.)*	hier: Freibeträge
beverage *(n.)*	Getränk
motor fuel *(n.)*	Kraftstoff
bets *(n.)*	Wetten
proceeds *(n.)*	Erlöse
boxing *(n.)*	Boxkämpfe
wrestling *(n.)*	Ringkämpfe
Business Taxes *(n.)* AE	etwa: Gewerbesteuer

Corporation Franchise Tax (n.) AE	etwa: Körperschaftssteuer	far-reaching (adj.)	weit reichend
Unrelated Business Income Tax (n.) AE	etwa: Nebenerwerbssteuer	laws (n.)	Gesetze
		states (n.)	Staaten
		earnings (n.)	Einkünfte
Corporation & UtilityTax (n.) AE	etwa: Körperschafts- und Betriebssteuer	intangible (adj.)	nicht greifbar
		interstate nature (n.)	zwischen- oder einzelstaatliche Natur
Petroleum Business Tax (n.) AE	etwa: Mineralölsteuer	base (n.)	Basis
Bank Tax (n.) AE	etwa: Bankensteuer	services tax (n.)	Dienstleistungssteuer
Insurance Tax (n.) AE	Versicherungssteuer	property tax (n.)	Vermögenssteuer
endless (n.)	endlos	statutes (n.)	Statuten
advent (n.)	Beginn	jurisdiction (n.)	hier: Gerichtsstand
established (adj.)	etabliert	to transact (v.)	durchführen, abschließen
electronic commerce (n.)	elektronischer Geschäftsverkehr	federal (adj.)	Bundes-,
to increase (v.)	steigen	issue (n.)	Sache, Angelegenheit
upwards of (prep.)	mehr als	state legislation (n.)	Rechtsprechung/ Gerichtsbarkeit eines Bundesstaates
infancy (n.)	Anfangsstadium, in den Kinderschuhen		
to recognize (v.)	erkennen	to adjust (v.)	justieren, abändern
tremendous (adj.)	ungeheuer	federal government (n.)	Bundesregierung
hitherto (adv.)	bisher		
data (n.)	Daten	communication services (n)	Kommunikations- und Vermittlungsdienste
voice (n.)	hier: Ton		
video transmissions (n.)	Videoübertragungen	broad (adj.)	breit, weit
		narrow (adj.)	eng, schmal
powerful (adj.)	stark, mächtig	unlike (prep.)	nicht wie, anders als
access (n.)	Zugang	VAT (n.)	
video on demand (n.)	Video auf Abruf	Value Added Tax	Mehrwertsteuer
cable TV (n.)	Kabelfernsehen	tax authority (n.)	Steuerbehörde, Finanzamt
education (n.)	Bildung(swesen)		
health care (n.)	Gesundheitswesen	rate (n.)	hier: Höhe, Prozentsatz
electronic bill payment (n.)	Bezahlung von Rechnungen auf elektronischem Wege		
		double taxation (n.)	Doppelbesteuerung
		down to earth (adj.)	bodenständig, alltäglich
customer services (n.)	Kundendienste		
		location (n.)	Standort
online stock trading (n.)	Online-Aktiengeschäfte; Online-Börse	vendor (n.)	Verkäufer
		to determine (v.)	feststellen, festlegen
		invoice (n.)	Rechnung
bulletin board (n.)	„schwarzes Brett", Notizbrett, Forum	to miss (v.)	verpassen, auslassen
		lack (n.)	Mangel
taxing (adj.)	anstrengend	to serve to (v.)	dienen zu

152

to strengthen *(v.)*	verstärken, bestärken	outside *(prep.)*	außerhalb
electorate *(n.)*	Wähler	to benefit *(v.)*	profitieren
aware *(adj.)*	(sich) bewusst	sources of revenue *(n.)*	Einnahmequellen
to discourage *(v.)*	entmutigen	nexus *(n.)*	Verknüpfung, Verflochtenheit
to impede *(v.)*	aufhalten, (ver)hindern	responsible *(adj.)*	verantwortlich
inopportune *(adj.)*	unpassend	to file *(v.)*	hier: einreichen
legislature *(n.)*	Legislatur, Gesetz(gebung)	tax returns *(n.)*	Steuererklärung
wary *(adj.)*	vorsichtig	use tax *(n.)*	Gebrauchssteuer
to predict *(v.)*	vorhersagen	to be sourced *(v.)*	seine Quelle haben (bei)
to all concerned	an alle Beteiligten	to be sited *(v.)*	seinen Standort haben (in)
source *(n.)*	Quelle	legislation *(n.)*	Gesetzgebung
growth rate *(n.)*	Wachstumsrate		
within *(prep.)*	innerhalb		

Reading for Gist

1. Match them up
Welche Satzteile gehören zusammen?

Example: 1 d

1. Taxation has always been
2. Caesar Augustus provided
3. The Sheriff of Nottingham imposed
4. The idea of progessive taxation
5. The imposition of unjust taxation
6. The State of New York has
7. Commercialisation of the electronic revolution
8. The income tax laws now have to apply
9. Taxes in the U.S. are not just
10. The lack of clarity serves to strengthen

a. to earnings from electronic commerce.
b. is still in its infancy.
c. strong anti-tax feelings.
d. a means of creating revenue.
e. an issue of single state legislation.
f. a retirement fund for the military.
g. was born in Britain.
h. oppressive taxes on the poor.
i. a seemingly endless list of taxes.
j. led to the American Revolution.

2. Odd one out
Welcher Begriff passt nicht zum jeweiligen Absatz des Artikels?

1. *A brief history of taxation* **a.** ancient times **b.** legendary characters **c.** communication services **d.** sales tax on slaves
2. *Modern times* **a.** boxing and wrestling **b.** endless list **c.** present-day state **d.** circumstances of war
3. *The advent of the digital age* **a.** powerful combination **b.** double taxation **c.** electronic commerce **d.** computers
4. *A taxing task* **a.** attractive growth rates **b.** the federal aspect **c.** intangible nature **d.** far-reaching consequences
5. *An opportunity too good to miss* **a.** enormous new sources **b.** in its infancy **c.** legislature is wary **d.** anti-tax feelings

3. True or false?
Welche der folgenden Aussagen sind richtig und welche nicht?

	True	False
Example: Taxation has never been a means of creating revenue.	☐	☑
1. Taxes were not levied on land and property until after the American Revolution.	☐	☐
2. The Romans created a tax to provide money for retired soldiers.	☐	☐
3. A progressive income tax introduced by Abraham Lincoln was later declared unconstitutional.	☐	☐
4. The State of New York imposes taxes on boxing and wrestling.	☐	☐
5. All American families now have home computers.	☐	☐
6. Digital technology has very little potential commercially.	☐	☐
7. Electronic commerce is an intangible business.	☐	☐
8. The U.S. federal government is not involved in taxation.	☐	☐
9. There is a very strong anti-tax feeling among the U.S. electorate.	☐	☐
10. Now that jurisdiction has been clarified, the tax question has been answered.	☐	☐

Reading for Language

1. The missing word
Setzen Sie bitte das richtige Wort aus der Liste in die Lücke.

> predict – earnings – progressive – benefit – commodities – impede – access – VAT – sales – jurisdiction – credits

Example:
The Egyptians imposed taxes on everyday ... *(commodities)*...

1. Caesar Augustus introduced a .... tax of 4% on slaves.

2. The idea of .... taxation was born in Britain.

3. Personal Income Tax involves a complicated system of tax brackets and ....

4. Digital technology provides instant .... to many useful services.

5. Income tax laws now have to apply to .... from electronic commerce.

6. The kind of tax that applies depends on state ....

7. The United States does not impose ....

8. Politicians do not wish to discourage or .... business.

9. The future of digital technology is hard to ....

10. The community as a whole needs to .... from the new technology.

2. True or false?
Welche der folgenden Definitionen sind richtig und welche falsch?

	True	False
Example: *An excise tax* is a method of trying out new tax systems.	☐	☑
1. A *poll tax* is a standard tax levied on every person.	☐	☐
2. *Personal income tax* depends on personal status.	☐	☐
3. An *inheritance tax* has to be paid when someone is born.	☐	☐
4. The *intangible nature* of electronic commerce means that all transactions are completed on paper.	☐	☐
5. *Commodities* are only used to make our lives comfortable.	☐	☐
6. *Progressive* taxation means that the tax system is very advanced.	☐	☐
7. If politicians *impede* business, they encourage new tax methods.	☐	☐
8. *Vendor* is another expression for customer.	☐	☐
9. *State legislation* means laws made by the state.	☐	☐
10. A *lack of clarity* means that things are very unclear.	☐	☐

3. Translation
Welche Übersetzung aus der zweiten Liste passt am besten zu den Begriffen in der ersten?

Example: 1 c

1. Income Tax
2. Excise Tax
3. Property Tax
4. Inheritance Tax
5. Corporation Tax
6. Petroleum Business Tax
7. Insurance Tax
8. Real Esate Transfer Tax
9. Sales Tax
10. Unrelated Business Income Tax

a. Verkaufssteuer
b. Versicherungssteuer
c. Einkommenssteuer
d. Nebenerwerbssteuer
e. Grunderwerbssteuer
f. Verbrauchssteuer
g. Vermögenssteuer
h. Erbschaftssteuer
i. Körperschaftssteuer
j. Mineralölsteuer

4. Crossword

Across
1 What belongs to you (8)
3 Another word for riches (6)
7 The money you need to pay tax on (6)
8 The people you pay your tax to are the tax .... (9)

Down
1 To say what is going to happen (7)
2 Paying money to the state (8)
4 Everyone must obey the ... (3)
5 Very, very old (7)
6 The person who sells something (6)

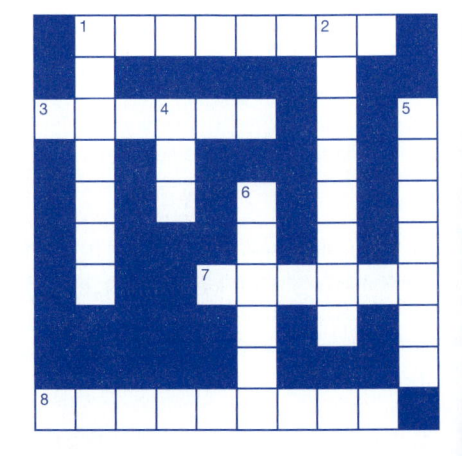

Reading for Understanding

1. Essential facts
Sind folgende Aussagen zum Textinhalt richtig oder falsch?

Example:	True	False
Taxation has been used since ancient times to raise money for the state.	☐	☑
1. Taxation systems have not changed since the time of the Athenians.	☐	☐
2. The Romans were responsible for destroying sales and property tax.	☐	☐

3. A progressive system of taxation means that the rich pay more and the poor pay less tax. ☐ ☐
4. A regressive tax system means that the rich pay all the taxes. ☐ ☐
5. The number of electronic machines in American homes has been decreasing slowly. ☐ ☐
6. Digital technology can combine text, sound and vision. ☐ ☐
7. The U.S. tax system is having great difficulty dealing with the new technology. ☐ ☐
8. All the U.S. states have decided to deal with the tax problem in the same way. ☐ ☐
9. The U.S. federal government has passed new laws dealing with all e-commerce transactions. ☐ ☐
10. Problems with federal legislation will mean that the states and businesses will have to work together to gain maximum benefit. ☐ ☐

2. What does it really mean?

Versuchen Sie folgende Fragen zu beantworten.

Example:
What is cyberspace? **a.** the place where computers are built **b.** the place where electronic messages exist — **b**

1. If the government imposes a poll tax, does it mean that **a.** every person in the country has to pay a tax? **b.** people have to pay a tax if they want to vote?
2. If the government imposes an excise tax on certain commodities, does it mean **a.** that people have to pay tax on what they buy? **b.** that people have to pay tax on what they earn?
3. What led to the American Revolution? Was it **a.** a poll tax imposed on foreigners? **b.** unfair taxes imposed by the British?
4. How does the State of New York earn revenue? **a.** by imposing a system of different taxes **b.** by employing digital technology
5. If the commercialisation of the electronic revolution is „still in its infancy", does it mean **a.** that only children will be able to understand it? **b.** that its true potential has not yet been realised?
6. If the task of solving the taxation problems is said to be *taxing*, does this mean **a.** that will cost a lot of money? **b.** that it will be very difficult?
7. If taxes in the U.S. are „not just an issue of state legislation", does this mean **a.** that all taxes in the U.S. have to be levied from Washington D.C.? **b.** that the federal goverment also responsible imposes certain taxes?
8. If the United States do not impose VAT, does this mean **a.** that there is no sales tax in America? **b.** that there is no general or national value added tax on sales or purchases?

3. What do you think?

Lesen Sie den Text nochmals durch. Wie stehen Sie jetzt zu der dort erläuterten Problematik? Versuchen Sie folgende Fragen zu beantworten.

> *Example:*
> Why do you think the Athenians refunded their taxes after the war was over?
> **a.** so that next time the citizens would be willing to pay taxes again
> **b.** because they didn't want the responsibilty of looking after the money   `a`

1. What may have been the reason, do you think, that Abraham Lincoln's progressive income tax was later declared unconstitutional? **a.** because the war was over and taxes were no longer necessary **b.** because the Constitution stated that all men should be treated equally
2. Why do you think that in modern times „taxation seems to know no bounds"? **a.** because governments cannot control public spending **b.** because the state needs more and more money to finance the services we have come to expect
3. Why do you think digital technology has tremendous commercial potential? **a.** because it provides customers and consumers with a new range of services **b.** because the consequences for the taxpayer are uncertain
4. Why do you think the problem of taxation is particularly difficult in the U.S.A? **a.** because of the federal system and the different responsibilities involved **b.** because there is so much strong anti-tax feeling among the electorate
5. Why do you think that, according to the text, the digital revolution is too good an opportunity to miss? **a.** because it will create a paperless world **b.** because it will generate a lot of business for both companies and government

Over to you

1. Value Added Tax

Stellen Sie nun Ihre Lesekompetenz erneut auf die Probe. Versuchen Sie, die Prinzipien einer „Mehrwertsteuer" zu erklären.

Try to explain the basic principles of VAT to your American colleagues (some American visitors) bearing in mind that they are not familiar with a national sales or purchase tax, but with different types of other taxes.

2. E-commerce tax

Versuchen Sie herauszufinden, wie das Steuersystem in Deutschland funktioniert.
Find out about the tax situation as regards *e-commerce* in Germany. Try www.bundesfinanzamt.com or a similar website.

Do the same problems occur? How are the problems mentioned in the text dealt with in Germany and the German federal states? Write a short report for your American colleagues. You might compare the German federal system with the American one.

Lösungen

Unit 1 Company Research
Reading for Gist
1 True or false?
1 true; 2 false; 3 false; 4 true; 5 true; 6 true; 7 false;
8 true; 9 true; 10 true
2 Match them up
1c; 2e; 3a; 4b; 5d; 6i; 7f; 8j; 9h; 10g

Reading for Language
1 True or false?
1 true; 2 false; 3 true; 4 true; 5 false; 6 true; 7 false;
8 true; 9 true; 10 true
2 Fill in the gaps
1 founded; 2 employees; 3 advertising; 4 subsidised;
5 company; 6 appreciate; 7 dress code; 8 annual;
9 in-house; 10 recruit
3 Form sentences
1 was founded; 2 was quoted; 3 are given; 4 is complemented; 5 will be used; 6 are employed; 7 have been satisfied; 8 can be earned; 9 has been subsidised;
10 is thought of
4 Language alternatives
1a; 2b; 3a; 4b; 5b; 6a; 7b; 8a; 9b; 10b

Reading for Understanding
1 Essential facts
1 M,L&P; 2 M,L&P; 3 M,L&P; 4 M,L&P; 5 M,L&P;
6 Joystix; 7 Joystix; 8 M,L&P; 9 Joystix; 10 M,L&P;
11 Joystix; 12 M,L&P; 13 M,L&P; 14 Joystix; 15 M,L&P
2 Understanding the text
1a; 2c; 3a; 4d; 5b,c
3 What do you think?
1B; 2A; 3B; 4B; 5A, 6A; 7B; 8A; 9B; 10B

Unit 2 Recruitment
Reading for Gist
1 True or false?
1 true; 2 true; 3 false; 4 false; 5 false; 6 true; 7 false;
8 false; 9 true; 10 true
2 Match them up
1c; 2a; 3d; 4e; 5b

Reading for Language
1 Fill in the gaps
1 prestigious; 2 fluent; 3 personnel; 4 freelance;
5 competence; 6 challenge; 7 hobbies; 8 graduate;
9 interview; 10 suited
2 What does it mean?
1a; 2a; 3b; 4b; 5a
3 Odd one out
1 sailing; 2 to photograph; 3 challenge; 4 employed;
5 CV
4 Translation
1 Werbeagentur; 2 Lebenslauf; 3 Bewerbung; 4 freiberuflich; 5 Herausforderung; 6 Verantwortung; 7 Redakteur;
8 Schulbildung; 9 Hochschulabsolvent; 10 Gelegenheit
5 Crossword
Across: 5 competence 6 graduate
Down: 1 freelance 2 education 3 account 4 executive

Reading for Understanding
1 Writing a letter of application
Falsch sind 6 und 8
2 Essential facts
1 Yes; 2 No; 3 Yes; 4 Yes; 5 No; 6 No; 7 Yes; 8 Yes
3 What do you think?
1a; 2a; 3a; 4b; 5a; 6a; 7b; 8a; 9b; 10b

Unit 3 Meetings
Reading for Gist
1 What's it all about?
1a; 2b; 3b; 4b; 5b; 6a; 7a; 8b; 9a; 10b
2 Match them up
1c; 2d; 3b; 4e; 5a
3 Odd one out
a)4; b)3; c)1; d)2
4 True or false?
1 false; 2 false; 3 true; 4 true; 5 true; 6 true; 7 false;
8 false; 9 false; 10 true

Reading for Language
1 The right meaning
1a; 2b; 3b; 4a; 5a; 6b; 7b; 8a; 9a; 10b

2 The right word
1 figures; 2 schedule; 3 expenditure; 4 prognosis;
5 complacency; 6 proposals; 7 analyse; 8 efficient;
9 implement; 10 failure
3 Translation
1e; 2f; 3g; 4a; 5i; 6j; 7d; 8c; 9h; 10b
4 Crossword
Across: 1 minutes 7 update 8 fallback
Down: 2 template 3 license 4 staff 5 mailing 6 backup

Reading for Understanding
1 Who or what?
1a; 2b; 3b; 4b; 5b; 6b
2 Why action points?
1c; 2g; 3d; 4h; 5b; 6f; 7a; 8e

Unit 4 Marketing
Reading for Gist
1 True or false?
1 true; 2 true; 3 false; 4 false; 5 true; 6 false; 7 false;
8 false; 9 true; 10 true
2 Match them up
1g; 2j; 3h; 4a; 5h; 6i; 7c; 8d; 9e; 10f

Reading for Language
1 True or false?
1 false; 2 false; 3 true; 4 false; 5 true; 6 false; 7 true;
8 false; 9 true; 10 false
2 What does it mean?
1b; 2b; 3a; 4a; 5b; 6b; 7b; 8a; 9b; 10b
3 Match them up
1d; 2e; 3h; 4j; 5g; 6a; 7i; 8f; 9b; 10c
4 Translate
1 Kundenbetreuung; 2 gemeinsames Ziel; 3 Richtlinie;
4 Mitarbeiter, (-innen); 5 Konkurrenz; 6 befriedigen;
7 bewerkstelligen; 8 Einzelhändler; 9 Außendienstmit-
arbeiter; 10 betreuen
5 Crossword
Across: 1 cash cow; 6 feedback; 7 identity; 8 promotion
Down: 2 segment; 3 freebie; 4 marketing; 5 analysis

Reading for Understanding
1 Essential facts
1b; 2b; 3a; 4b; 5b; 6a; 7b; 8b; 9a; 10a
2 What does it really mean?
1 yes; 2 yes; 3 yes; 4 yes; 5 yes; 6 no; 7 no; 8 no; 9 no;
10 no
3 What do you think?
1b; 2a; 3a; 4b; 5b; 6b; 7a; 8a; 9b; 10b

Unit 5 Contracts
Reading for Gist
1 True or false?
1 true; 2 true; 3 true; 4 false; 5 false; 6 false: 7 true;
8 true; 9 true; 10 false
2 Match them up
1i; 2j; 3h; 4f; 5d; 6g; 7a; 8e; 9c; 10b; 11l; 12k

Reading for Language
1 Odd one out
1d; 2e; 3e; 4a
2 Translate
1 Lizenznehmer; 2 Markenzeichen; 3 Nebenrechte;
4 Erlös; 5 Abrechnung; 6 Gewährleistung; 7 Verstoß;
8 Schadensersatz; 9 bankrott; 10 Klausel
3 Match the meaning
1c; 2g; 3a; 4f; 5h; 6e; 7d; 8b
4 The right verb
1b; 2b; 3b; 4a; 5a
5 Contract-speak
1b; 2d; 3a; 4c; 5e
6 Crossword
Across: 2 expense 6 subsidiary 7 rectify 8 bankrupt
Down: 1 terms 3 permission 4 copyright 5 claim
7 What does it mean?
1a; 2b; 3b; 4a; 5b

Reading for Understanding
1 What does it mean?
1a; 2b; 3a; 4b; 5a; 6b; 7b; 8b; 9a; 10b
2 Key features of the contract
1d; 2g; 3f; 4j; 5i; 6b; 7e; 8h; 9a; 10c
3 Who is responsible?
1a; 2a; 3b; 4a; 5b; 6b; 7b; 8a; 9a; 10a
4 Perspectives
1b; 2a; 3a; 4b; 5a; 6a; 7a; 8a; 9b;10a; 11b; 12b

Unit 6 Invoices
Reading for Gist
1 True or false?
1 true; 2 false; 3 false; 4 true; 5 true; 6 false; 7 true;
8 true; 9 false; 10 true
2 Match them up
1f; 2i; 3e; 4j; 5a; 6b; 7c; 8d; 9g; 10h

Reading for Language
1 Fill in the gaps
1 ingredient; 2 delivery; 3 ownership; 4 abbreviations;
5 cash-flow; 6 guarantees; 7 conscientious; 8 prudent;
9 insurance; 10 gross
2 What do they mean?
1b; 2a; 3a; 4a; 5b; 6a; 7b; 8a; 9b; 10b; 11a; 12b

3 Match them up
1f; 2c; 3a; 4h; 5d; 6j; 7m; 8i; 9b; 10e; 11l; 12g; 13k
4 Odd one out
1e; 2d; 3b; 4c
5 Crossword
Across: 3 risk; 5 invoice; 7 reference 8 VAT; 9 freight
Down: 1 incoterm; 2 discount; 4 shipment; 6 credit

Reading for Understanding
1 Essential facts
1c; 2d; 3b; 4a
2 Understanding the text
1a; 2a; 3a; 4b; 5b; 6b; 7b; 8a; 9a, 10b
3 What do you think?
1 Customer; 2 Supplier; 3 Customer; 4 Customer;
5 Customer; 6 Customer; 7 Supplier; 8 Supplier;
9 Customer; 10 Customer

Unit 7 Company Finance
Reading for Gist
1 Match them up
1B; 2B; 3B; 4A; 5A; 6A; 7B; 8B; 9B; 10A
2 Odd one out
1d; 2a; 3c; 4c
3 True or false?
1 true; 2 true; 3false; 4 false; 5 false; 6 false; 7 true;
8 true; 9 true; 10 false

Reading for Language
1 Match them up
1g; 2e; 3f; 4h; 5c; 6i; 7j; 8b; 9d; 10a
2 The right meaning
1a; 2b; 3a; 4b; 5b; 6a; 7a; 8a; 9b; 10b
3 Match them up
1h; 2j; 3a; 4b; 5c; 6d; 7i; 8e; 9f; 10g
4 Crossword
Across: 1 assets; 4 profit; 6 loan; 8 tax; 9 turnover;
10 loss
Down: 2 stock; 3 outlay; 5 interest; 7 annual

Reading for Understanding
1 Essential facts
1 true; 2 true; 3 false; 4 false; 5 false; 6 true; 7 false;
8 false; 9 true; 10 false
2 What does it really mean?
1b; 2b; 3a; 4b; 5a; 6a; 7b; 8b; 9a; 10a
3 What do you think?
1a; 2a; 3a; 4a; 5b; 6a

Unit 8 Stock Markets
Reading for Gist
1 True or false?
1 false; 2 true; 3 true; 4 false; 5 true; 6 true; 7 true;
8 false; 9 true; 10 false
2 Match them up
1d; 2g; 3h; 4j; 5e; 6b; 7f; 8c; 9i; 10a

Reading for Language
1 Fill in the gap
1b; 2b; 3a; 4b; 5b; 6a; 7b; 8a
2 Odd one out
1a; 2d; 3d; 4a
3 The right meaning
1b; 2b; 3b; 4a; 5a; 6b; 7b; 8a
4 Translate
1 Vertrauen; 2 Wachstum; 3 Handy; 4 Makler;
5 Verbraucher; 6 verdächtig; 7 Buchführung;
8 empfehlen; 9 ehrlich; 10 Steuerhinterziehung
5 Crossword
Across: 2 tax 5 broker 6 index 7 bulls
Down: 1 confidence 2 target 3 worthless 4 investor
7 bears

Reading for Understanding
1 Essential facts
1 Ursache; 2 Ursache; 3 Auswirkung; 4 Ursache;
5 Auswirkung; 6 Ursache; 7 Ursache; 8 Ursache;
9 Auswirkung; 10 Ursache; 11 Ursache; 12 Auswirkung
2 Understanding the text
1a; 2b; 3b; 4b; 5a; 6a; 7b; 8a; 9b; 10a
3 What do you think?
1b; 2a; 3b; 4a; 5a

Unit 9 Takeovers
Reading for Gist
1 Match them up
1h; 2 j; 3g; 4a; 5b; 6i; 7d; 8e; 9c; 10f

Reading for Language
1 What does it mean?
1b; 2b; 3b; 4a; 5a

Reading for Understanding
1 Essential facts
1 false; 2 true; 3 false; 4 true; 5 true
2 What does it really mean?
1a; 2b; 3a; 4b; 5a
3 What do you think?
1b; 2b; 3b; 4a; 5b

Unit 10 Trade Fairs
Reading for Gist
1 Match them up
1h; 2f; 3j; 4b; 5a; 6d; 7i; 8c; 9e; 10g
2 True or false?
1 false; 2 true; 3 true; 4 false; 5 false; 6 false; 7 true;
8 false; 9 true; 10 true

Reading for Language
1 Match them up
1d; 2h; 3f; 4g; 5a; 6e; 7b; 8c
2 True or false?
1 true; 2 false; 3 true; 4 true; 5 false; 6 true; 7 true;
8 false; 9 false; 10 true
3 Translation
1 Messezentrum; 2 Zeitplanung; 3 persönliche Unterredung; 4 thematischer Schwerpunkt; 5 zentrale Punkte
4 Crossword
Across: 2 space; 5 trade fair; 6 commercial; 7 venue; 8 cafeteria
Down: 1 contacts; 3 conference; 4 journal

Reading for Understanding
1 Essential facts
1a; 2b; 3b; 4b; 5 b
2 What does it really mean?
1b; 2 b; 3a; 4b; 5a
3 What do you think?
1b; 2b; 3a; 4b

Unit 11 International Business Relations
Reading for Gist
1 Match them up
1d; 2f; 3g; 4i; 5b; 6h; 7c; 8j; 9e; 10a
2 True or false?
1 false; 2 true; 3 false; 4 true; 5 true; 6 true; 7 true;
8 false; 9 false; 10 true
3 Headlines
1b; 2a; 3b; 4a; 5b

Reading for Language
1 True or false?
1 true; 2 false; 3 true; 4 false; 5 true; 6 false; 7 true;
8 true; 9 false; 10 true
2 Match them up
1h; 2j; 3b; 4a; 5i; 6c; 7d; 8f; 9e; 10g
3 What does it mean?
1a; 2b; 3b; 4b; 5b; 6b; 7a; 8b
4 Odd one out
1e; 2e; 3b; 4a; 5d

5 Crossword
Across: 1 speech; 5 division; 6 global; 7 brash; 8 terms
Down: 2 praise; 3 consultant; 4 linear

Reading for Understanding
1 Essential facts
3; 6; 10; 14; 16
2 Understanding the text
1b; 2b; 3a; 4a; 5b; 6a; 7b; 8a
3 What do you think?
1b; 2b; 3a; 4b; 5a; 6b

Unit 12 Multinationals
Reading for Gist
1 Headlines
1b; 2b; 3a; 4b
2 True or false?
1 false; 2 true; 3false; 4 true; 5 true; 6 true; 7 false;
8 true; 9 true; 10 false; 11 true; 12 false
3 Match them up
1e; 2f; 3g; 4i; 5b; 6h; 7d; 8j; 9a; 10c

Reading for Language
1 Match them up
1f; 2g; 3i; 4j; 5b; 6h; 7d; 8c; 9e; 10a
2 True or false?
1 true; 2 false; 3 true; 4 true; 5 true; 6 false; 7 false;
8 true; 9 true; 10 true
3 Odd one out
1d; 2b; 3d; 4a; 5d; 6a
4 Translation
1 Teilnchmer; 2 im Durchschnitt; 3 wirkliche Macht;
4 Beweis; 5 Menschenrechte; 6 Darlehen; 7 Fluggesellschaft; 8 Gesundheit; 9 Verdacht; 10 Credo, Glaube
5 Crossword
Across: 1 health; 5 enterprise; 7 century; 8 criticism
Down: 2 airline; 3 creed; 4 democracy; 6 summit

Reading for Understanding
1 Essential facts
Falsch sind: 1; 3; 6; 7; 9
2 What does it really mean?
1b; 2a; 3b; 4b; 5a; 6b; 7a; 8a; 9b; 10b
3 What do you think?
1a; 2b; 3b; 4a; 5a

Unit 13 New Technologies
Reading for Gist
1 Match them up
1g; 2d; 3j; 4a; 5b; 6i; 7c; 8e; 9h; 10f
2 Headlines
1c; 2d; 3a; 4b; 5d
3 True or false?
1 false; 2 fakse; 3 true; 4 true; 5 true; 6 true; 7 false;
8 false; 9 false; 10 true

Reading for Language
1 Match them up
1e; 2i; 3g; 4h; 5d; 6b; 7c; 8j; 9f; 10a
2 Odd one out
1d; 2a; 3c; 4b; 5c
3 What does it mean?
1b; 2a; 3b; 4a; 5b; 6b; 7a; 8b; 9b; 10b
4 Crossword
Across: 1 security; 7 savings; 8 credit; 9 debit
Down: 2 investment; 3 account; 4 password; 5 device;
6 PIN

Reading for Understanding
1 Essential facts
1 true; 2 true; 3 true; 4 true; 5 false; 6 true; 7 false;
8 false; 9 false; 10 true
2 What does it really mean?
Advantage: 1; 5; 8; 10
Disadvantage: 2; 3; 4; 6; 7; 9
3 What do you think?
1a; 2b; 3a; 4a; 5a; 6b; 7a; 8a

Unit 14 Environmental Issues
Reading for Gist
1 True or false?
1 true; 2 false; 3 false; 4 true; 5 true; 6 false; 7 true;
8 true; 9 false; 10 true
2 Match them up
1e; 2g; 3j; 4f; 5b; 6i; 7h; 8a; 9d; 10c
3 Headlines
1c; 2a; 3b; 4b; 5c; 6a

Reading for Language
1 Choose the right word
1c; 2b; 3c; 4b; 5a
2 Match them up
1f; 2i; 3E; 4h; 5a; 6c; 7j; 8b; 9d; 10g
3 True or false?
1 true; 2 true; 3 false; 4 false; 5 true; 6 true; 7 false;
8 true; 9 true; 10 true
4 Odd one out
1d; 2c; 3a; 4b; 5a; 6b; 7c; 8b

5 Crossword
Across: 1 energy; 5 shortage; 6 damage; 8 pollute
Down: 2 geothermal; 3 island; 4 solar; 7 plant

Reading for Understanding
1 Essential facts
1 true; 2 false; 3 false; 4 true; 5 true; 6 false; 7 true;
8 false; 9 true; 10 false
2 What does it mean?
1a; 2b; 3b; 4b; 5b; 6a; 7b; 8a
3 What do you think?
1b; 2a; 3b; 4a; 5a

Unit 15 Taxation
Reading for Gist
1 Match them up
1d; 2f; 3h; 4g; 5j; 6i; 7b; 8a; 9e; 10c
2 Odd one out
1c; 2d; 3b; 4a; 5b
3 True or false?
1 false; 2 true; 3 true; 4 true; 5 false; 6 false; 7 true;
8 false; 9 true; 10 false

Reading for Language
1 The missing word
1 sales; 2 progressive; 3 credits; 4 access; 5 earnings;
6 jurisdiction; 7 VAT; 8 impede; 9 predict; 10 benefit
2 True or false?
1 true; 2 true; 3 false; 4 false; 5 false; 6 false; 7 false;
8 false; 9 true; 10 true
3 Translation
1c; 2f; 3g; 4h; 5i; 6j; 7b; 8e; 9a; 10d
4 Crossword
Across: 1 property; 3 wealth; 7 income; 8 authority
Down: 1 predict; 2 taxation; 4 law; 5 ancient; 6 vendor

Reading for Understanding
1 Essential facts
1 false; 2 false; 3 true; 4 false; 5 false; 6 true; 7 true;
8 false; 9 false; 10 true
2 What does it really mean?
1a; 2a; 3b; 4a; 5b; 6b; 7b; 8b
3 What do you think?
1b; 2b; 3a; 4a; 5b

Glossar

Die Zahlen beziehen sich auf die *Units*.

A

abbreviate *(v.)*	abkürzen	6	agreement *(n.)*	Vertrag	3
ability *(n.)*	Fähigkeit	1		Übereinkunft, Einverständnis	11
access *(n.)*	Zugang	4; 11; 15	agriculture *(n.)*	Landwirtschaft	14
accommodate *(v.)*	akzeptieren	11	aid *(v.)*	helfen, unterstützen	14
account *(n.)*	Konto	13	air-conditioned *(adj.)*	mit Klimaanlage	1; 10
account *(n.)*	Konto; hier: Auftrag	2	airline *(n.)*	Fluggesellschaft	12
account details *(n.)*	Einzelheiten, Angaben zum Konto	13	airline stocks *(n.)*	Aktien der Fluggesellschaften	8
account executive *(n.)*	hier: Projektleiter	1; 2	Aladdin's cave *(n.)*	die Höhle des Aladdin, märchenhafte Schätze	13
accounting *(n.)*	Abrechnung, Rechnungslegung	5	all concerned *(n.)*	alle Beteiligten	14
achieve *(v.)*	erreichen	14	alleged *(adj.)*	angeblich	8
acknowledgement *(n.)*	Quellennachweis	5	all-time *(adj.)*	historisch, Rekord-	8
acquire *(v.)*	erwerben, anschaffen	9	altruistic *(adj.)*	altruistisch	4
acquisition *(n.)*	Kauf, Übernahme	9	ambition *(n.)*	Ambition	1
action points *(n.)*	zu erledigende Punkte	3	analysis *(n.)*	Analyse	4; 12
actual *(adj.)*	tatsächlich, wirklich	11; 12	announce *(v.)*	bekannt geben	1
acute *(adj.)*	akut	9; 14	announcement *(n.)*	(Presse-)Meldung	9
adapt *(v.)*	(sich) anpassen	11	annoyance *(n.)*	Ärgernis	13
added *(adj.)*	zusätzlich	9	annual *(adj.)*	jährlich	1; 7; 9
adequate *(adj.)*	adäquat, angemessen	1	annually *(adv.)*	jährlich	5
adjust *(v.)*	sich anpassen	8; 15	anonymously *(adv.)*	anonym	4
adopt *(v.)*	annehmen	11	AOB *(n.) (abbrev.)* (Any Other Business)	sonstige Punkte	3
advantage *(n.)*	Vorteil	9; 10; 12	apart from *(adv.)*	abgesehen von	2
advent *(n.)*	Beginn	15	appearance *(n.)*	Aussehen, Aufmachung Anmutung	4
advertise *(v.)*	Werbung machen für, ankündigen	10	applicant *(n.)*	Bewerber(in)	2
advertisement *(n.)*	Anzeige	2	application *(n.)*	Bewerbung	2
advertising *(n.)*	Werbung	3		Anwendung	4
advertising agency *(n.)*	Werbeagentur	1; 2	application form *(n.)*	Anmeldeformular	13
advice *(n.)*	Rat(schlag), Beratung	11; 13	apply *(v.)*	sich bewerben	2
affect *(v.)*	beeinflussen	10	appointment *(n.)*	(Besprechungs-)Termin	10
afoot *(adv.)*	in der Mache	14	appreciably *(adv.)*	beträchtlich	1
after-sales back-up *(n.)*	Kundendienst (-unterstützung)	7	appreciate *(v.)*	schätzen	1
age *(n.)*	Zeitalter, Ära	4		verstehen	9
agenda *(n.)*	Tagesordnung	3	approach *(n.)*	Betrachtungsweise, Ansatz	11; 14
AGM *(abbrev.)* (Annual General Meeting)	Jahresversammlung	1	appropriate *(adj.)*	passend, entsprechend	5
			approve *(v.)*	bewilligen	9
agree to differ *(v.)*	sich einigen, dass man unterschiedlicher Meinung ist	11	area of operation *(n.)*	Absatzgebiet, Tätigkeitsbereich	9
			art-form *(n.)*	Kunstform	1
			artificially *(adv.)*	künstlich	8
			as follows *(adv.)*	wie folgt	9

164

a.s.a.p. *(abbrev.)*	möglichst bald 3	
as soon as possible		
as yet *(adv.)*	bisher 3	
assess *(v.)*	(ein)schätzen 9	
assessment *(n.)*	Einschätzung, Beurteilung 9	
assets *(n.)*	Vermögen, Finanzreserven 9	
assets and liabilities *(n.)*	Aktiva und Passiva 7	
assimilation *(n.)*	Assimilierung, Integration 9	
at least *(adv.)*	wenigstens 2	
attend *(v.)*	besuchen, teilnehmen an 10	
attitude *(n.)*	Haltung; Einstellung 1	
audience concentration *(n.)*	Konzentration des Publikums 10	
audit *(n.)*	Buchprüfung 7	
available *(adj.)*	verfügbar, erhältlich, vorhanden, zugänglich 9; 10; 14	
average *(v.)*	sich im Durchschnitt belaufen auf 1	
avoid *(v.)*	vermeiden, aussparen 13	
aware *(adj.)*	(sich) bewusst 15	

B

background *(n.)*	Hintergrund 1	
backup strategy *(n.)*	Plan für den Notfall 3	
balance sheet *(n.)*	Finanzbericht 6	
	Bilanz, Jahresabschluss 7	
bank charges *(n.)*	Bankgebühren 13	
bank clerk *(n.)*	Bankangestellte(r) 13	
bank loan *(n.)*	Bankdarlehen 7	
bank staff *(n.)*	Mitarbeiter der Bank 13	
Bank Tax *(n.)* AE	etwa: Bankensteuer 15	
bankrupt *(adj.)*	bankrott 5	
barrier *(n.)*	Hürde, Barriere, Sperre 4; 11	
base *(n.)*	Basis 15	
base *(n.)*	Standort 13	
based on (to be)*(v.)*	basieren auf 15	
basement *(n.)*	Untergeschoss, Keller 1	
basic *(adj.)*	grundsätzlich 11	
bear *(v.)*	tragen 6	
bears *(n.)*	Baisse (Ausdruck für fallende Aktienpreise, negative Entwicklung) 8	
beforehand *(adv.)*	vorher 6	
behaviour patterns *(n.)*	Verhaltensmuster 11	
behind the scenes *(adv.)*	hinter den Kulissen 11	
belief *(n.)*	Glaube 10	
benefit *(n.)*	Vorteil 14	
benefit *(v.)*	profitieren 15	
benefits *(n.pl.)*	Vorteile 12	
bets *(n.)*	Wetten 15	
beverage *(n.)*	Getränk 15	
beware *(v.)*	sich in Acht nehmen 13	
beyond recognition	so, dass man es kaum wiedererkennt 12	
bill *(n.)* BE	Rechnung 6	
blame *(v.)*	jmd die Schuld geben 12	

blank *(adj.)*	leer, ausdruckslos 11	
board *(n.)*	Vorstand 3	
board meeting *(n.)*	Direktorenkonferenz, Vorstandssitzung 9	
boardroom *(n.)*	Konferenzraum 3	
boast *(v.)*	hier: vorzeigen 1	
bogus *(adj.)*	falsch, erfunden 13	
bounce back *(v.)*	zurückspringen 8	
boxing *(n.)*	Boxkämpfe 15	
branch *(n.)*	Bereich 8	
	Niederlassung, Filiale, Zweigstelle 9	
brand loyalty *(n.)*	Markentreue 4	
brash *(adj.)*	rau, unkultiviert, frech 11	
breach *(n.)*	Verstoß, Bruch 5	
breakdown *(n.)*	Panne, Fehler, Versagen 3	
broad *(adj.)*	breit, weit 15	
brochure *(n.)*	Broschüre 10	
broker *(n.)*	Kaufmann, (Börsen-)Makler 8	
bull market *(n.)*	positiver, zur Hausse tendierender Markt 8	
bulletin board *(n.)*	„schwarzes Brett", Notizbrett, Forum 15	
bulls *(n.)*	Hausse (Ausdruck für steigende Aktienpreise, positive Entwicklung) 8	
burden *(n.)*	Last, Belastung 15	
Business Taxes *(n.)* AE	etwa: Gewerbesteuer 15	

C

cable TV *(n.)*	Kabelfernsehen 15	
capitalism *(n.)*	Kapitalismus 12	
careful *(adj.)*	vorsichtig 11	
carrier *(n.)*	Transportfirma, Spediteur 6	
case *(n.)*	Fall 13	
cash cow *(n.)*	etwa: „Gans, die goldene Eier legt", „Goldesel", sehr erfolgreiches Produkt als sichere Geldquelle 4	
cash dispenser *(n.)*	Geldautomat 13	
cash in hand *(n.)*	verfügbare Geldmittel 7	
cash-flow *(n.)*	Cashflow 6	
cater for *(v.)*	betreuen, bedienen 4	
cell-phone *(n.)*	Mobiltelefon, Handy 8	
century *(n.)*	Jahrhundert 12; 15	
CEO *(abbrev.* Chief Executive Officer.*)*	Firmenleiter, Generaldirektor 9; 10	
CFR (Cost and freight)	Kosten und Fracht bis (Ortsname) 6	
chair *(n.)*	Vorsitz 3	
challenge *(n.)*	Herausforderung 2	
cheque *(n. BE)*	Scheck 13	
choice *(n.)*	Wahl 10	
CIF (Cost, insurance and freight)	Kosten, Versicherung und Fracht bis (Ortsname) 6	
CIP (Carriage and insurance paid to)	Fracht und Versicherung bis (Ortsname) 6	

G

circle the square (v.)	aus dem Quadrat einen Kreis machen (hier: in Einklang bringen)	4	
circumstances (n.)	Umstände	15	
civil action (n.)	zivilrechtlicher Prozess	5	
claim (n.)	Anspruch, Forderung	5	
clamour (v.)	lauthals bitten	12	
clause (n.)	Klausel	5	
clear the air (v.)	die Luft reinigen	6	
client (n.)	Klient	1	
clientele (n.)	Klientel	9	
clinch a deal (v.)	ein Geschäft abschließen	11	
clone (n.)	Klon	13	
co-branding (n.)	Partnerschaft zwischen Firmen	4	
combined (adj.)	kombiniert	14	
comfort (n.)	Komfort, Bequemlichkeit, Behaglichkeit	13	
commercial (adj.)	kommerziell, kaufmännisch	6	
commit oneself (v.)	sich festlegen	9	
commitment (n.)	Verpflichtung, Engagement	14	
commodity (n.)	Ware, Erzeugnis	15	
common aim (n.)	gemeinsames Ziel	4	
communication services (n.)	Kommunikations- und Vermittlungsdienste	15	
communication skills (n.)	Kommunikationsfähigkeiten	2	
community (n.)	Gemeinschaft	14	
company car (n.)	Firmenwagen	1	
comparatively (adv.)	vergleichsweise	6	
compare (v.)	vergleichen	14	
compatible (adj.)	kompatibel, verträglich	1	
competence (n.)	Kompetenz, Beherrschung	2	
competition (n.)	Konkurrenz	4	
competitive (adj.)	wettbewerbsbetont, wettbewerbsfähig	4	
complacency (n.)	Bequemlichkeit	3	
complain (v.)	sich beschweren	13	
complaint (n.)	Beschwerde	3	
complement (v.)	ergänzen	1	
complicated (adj.)	kompliziert	12	
complimentary (adj.)	kostenlos	5	
comply (v.)	entsprechen, erfüllen	5	
compound (v.)	verstärken	8	
comprehensive school (n.)	Gesamtschule	2	
computer literate (adj.)	PC-erfahren	2	
conceal (v.)	verdecken	11	
conclude (v.)	folgern, zur Schlussfolgerung kommen	12	
condemn (v.)	verdammen, verurteilen	12	
conference room (n.)	Konferenzraum	10	
confidence (n.)	Vertrauen	8	
confidential (adj.)	vertraulich	9	
confirm (v.)	bestätigen	9; 13	
conscientious (adj.)	gewissenhaft	6	
consensus (n.)	Konsens	12	
consider (v.)	in Betracht ziehen	13	
considerably (adv.)	beträchtlich	9	
construe (v.)	auffassen, deuten, ableiten	5; 11	
consultancy service (n.)	Beratungsdienst	7	
consultant (n.)	Fachberater, Beratungsdienst	9; 11	
consumer (n.)	Verbraucher	8	
consumer spending (n.)	Verbraucherausgaben	8	
continue (v.)	fortfahren, fortsetzen	14	
continuously (adv.)	kontinuierlich, fortlaufend	13	
convenience (n.)	Annehmlichkeit	13	
convenient (adj.)	praktisch, zweckmäßig, passend, akzeptabel	2; 13	
convincing (adj.)	überzeugend	10	
cooking oil (n.)	Speiseöl	15	
cooperation (n.)	Zuammenarbeit, Kooperation	14	
copy editor (n.)	Redakteur(in)	2	
copyright (n.)	Urheberrecht	5	
corporate identity (n.)	einheitliches Firmenimage	4	
corporate industry (n.)	Welt der Industrieunternehmen	12	
corporate scandal (n.)	Firmenskandal	8	
Corporation & Utility Tax (n.) AE	etwa: Körperschafts- und Betriebssteuer	15	
Corporation Franchise Tax (n.) AE	etwa: Körperschaftssteuer	15	
counter (n.)	Schalter	13	
court (n.)	Gericht	6	
cover (v.)	abdecken	6	
coverage (n.)	hier: Berichterstattung	3	
cover-up (n.)	Vertuschung	8	
CPT (Carriage paid to)	Fracht bezahlt bis (Ortsname)	6	
create (v.)	kreieren, schaffen	15	
credit balance (n.)	Kontostand, (Haben-)Saldo	13	
credits (n.)	Freibeträge	15	
creditworthiness (n.)	Kreditwürdigkeit	6	
creed (n.)	Credo, Glaube	12	
criminal prosecution (n.)	strafrechtliche Verfolgung	5	
criticism (n.)	Kritik	11; 12	
currency (n.)	Währung	6; 13	
current (adj.)	aktuell	10	
current account (n.)	Girokonto, Kontokorrent	13	
current assets (n.)	Umlaufvermögen	7	
current liabilities (n.)	laufende Verbindlichkeiten	7	
custodial body (n.)	Aufsichtsbehörde	12	
customer (n.)	Kunde, Kundin	13	
customer services (n.)	Kundendienste	15	
customer-care (n.)	Kundenservice, -betreuung	4	

CV (curriculum vitae)	Lebenslauf	2	
cyberspace (n.)	virtueller Raum, wo sich elektronische Informationen befinden	15	

D

DAF (Delivered at frontier)	geliefert bis Grenze (Ortsname)	6
daily menue (n.)	Tages(speise)karte	1
damage (n.)	Beschädigung	6
damages (n.)	Schadensersatz	5
data (n.)	Daten	15
data protection act (n.)	Datenschutzgesetz	13
database (n.)	Datenbank	3
Dax (n.)	deutscher Börsenindex	8
DDP (Delivered duty paid)	Lieferung inkl. Zahlung von Zollgebühren	6
DDU (Delivered duty unpaid)	Lieferung ohne Zahlung von Zollgebühren	6
deal (n.)	Geschäft, Handel	9
deal with (v.)	bearbeiten, sich beschäftigen mit erledigen	4; 11 / 6
debts (n.pl.)	Schulden	7
decade (n.)	Jahrzehnt	1
decision (n.)	Entscheidung	11
decision-maker (n.)	Entscheidungsträger	10
declare (v.)	erklären	15
deduction (n.)	Abzug	5
define (v.)	definieren	11
delay (n.)	Verzögerung, Wartezeit	13
delegation (n.)	Delegation, Mannschaft	11
democracy (n.)	Demokratie	12
deny (v.)	abstreiten	6
depreciation (n.)	Wertminderung, hier: Abschreibung	7
depth (n.)	Tiefe	14
DEQ (Delivered ex quay)	geliefert ab Kai (Ortsname)	6
DES (Delivered ex ship)	geliefert ab Schiff (Ortsname)	6
desalination plant (n.)	Entsalzungsanlage	14
design (n.)	Design; Kunstgewerbe	1
despatch (v.)	versenden	6
despite (prep.)	trotz	15
destined to (adj./p.p.)	bestimmt für	4
determine (v.)	bestimmen, festlegen	4; 6; 15
development (n.)	Entwicklung	12
device (n.)	hier: Vorwand, Trick Gerät	11 / 13
devil (n.)	Teufel	12
differ (v.)	sich unterscheiden	9
diminish (v.)	sich verringern, mindern	8
dip (v.)	sinken, nach unten gehen	8
direct mail (n.)	direktes Anschreiben per Post	10
disadvantage (n.)	Nachteil	9
discount (n.)	Skonto, Rabatt	5; 6
discourage (v.)	entmutigen	15
discretion (n.)	Diskretion	9
disguise (n.)	Verkleidung	12
dismissive (adj.)	abweisend	4
dispose of (v.)	verfügen über	5
disruption (n.)	Störung	9
distribution (n.)	Vertrieb	4
divide (v.)	teilen	7
dividend (n.)	Dividende	7
division (n.)	Trennung, Teilung	11
divisive (adj.)	verfremdend, trennend	11
dodgy (adj. infml.)	verdächtig, suspekt	8
door-to-door leafleting (n.)	Werbeblätter an alle Haushalte, Postwurfsendungen	4
double taxation (n.)	Doppelbesteuerung	15
dour (adj.)	mürrisch, stur	11
Dow Jones (n.)	amerikanischer Börsenindex	8
down (to be) (v.)	niedriger ausfallen	9
down to earth (adj.)	hier: alltagsrelevant	15
downside (n.)	die negative Seite	13
dress code (n.)	Kleidungsordnung	1
drinking water (n.)	Trinkwasser	14
due to (prep.)	aufgrund, wegen	9
duly (adv.)	ordnungsgemäß	3
duties (n.)	(Zoll-)Gebühren, (indirekte) Steuern	5; 12

E

earnings (n.)	Ertrag, Verdienst Einkünfte	7 / 15
Earth Summit (n.)	Gipfeltreffen zum Thema Umwelt	12
earth's crust (n.)	Erdkruste	14
e-commerce (n.)	elektronischer Handel	13
economic (adj.)	wirtschaftlich	4; 12
edition (n.)	Ausgabe	2
education (n.)	Schulbildung Bildung(swesen)	2 / 15
effectiveness (n.)	Effektivität	3
efficient (adj.)	effizient	10
effort (n.)	Anstrengung	14
egocentric (adj.)	egozentrisch	4
electorate (n.)	Wähler(schaft)	15
electronic bill payment (n.)	Bezahlung von Rechnungen auf elektronischem Wege	15
electronic commerce (n.)	elektronischer Geschäftsverkehr	15
elsewhere (adv.)	anderswo	14
empathize (v.)	sich einfühlen	1
Empire (n.)	Reich	15
employ (v.)	beschäftigen; einsetzen, anwenden	4
employee (n.)	Arbeitnehmer(in), Angestellte(r)	1; 7

G

employment (preview) (n.)	bisherige Beschäftigung(en)	2	
enable (v.)	es jmd ermöglichen	10	
enclosed (adj.)	beigefügt	10	
encourage (v.)	ermuntern, anregen	6	
endless (n.)	endlos	15	
end-user licence (n.)	Endverbraucherlizenz	5	
energy (n.)	Energie	14	
energy source (n.)	Energiequelle	14	
enormously (adv.)	enorm	4	
ensuing (adj.)	daraus resultierend	6	
ensure (v.)	sicherstellen	3; 4; 14	
enterprise (n.)	Unternehmen	12	
enterprises (n.)	Unternehmen (hier als Firmennamen)	3	
entitled (p.p.)	genannt	5	
environment (n.)	Umgebung, Umfeld, Situation	4; 11	
	Umwelt	12; 13	
environmental (adj.)	Umwelt-	14	
environmental damage (n.)	Umweltschäden	14	
environmentally friendly (adj.)	umweltfreundlich	14	
equipment (n.)	Geräte, Einrichtung, Ausstattung; hier: Inventar	7	
error (n.)	Fehler	3	
essential (adj.)	wesentlich	4; 6	
established (adj.)	etabliert	15	
Estate Tax (n.) AE	Erbschaftssteuer	15	
estimate (v.)	schätzen	9; 14	
ethics (n.)	Ethik	8	
Eurex (n.)	Frankfurter Online-Börse	8	
even (adv.)	noch	15	
eventually (adv.)	schließlich	15	
everything else	alles andere	15	
evil (adj.)	böse	14	
excesses (n.)	Exzesse	8	
excessive (adj.)	übermäßig	13	
exchange rate (n.)	Wechselkurs	13	
excise tax (n.)	Verbrauchssteuer	15	
executive (n.)	Manager	2	
exhibition centre (n.)	Messe(zentrum)	10	
exhibition hall (n.)	Messehalle	10	
exhibition stand (n.)	Messestand	10	
exhibitor (n.)	Aussteller	10	
expand (v.)	expandieren	2; 9	
expansion (n.)	Vergrößerung, Ausdehnung, Expansion	9	
expect (v.)	erwarten	9	
expenditure (n.)	Ausgaben, Auslagen	3; 7	
expense (n.)	Kosten	5	
experience (n.)	Erfahrung	2; 11	
experienced (adj.)	erfahren	1	
expert knowledge (n.)	Fachwissen	4	
explanation (n.)	Erklärung	11	
expose (v.)	enthüllen	12	
extension (n.)	Durchwahl	6	
exterior (n.)	Außenseite, Äußeres	11	
extraordinary (adj.)	außergewöhnlich	13	
EXW (Ex works)	ab Werk (Ortsname)	6	

F

face (v.)	konfrontieren	11
face-to-face communication (n.)	persönliche Kontakte	10
facilitate (v.)	vereinfachen, erleichtern	5
facilities (n.)	Einrichtungen	3; 10
	Dienstleistungen	13
failure (n.)	Versagen	3
fairly (adv.)	ziemlich	9
fallback (n.)	Notplan, Reserve	3
false (adj.)	falsch	13
Far East (n.)	Fernost	11
far-reaching (adj.)	weit reichend	15
FAS (Free alongside ship)	frei Längsseite Schiff (Ortsname)	6
fascinating (adj.)	faszinierend	4
faulty (adj.)	fehlerhaft	6
favorable (adj.)	günstig	3
FCA (Free carrier)	frei Frachtführer (Ortsname)	6
fear (n.)	Angst, Befürchtung	13
feasibility study (n.)	Machbarkeitsstudie	9
federal (adj.)	Bundes-	15
federal government (n.)	Bundesregierung	15
fee (n.)	Gebühr, Vergütung	5
feedback (n.)	Rückmeldung(en)	3; 4
felon (n.)	(Schwer-)Verbrecher	13
felt (p.p. to feel)	gespürt	10
fictitious (adj.)	erfunden, nicht wirklich	8
fight (v.)	bekämpfen	15
file (v.)	einreichen	15
finance director (n.)	Finanzdirektor	9
financial reserves (n.)	Finanzreserven, Rücklagen, Gesamtvermögen	7
fixed assets (n.)	Anlagevermögen	7
flesh (n.)	Fleisch	15
flexi-time (n.)	Gleitzeit	1; 3
floor-trading (n.)	Geschäfte direkt an der Börse selbst	8
fluctuation (n.)	Fluktuation, Schwankung	3
fluent (adj.)	fließend	2
fluids (n.)	Flüssigkeiten	14
FOB (Free on board)	frei an Bord (Ortsname)	6
focus group (n.)	Arbeitsgruppe	4
follow (v.)	daraus folgen	14
follow-up (n.)	Nachhakaktion	4
food (n.)	hier: Nahrungsmittel	15
foreign (adj.)	ausländisch	11
foresee (v.)	voraussehen	9
forever (adv.)	immer und ewig	11
forewarn (v.)	vorwarnen	3
formal (adj.)	formell	11
formality (n.)	Formalität	6
forward (adv.)	nach vorn	14

G

forward-looking *(adj.)*	vorwärts schauend, progressiv denkend		9
found *(v.)*	gründen		1; 9
fraud *(n.)*	Betrug		8
freebies *(n.)*	kostenlose Werbegeschenke		4
freelance *(adj..)*	freiberuflich		2
freight *(n.)*	Fracht		6
frequent *(adj.)*	häufig		11
friendship *(n.)*	Freundschaft		11
FTSE *(n.)*	britischer Börsenindex		8
funding *(n.)*	Finanzierung		14
funds *(n.)*	Gelder		6; 13
future *(n.)*	Zukunft		9
futures *(n.)*	Termingeschäfte, Futures		8

G

gain *(v.)*	gewinnen, hier: erobern		15
gain access *(v.)*	sich Zugang verschaffen		13
gather *(v.)*	sammeln		10
	zusammenkommen		15
generalisation *(n.)*	Verallgemeinerung		11
generality *(n.)*	Allgemeinheit		6
generate *(v.)*	erzeugen		14
generous *(adj.)*	großzügig		1
genuine *(adj.)*	echt		13
geothermal *(adj.)*	geothermal		14
giant *(n.)*	Riese		15
gilt edge stocks *(n.)*	britische Regierungsfonds, Staatspapiere		8
give rise to *(v.)*	verursachen		5
globalisation *(n.)*	Globalisierung, das Zusammenwachsen der Erde		11; 12
go ahead *(v.)*	durchgehen, gelingen		9
go through *(v.)*	durchgehen, gelingen		6
goods *(n.)*	Güter, Waren		6
governing law *(n.)*	anwendbares Recht		5
government *(n.)*	Regierung		12
government bonds *(n.)*	Regierungswertpapiere		8
grade *(n.)*	Stufe		15
graduate trainee *(n.)*	Auszubildende(r) mit Hochschulabschluss		1
grain *(n.)*	Getreide		15
grant *(v.)*	gewähren, erlauben		5; 6
Greek *(n.)*	Grieche, Griechin		14
gross amount payable *(n.)*	zu zahlende Gesamtsumme		6
groundwater table *(n.)*	Grundwasserspiegel		14
growth *(n.)*	Wachstum		8
growth prospects *(n.)*	Wachstumserwartungen		9
growth rate *(n.)*	Wachstumsrate		15
guarantee *(n.)*	Garantie		6
guidance *(n.)*	Leitung, Beratung		3
guideline *(n.)*	Richtschnur, -linie		4
gymnasium *(n.)*	Sport- und Fitnessraum		1

H

hacker *(n.)*	Hacker		13
hands-on *(adj.)*	anpackend		1
Hang Seng *(n.)*	Hong Kong Börsenindex		8
hard center *(n.)*	harter Kern		11
hard or soft sell *(n.)*	aggressive oder „weichere" Verkaufsmethoden		4
hard-pressed *(adj.)*	stressgeplagt		12
harnessing *(n.)*	Nutzen, nutzbar machen		14
have it on good authority	aus verlässlicher Quelle wissen		9
have sb believe *(v.)*	jmd im Glauben lassen		12
head office *(n.)*	Zentralbüro, Zentrale		9
health *(n.)*	Gesundheit		12
health care *(n.)*	Gesundheitswesen		15
health insurance *(n.)*	Krankenversicherung		1
hereby *(adv. fml)*	hiermit		5
hereinafter *(adv. fml)*	im Folgenden		5
hidden *(adj.)*	geheim gehalten		11
	versteckt, verborgen		13
hierarchy *(n.)*	Hierarchie, Firmenstruktur, Rangordnung		11
high-grade *(adj.)*	hochwertig		2
highly respected *(adj.)*	hoch geschätzt		9
highly valued *(adj.)*	hoch geschätzt		1
high-pressure *(adj.)*	Hochleistungs-, anspruchsvoll		1
hinder *(v.)*	(ver)hindern		12
hitherto *(adv.)*	bisher		15
hobbies *(n.)*	Freizeitinteressen, Hobbys		2
hold true *(v.)*	wahr sein		11
honest *(adj.)*	ehrlich, redlich		8
huge *(adj.)*	riesig		14
human rights *(n.)*	Menschenrechte		12

I

idiosyncrasies *(n.pl.)*	Eigenheiten, Eigentümlichkeiten		11
ignore *(v.)*	ignorieren		12
image *(n.)*	Vorstellung		11
impede *(v.)*	aufhalten, (ver)hindern		15
implement *(v.)*	bewerkstelligen		3; 4
impose *(v.)*	hier: erheben, mit …belegen		15
imposition *(n.)*	Erhebung, Auferlegung		15
impressive *(adj.)*	beeindruckend		10
imprint *(n.)*	Markenzeichen, Firmennamen		5
improve *(v.)*	(sich) verbessern		12
in ancient times *(adj.)*	in der Antike		15
in excess of *(prep.)*	über		6
in fact *(adv.)*	in Wirklichkeit		12
in his seventies	in den Siebzigern, schon über siebzig		9
in particular *(adv.)*	insbesondere		13
in pursuit of	auf der Jagd nach		12

169

G

in stock *(adv.)*	vorrätig	5
in succession *(adv.)*	hintereinander	9
in the region of *(prep.)*	ungefähr, nahezu	9
in western terms *(adv.)*	nach westlichen Maßstäben	11
in writing *(adv.)*	in schriftlicher Form	5
incentive *(n.)*	Anreiz	1
include *(v.)*	mit einschließen	10
income *(n.)*	Einkommen, Einnahmen	4; 7; 12; 15
income tax *(n.)*	Einkommenssteuer	15
Incoterms *(n.)* International commercial terms	Internationale Regeln für die Auslegung handelsüblicher Vertragsformeln	6
increase *(n.)*	Erweiterung	3; 14
increase *(v.)*	wachsen	14
	steigen	15
incur *(v.)*	zuziehen, machen	5
indeed *(adv.)*	in der Tat	14
indemnify *(v.)*	absichern, schadlos halten	5
indemnity *(n.)*	Schadloshaltung; Absicherung	5
independent *(adj.)*	unabhängig	1; 2; 9; 12
in-depth *(adj.)*	eingehend, gründlich	9; 10
index *(n.)*	Index, Verzeichnis	8
individual *(n.)*	Einzelne(r)	15
industrial relations *(n.)*	hier: Betriebsklima	9
infancy *(n.)*	Anfangsstadium, in den Kinderschuhen	15
infomercial *(n.)*	Werbung mit Information (information und commercial)	4
informal *(adj.)*	informell	11
infuriating *(adj.)*	äußerst ärgerlich	11
ingredient *(n.)*	Bestandteil	6
inheritance tax *(n.)*	Erbschaftssteuer	15
in-house *(adj.)*	hausintern	1
initiate *(v.)*	einleiten	9
inject *(v.)*	einspritzen	14
innovative *(adj.)*	innovativ	14
inopportune *(adj.)*	unpassend	15
insider dealing *(n.)*	(illegale) Insider-Geschäfte	8
insincere *(adj.)*	unaufrichtig	11
instead of *(prep.)*	anstatt	11
insurance *(n.)*	Versicherung(swesen)	6; 13; 14
insurance quotation *(n.)*	Versicherungsangebot	13
Insurance Tax *(n.)* AE	Versicherungssteuer	15
intangible *(adj.)*	nicht greifbar	15
intend *(v.)*	beabsichtigen	11
interest *(n.)*	Zins	7
interest rate *(n.)*	Zinssatz	13
internally *(adv.)*	intern	11
interpret *(v.)*	deuten, auslegen; interpretieren	5; 11
interstate nature *(n.)*	zwischen den US-Bundesstaaten bestehende Art	15
introduce *(v.)*	einführen	15
inventiveness *(n.)*	Einfallsreichtum	4
investigation *(n.)*	Untersuchung	9
investment *(n.)*	Investition	9
	Anlage	13
investment sources *(n.)*	Kapitalanlagen	7
investors *(n.)*	Investoren	8
invoice *(n.)* fml.	Rechnung	6; 15
involve *(v.)*	involvieren, mitbeteiligen	12
involvement *(n.)*	Beteiligung, Verwicklung	8
irrigation *(n.)*	Bewässerung	14
irritation *(n.)*	Verärgerung	11
island *(n.)*	Insel	14
issue *(n.)*	Angelegenheit	8; 12; 15
it pays *(v.)*	es macht sich bezahlt	11

J

Janus *(n.)*	Janus (altgriechischer Gott mit zwei Gesichtern)	13
jewel *(n.)*	Juwel	13
job losses *(n.)*	Arbeitsplatzverluste, Entlassungen	9
judge *(v.)*	(be)urteilen	11
jurisdiction *(n.)*	Rechtsprechung, Rechtssystem	13
	Gerichtsstand	15
justified *(adj.)*	gerechtfertigt	12

K

key *(n.)*	Schlüssel	6
key area *(n.)*	Schlüsselbereich	4
key issues *(n.)*	die wichtigsten Fragen	10
know no bounds *(v.)*	keine Grenzen kennen	15

L

lack *(n.)*	Mangel	15
ladder *(n.)*	Leiter	11
lapse *(v.)*	erlöschen	5
latest *(adj.)*	neueste(r, s)	13
launch *(v.)*	auf den Markt bringen	4
	starten	14
laws *(n.)*	Gesetze	15
lay the blame *(v.)*	die Schuld geben	12
leading *(adj.)*	führend	10
led to believe (to be) *(v.)*	glauben lassen	13
legal *(adj.)*	juristisch	12; 13
legendary *(adj.)*	legendär	15
legislation *(n.)*	Gesetzgebung	15
legislature *(n.)*	Legislatur, Gesetz(gebung)	15
letter of credit *(n.)*	Kreditbrief, Akkreditiv	6
level *(n.)*	Ebene, Niveau	12; 13; 14; 15
levy *(v.)*	erheben, einziehen	15

liable *(adj.)*	hier: möglicherweise imstande	5	
liaise *(v.)*	kommunizieren, kooperieren	3	
liaison *(n.)*	Zusammenarbeit, Verbindung	4	
license *(n.)* AE (BE licence)	Lizenz	3	
licensee *(n.)*	Lizenznehmer	5	
licensing *(n.)*	Lizenzgeschäfte	3	
licensor *(n.)*	Lizenzgeber	5	
limited to *(adj.)*	begrenzt auf	11	
linear *(adj.)*	gradlinig	11	
linger *(v.)*	bleiben, fortbestehen	4	
literally *(adv.)*	wörtlich	11	
living standards *(n.pl.)*	Lebensstandard	12	
loan *(n.)*	Darlehen	12	
local *(adj.)*	lokal, örtlich	13	
local branch *(n.)*	örtliche Zweigstelle, Niederlassung	13	
location *(n.)*	Standort	15	
lock into *(v.)*	einschließen, einsperren	4	
long since *(adv.)*	schon längst	11	
long-distance *(adj.)*	über eine weite Strecke	6	
long-term *(adj.)*	langfristig	14	
long-term debts (n)	langfristige Verbindlichkeiten	7	
look into *(v.)*	untersuchen	9	
lookout (to be on the ... for) *(v.)*	Ausschau halten nach	10	
loop *(n.)*	Schleife	11	
loophole *(n.)*	Lücke, Schlupfloch, Winkel	12	
loss *(n.)*	Verlust	6; 9	
lunch *(n.)*	Mittagessen	13	

M

mailing *(n.)*	Werbeaktion per Post, Mailing	3; 4	
maintain *(v.)*	aufrechterhalten	13	
maintenance *(n.)*	Instandhaltung	7	
majority holding *(n.)*	Mehrheitsanteil	9	
make the big time *(infml.)*	groß einsteigen	1	
malfunction *(n.)*	Fehlfunktion	3	
manage to *(v.)*	jmd gelingen, es schaffen	9	
managing director *(n.)*	Generaldirektor, Firmenchef, Geschäftsführer	1; 9	
Manchester-based *(adj.)*	mit Sitz in Manchester	9	
manipulate *(v.)*	manipulieren	13	
manners *(n.)*	Sitten, Manieren	11	
manufacture *(v.)*	herstellen, verarbeiten	4	
manufacturer *(n.)*	Hersteller, Produktionsfirma	6	
mark *(v.)*	markieren, kennzeichnen	9	

market niche *(n.)*	Marktnische	9	
market outlet *(n.)*	Marktbereich	9	
market presence *(n.)*	Marktpräsenz	4	
marketing executive *(n.)*	Marketing-Manager	4	
matter *(n.)*	Angelegenheit	9	
means *(n.)*	Mittel	13; 14	
measure *(n.)*	Maßnahme	4; 12	
meat *(n.)*	Fleisch	15	
meet half way *(v.)*	auf halbem Wege treffen, entgegenkommen	11	
meet the needs	Bedürfnisse befriedigen	14	
member *(n.)*	Mitglied	15	
mere *(adj.)*	bloß	6; 14	
merger *(n.)*	Zusammenschluss, Fusion	9	
Middle Ages *(n.)*	Mittelalter	15	
middle-men *(n.)*	Mittelsmänner, Zwischenhändler, Vermittler	13	
military *(n.)*	Militär	15	
mind *(n.)*	Geist	15	
minutes *(n.)*	Protokoll	3	
misinterpretation *(n.)*	Fehldeutung	11; 13	
miss *(v.)*	verpassen, auslassen	11; 15	
mistaken *(adj.)*	verfehlt, fehlerhaft	12	
misunderstand *(v.)*	missverstehen	13	
misunderstanding *(n.)*	Missverständnis	11	
monies (n.pl)	Gelder, Beträge	5; 7	
monies owed to the company *(n.)*	Außenstände	7	
monies payable by the company *(n.)*	eigene finanzielle Verpflichtungen, Verbindlichkeiten	7	
monitor *(v.)*	beobachten, kontrollieren, verfolgen	3; 4; 13	
motor fuel *(n.)*	Kraftstoff	15	
move on *(v.)*	weitergehen, weitermachen	11	
mutual *(adj.)*	gemeinsam, gegenseitig	14	
mutually *(adv.)*	gegenseitig, gemeinsam	5	

N

nagging *(adj./pr.p.)*	quälend, keine Ruhe lassend	6	
narrow *(adj.)*	eng, schmal	15	
Nasdaq *(n.)*	amerikanischer Börsenindex	8	
nearer to home *(adv.)*	näher liegend, vordergründiger	11	
necessarily *(adv.)*	notwendigerweise	4; 11	
née *(adj.)*	geborene	2	
needs *(n.)*	Bedürfnisse	4	
neglect to *(v.)*	etwas nicht tun, unterlassen, vergessen	9	
negotiations *(n.)*	Verhandlungen	11	
net *(adj.)*	Netto	7	
nexus *(n.)*	Verknüpfung, Verflochtenheit	15	

no longer *(adv.)*	nicht mehr	9	
no wonder	kein Wunder	1	
no-nonsense *(adj.)*	sachlich	1	
null and void *(adj.)*	null und nichtig	5	
numerous *(adj.)*	viele, zahlreiche	13	

O

obscure *(adj.)*	unbekannt, obskur	13	
observe *(v.)*	beobachten	3	
obtain *(v.)*	erhalten, bekommen	5; 9; 10	
obvious *(adj.)*	deutlich	11	
occur *(v.)*	vorkommen	11	
of its kind	dieser Art	14	
of the one part *(adv.fml)*	einerseits	5	
of the other part *(adv. fml)*	andererseits	5	
offset *(p.p.)*	ausgeglichen, kompensiert	3	
omnipresent *(adj.)*	allgegenwärtig	12	
on average *(adv.)*	im Durchschnitt	12	
on behalf of *(prep.)*	im Auftrag/Namen von	5; 15	
on display *(adv.)*	ausgestellt	10	
on the other hand *(adv.)*	andererseits	11	
on the union front *(adv.)*	auf Seiten der Gewerkschaften	9	
one-stop-shop *(n.)*	eine Firma, die alle Produkte für ein bestimmtes Marktsegment anbietet	4	
ongoing *(adj.)*	in Arbeit	4	
online stock trading *(n.)*	Online-Aktiengeschäfte; Online-Börse	15	
operating profit *(n.)*	Betriebsgewinn	7	
operational outlay *(n.)*	Betriebskosten	7	
opportunity *(n.)*	Gelegenheit, Chance	2; 9; 11	
opposition *(n.)*	Einspruch, Gegenwehr	9	
oppressive *(adj.)*	erdrückend, repressiv	15	
organigram *(n.)*	Organigramm (Organisationsdiagramm)	3	
other trading income *(n.)*	sonstige Einkünfte	7	
out of hand *(adv.)*	voreilig	12	
outcome *(n.)*	Ergebnis	9	
outlet *(n.)*	Absatzmöglichkeit	9	
outline *(v.)*	umreißen	3	
outside *(prep.)*	außerhalb	15	
overall *(adj.)*	gesamt, übergreifend, umfassend	3; 4	
overestimate *(v.)*	überschätzen	12	
overlap *(v.)*	überlappen, sich überschneiden	9	
overseas *(adv.)*	im Ausland, in Übersee	6	
overtly *(adv.)*	offenkundig, vordergründig	11	
owe *(v.)*	schulden	7	
ownership *(n.)*	Besitz	6	

P

p.a. *(per annum) (adv.)*	jährlich	1	
PA *(abbrev.)* (Personal Assistant) *(n.)*	Assistent(in), Sekretär(in)	2	
package *(v.)*	präsentieren, verpacken	4	
pain *(n.)*	Schmerz	14	
painstaking *(adj.)*	sorgfältig, peinlich genau	4	
paperwork *(n)*	Schreibarbeit, „Papierkrieg"	13	
participants *(n.pl.)*	Teilnehmer	3; 12	
participation *(n.)*	Teilnahme	10	
particular *(adj.)*	besondere(r,s)	9	
particularly *(adv.)*	insbesondere	11	
partnership *(n.)*	Partnerschaft	14	
password *(n.)*	Passwort	13	
payable *(adj.)*	zahlbar	6; 7	
pension scheme *(n.)*	Pensionskasse	1	
per capita	pro Kopf, individuell	12	
perceive *(v.)*	wahrnehmen	11	
perks *(n.)*	Vergünstigungen	1	
permission *(n.)*	Erlaubnis, Genehmigung	5	
Personal Income Tax *(n.)* AE	persönliche Einkommenssteuer	15	
personnel manager *(n.)*	Personalchef	2	
Petroleum Business Tax *(n.)* AE	etwa: Mineralölsteuer	15	
phasing *(n.)*	Zeitplanung	4	
phenomena *(n.pl.)*	Phänomene	4	
photography *(n.)*	Fotografieren	2	
pick up *(n.)*	empfangen	11	
piggy-back mailshot *(n.)*	eine Werbeaktion, die mit einer anderen größeren Aktion mitläuft	4	
pillar *(n.)*	Säule	8	
pitfall *(n.)*	Falle, Fallstrick, Hauptschwierigkeit	6	
place *(v.)*	hier: auferlegen	15	
placement *(n.)*	hier: Vereinbarungen	4	
platform *(n.)*	Plattform, Basis	10	
plc *(Public Limited Company) (n.)*	AG (Aktiengesellschaft)	7	
pleasure *(n.)*	Vergnügen	14	
plentiful *(adj.)*	ergiebig, reichlich	14	
ploy *(n.)*	Strategie, Trick	4; 6	
policy *(n.)*	Plan, Strategie (Haus-)Politik	3 12	
poll tax *(n.)*	etwa: Personen- oder Kopfsteuer	15	
pollute *(v.)*	verunreinigen	14	
population *(n.)*	Bevölkerung	12; 14	
port of shipment *(n.)*	Verladungshafen	6	
positive thinking *(n.)*	positives Denken	14	
possibility *(n.)*	Möglichkeit	14	
post *(adj.)*	nach	8	

G

post *(n.)*	Posten, Position	2
post-modern *(adj.)*	post-modern	4
poverty *(n.)*	Armut	12
powerful *(adj.)*	stark, mächtig	15
PR *(abbrev.)(n.)* Public Relations	Öffentlichkeitsarbeit	9
pragmatic *(adj.)*	pragmatisch	14
praise *(n.)*	Lob	11
predict *(v.)*	vorhersagen	15
preferably *(adv.)*	vorzugsweise	2
prejudice *(n.)*	Vorurteil	11
preliminaries *(n.)*	Vorbereitungsarbeiten	10
preparation *(n.)*	Vorbereitung	10
prepare *(v.)*	vorbereiten	9
presence *(n.)*	Anwesenheit	10
present *(adj.)*	gegenwärtig	9
present-day *(adj.)*	heutig	15
prestigious *(adj.)*	mit hohem Prestigewert	1; 2
pre-tax profit *(n.)*	Gewinn vor Steuer	1
previous *(adj.)*	früher, vorherig	11
previously *(adv.)*	vorherig	14
principle *(n.)*	Prinzip	4
print-out *(n.)*	Ausdruck	10
prior *(adj.)*	vorherig	5
procedure *(n.)*	Verfahren	8
proceeds *(n.)*	Erlöse	15
process *(n.)*	Verfahren	15
process *(v.)*	bearbeiten	13
product developer *(n.)*	Produktentwickler	4
Profit & Loss Account *(n.)*	Gewinn- und Verlustrechnung	7
profit before tax *(n.)*	Gewinn vor Steuern	7
profit sharing *(n.)*	Gewinnbeteiligung	1
profitable *(adj.)*	rentabel, lohnend	14
profits *(n.)*	Gewinn	9
prognosis *(n.)*	Prognose, Vorhersage	3
progressive taxation *(n.)*	progressives (gestaffeltes) Steuersystem	15
prohibitive *(adj.)*	untragbar	14
project development *(n.)*	Projektentwicklung	11
promise *(n.)*	Versprechen	13
promotion *(n.)*	Beförderung Werbung, Werbemaßnahmen	1; 3 4
promptly *(adv.)*	prompt, umgehend	6
proof *(n.)*	Beweis	12
property *(n.)*	Besitz, Eigentum; hier: Immobilien	6; 15 7
property tax *(n.)*	Vermögenssteuer	15
Property Transfer Tax *(n.)* AE	etwa: Immobilienverkaufssteuer, Grunderwerbssteuer	15
proposal *(n.)*	Vorhaben, Vorschlag	3; 9
prospective *(adj.)*	interessiert, in Frage kommend	6
prospectus *(n.)*	Prospekt	9
protect *(v.)*	schützen	12
proud *(adj.)*	stolz	1
proven *(adj.)*	nachgewiesen, bewährt	13
provide *(v.)*	sorgen für, bereitstellen, liefern, zur Verfügung stellen	4; 12; 14; 15
provisional *(adj.)*	vorläufig	9
prudent *(adj.)*	klug, umsichtig	6
psychological *(adj.)*	psychologisch	4
public *(adj.)*	öffentlich	14
public eye *(n.)*	Öffentlichkeit	12
publicity material *(n.)*	Werbematerialien	9
pursuit *(n.)*	Streben, Jagd (nach)	14
purveyor *(n. fml.)*	Händler, Lieferant	6
push aside *(v.)*	zur Seite schieben	12

Q

quarter *(n.)*	Quartal	3
quench *(v.)*	stillen	14
questionnaire *(n.)*	Fragebogen(aktion)	4
queue *(n.)*	Schlange	13

R

raise *(v.)*	hier: erheben	15
rally *(v.)*	sich erholen	8
rallying-cry *(n.)*	Sammelruf	12
range (of products) *(n.)*	Reihe Produktpalette	3 9
rate *(n.)*	hier: Satz	15
reach *(v.)*	erreichen	9
reach agreement *(v.)*	sich einigen	12
Real Estate Transfer Tax *(n.)* AE	etwa: Grunderwerbssteuer	15
reasonable *(adj.)*	hier: (recht) ordentlich	2
reassuring *(adj.)*	beruhigend	6
recede *(v.)*	zurückgehen	14
recent *(adj.)*	jüngste(r,s), neueste(r,s)	13
recipe *(n.)*	Rezept	1
recognize *(v.)*	erkennen	13; 15
recommend *(v.)*	empfehlen	8
recommendation *(n.)*	Empfehlung	9
reconsider *(v.)*	erneut überlegen	11
record *(n.)*	Vorgeschichte	13
recover *(v.)*	sich erholen	14
recovery *(n.)*	Erholung	8
recruit *(v.)*	rekrutieren, einstellen	1
recruitment *(n.)*	Einstellung, Rekrutierung	2
rectify *(v.)*	berichtigen	5
redefine *(v.)*	neu definieren	12
redistribute *(v.)*	neu verteilen	8
reference *(n.)*	Referenz	6
refund *(v.)*	zurückerstatten	15
regressive *(adj.)*	regressiv, rückläufig	15
regularly *(adv.)*	regelmäßig	13
regulate *(v.)*	kontrollieren, regulieren, verwalten	12

173

G

regulation (n.)	Kontrolle	3
regulations (n.)	Verordnungen, Vorschriften	14
re-launch (n.)	neuer Versuch, ein Produkt auf den Markt zu bringen	4
relieve (v.)	erleichtern	12
rely on (v.)	sich verlassen auf	12
remind (v.)	erinnern	10
remote (adj.)	fern(gesteuert)	8
remove (v.)	entfernen, hier: überflüssig machen	13
request (n.)	Bitte	6
require (v.)	benötigen	5
research department (n.)	Forschungsabteilung	4
reserved (adj.)	reserviert	11
resources (n.)	Ressourcen	9
respective (adj.)	jeweilig	6
response (in ...) (n.)	in Beantwortung	2
responsibility (n.)	Verantwortung, Zuständigkeit	2; 12; 15
responsible (adj.)	verantwortlich; zuständig	5; 15
result (n.)	Ergebnis	11
result (v.)	sich ergeben	7
result in (v.)	hinauslaufen auf	14
retailer (n.)	Einzelhändler	4
retain (v.)	(ein)behalten	7
retention of ownership (n.)	Eigentumsvorbehalt	6
retirement fund (n.)	Pensionskasse	15
revenue (n.)	Einkünfte, Einnahmen	7; 15
revert (v.)	zurückgehen	5
RF, PLM etc. (brit./amer. Form)	Initialen als Namenskürzel	3
rights (n.)	Rechte	5
rise (v.)	steigen	12
risk (n.)	Risiko	6
rival (n.)	Rivale	9
role model (n)	Vorbild	11
Roman (n.)	Römer	15
royalty (n.)	Honorar, Tantieme	3; 5
rumour (n.)	Gerücht	9
rumour has it (v.)	man munkelt	9
run (v.)	leiten	9
	betreiben, unterhalten	14
rung (n.)	Sprosse	11
running costs (n.)	Unterhaltskosten	14

S

sabbatical (n.)	Sonderurlaub	1
sailing (n.)	Segeln	2
salary (n.)	Gehalt	7
Sales & Use Tax (n.) AE	etwa: Verkaufs- und Verbrauchssteuer	15
sales (n.)	Verkäufe, Umsatz	7
sales reps (n.) (representatives)	Außendienstmitarbeiter/Verkäufer im Außendienst	3; 4
sales tax (n.) AE	Verkaufssteuer	15
satisfy (v.)	befriedigen, zufrieden stellen	4
save (v.)	retten, sparen	14
savings (n.)	hier: Sparkonten	13
scale (n.)	Größenordnung	6; 12
scale down (v.)	verkleinern, reduzieren	12
scapegoat (n.)	Sündenbock	12
scheme (n.)	Plan, Vorhaben	14
scourge (n.)	Geißel	12
screen-based (adj.)	bildschirmgesteuert, online	8
seasonal (adj.)	saisonbedingt	8
security (n.)	Sicherheit	13
see eye to eye (v.)	sich verstehen	9
segment (n.)	Segment, Bereich	3; 4
self-assertion (n.)	Selbstbehauptung	4
self-explanatory (adj.)	selbsterklärend	6
self-fulfilling prophecy (n.)	eine Vorhersage, die das Vorhergesagte selbst auslöst	12
self-fulfillment (n.)	Selbstverwirklichung	4
sense (n.)	Sinn	12
separate (adj.)	getrennt	10
serve to (v.)	dienen zu	15
services tax (n.)	Dienstleistungssteuer	15
set (n.)	Satz	13
set up (v.)	arrangieren	9
several (adj.)	mehrere	12
severely (adj.)	ernsthaft	8
share (n.)	Aktie	7; 9; 13
share (v.)	teilen	10
share capital (n)	Aktienkapital	7
share prices (n.)	Aktienpreise	8
shareholder (n.)	Aktionär	7
shipment (n.)	Verschiffung, Versendung	6
shortage (n.)	Knappheit	14
short-term (adj.)	kurzfristig	9
show one's hand (v.)	seine Karten zeigen, auf den Tisch legen	9
showcase (v.)	ausstellen	10
sign (n.)	Zeichen	11
significant (adj.)	bedeutsam	12
sited (to be)(v.)	seinen Standort haben (in)	15
sixth form college (n.)	Oberstufe/Kollegstufe	2
skill (n.)	Fähigkeit, Fertigkeit	2
skilled (adj.)	mit Fachausbildung	9
slave (n.)	Sklave	15
snackbar (n.)	Imbissstube	10
snag (n.)	Haken, Schwierigkeit	6
solar installations (n.)	Sonnenkraftwerke	14
solar power (n.)	Sonnenkraft, -energie	14
solve (v.)	lösen	6
soonest (adv.)	möglichst bald	3
sophisticated (adj.)	raffiniert, klug	13

sort out *(v.)*	in Ordnung bringen	6	
sound *(adj.)*	gesund	14	
source *(n.)*	Quelle	9; 13; 15	
source codes *(n.)*	Quell-Codes	5	
sourced (to be)*(v.)*	seine Quelle haben (bei)	15	
sources of revenue *(n.)*	Einnahmequellen	15	
sovereignty *(n.)*	Hoheitsrechte	15	
space *(n.)*	Ausstellungs- oder Standfläche	10	
	Raum, Platz	12	
space of time *(n.)*	Zeitraum	10	
spacious *(adj.)*	geräumig	10	
spam *(n.)*	Werbung per E-Mail	4	
specialist journal *(n.)*	Fachzeitschrift	10	
speculation *(n.)*	Spekulation	8	
speech *(n.)*	Sprache	11	
spoils *(n.)*	Kriegsbeute	15	
spokesman *(n.)*	Sprecher	10	
staff *(n.)*	Mitarbeiter(innen), Belegschaft	4; 9	
staff cuts *(n.)*	(Mitarbeiter)Kündigungen, Entlassungen	9	
staff situation *(n.)*	Personalstand	3	
stage *(n.)*	Stadium, Stufe	9; 11	
stand construction *(n.)*	Standaufbau	10	
standing *(n.)*	Ruf, Reputation	9	
starting capital *(n.)*	Startkapital	7	
state legislation (single...) *(n.)*	Rechtsprechung/Gerichtsbarkeit eines einzelnen Bundesstaates	15	
states *(n.)*	Staaten	15	
stateside *(adv.)*	in den Staaten (USA)	8	
statutes *(n.)*	Statuten	15	
steel *(n.)*	Stahl	15	
sterling *(n.)*	brit. Währung	1; 7	
stigma *(n.)*	Stigma, negatives Merkmal	12	
stock *(n.)*	hier: Lagerbestand	7	
stock exchange *(n.)*	Börse	8; 13	
stock market *(n.)*	Aktienmarkt, Börse	8	
strengthen *(v.)*	verstärken; bestärken	10; 15	
study *(n.)*	Studie	9	
style *(n.)*	Stil	11	
subject *(n.)*	Schulfach	2	
subject to *(prep.)*	basierend auf	5	
subscriber *(n.)*	hier: Kunde, Teilnehmer	8	
subsidiary *(adj.)*	Tochter-	1	
subsidiary rights *(n.)*	Nebenrechte	5	
subsidised *(adj.)*	bezuschusst	1	
subsidy *(n.)*	Subvention	12; 14	
substantial *(adj.)*	erheblich, substanziell	14	
subtle *(adj.)*	subtil	11	
success rate *(n.)*	Erfolgsquote	13	
suffer *(v.)*	leiden	14	
sufficient *(adj.)*	ausreichend	14	
suit *(v.)*	sich eignen für, passen	2	
sum received *(n.)*	Erlös	5	
superficially *(adv.)*	oberflächlich	11	
supersede *(v.)*	ersetzen	5	
supplement *(v.)*	ergänzen	9	
supplier *(n.)*	Lieferant	6	
supply *(n.)*	Lieferung	5	
	Vorrat	14	
support *(n.)*	Unterstützung	14	
survey *(n.)*	Übersicht; Untersuchung, Umfrage	13	
suspect *(adj.)*	verdächtig	8	
suspicion *(n.)*	Verdacht	12	
sustainable *(adj.)*	haltbar, anhaltend	14	
swift *(adj.)*	rasch, schnell	6	
switch *(v.)*	hier: verlegen	3	
synergy *(n.)*	Synergie	9	
synonymous *(adj.)*	gleichbedeutend, synonym	11	

T

tailor-made *(adj.)*	maßgeschneidert	9	
take care of sb. *(v.)*	sich um jmd. kümmern	1	
takeover *(n.)*	Übernahme	9	
takeover bid *(n.)*	Kaufversuch, Übernahmeangebot	9	
tap into *(v.)*	anzapfen	14	
target *(n.)*	Ziel	8; 9	
targeted *(adj.)*	gezielt	10	
tariff *(n.)*	Zolltarif	12	
task *(n.)*	Aufgabe	12	
tax *(n.)*	Steuer	12	
tax *(v.)*	besteuern, mit einer Steuer belegen	15	
tax authority *(n.)*	Steuerbehörde, Finanzamt	15	
tax bracket *(n.)*	Steuergruppe	15	
tax deduction *(n.)*	Steuerabzug	13	
tax evasion *(n.)*	Steuerhinterziehung	8	
tax returns *(n.)*	Steuererklärung	15	
taxing *(adj.)*	anstrengend	15	
teaser ad *(n.)*	Werbestrategie mit nur wenig Information, „Appetitanreger"	4	
television commercials *(n.)*	Fernsehwerbung	10	
tempered *(p.p.)*	abgeschwächt	3	
template *(n.)*	Schablone, Muster	3	
tend to *(v.)*	neigen zu	11	
termination *(n.)*	Beendigung	5	
terms *(n.)*	Bedingungen	5; 11	
terms of credit *(n.)*	Kreditbedingungen	6	
terms of delivery *(n.)*	Lieferbedingungen	6	
terms of payment *(n.)*	Zahlungsbedingungen	6	
the lows *(n.)*	Tiefpunkte	8	
the poor *(n.)*	die Armen	15	
the twain *(n.)*	*altmodisch* die zwei, die beiden	11	
theft *(n.)*	Diebstahl	13	
theme focus *(n.)*	thematischer Schwerpunkt	10	

There's no such things as.	So etwas wie ... gibt es nicht	13	up-and-coming *(adj.)*	aufstrebend	1
thereafter *(adv.)*	danach	5	update *(n.)*	Aktualisierung	3
third party *(n.)*	Dritte(r)	5	update *(v.)*	auf den neuesten Stand bringen	13
thirst *(n.)*	Durst	14	upwards of *(prep.)*	mehr als	15
this time around *(adv.)*	diesmal	10	use tax *(n.)*	Gebrauchssteuer	15
thorough *(adj.)*	gründlich	10	utilise *(v.)*	nutzen	14
throughout *(prep.)*	während, im Laufe des ...	15	**V**		
throw out the baby with the bathwater	das Kind mit dem Bade ausschütten	14	vacation *(n.)*	Urlaub	3
tick off *(v.)*	als erledigt abhaken	11	valuable *(adj.)*	wertvoll	11
timetabling *(n.)*	Zeitplanung	10	VAT *(abbrev.)* Value Added Tax	Mehrwertsteuer	6; 15
to all concerned	allen Beteiligten	15	vendor *(n.)*	Verkäufer	15
to date *(adv.)*	bisher	3	venue *(n.)*	Treffpunkt	10
to that effect *(adv.)*	entsprechend, diesbezüglich	9	verdict *(n.)*	Urteil, Beurteilung	4; 11
total net price *(n.)*	Gesamtnettopreis	6	vicinity *(n.)*	Nähe	9
trade fair *(n.)*	Fachmesse	10	video on demand *(n.)*	Video auf Abruf	15
tragedy *(n.)*	Tragödie	12	video transmissions *(n.)*	Videoübertragungen	15
transact *(v.)*	durchführen, abschließen	15	violation *(n.)*	Verletzung	5
transaction *(n.)*	Transaktion	13	voice *(n.)*	hier: Ton	15
transfer *(n.)*	Überweisung	6	**W**		
transport *(n.)*	Transport	6	wares *(n. fml.)*	Waren	6
transportation services *(n.)*	öffentliche Verkehrsmittel	15	warranty *(n.)*	Gewähr(leistung)	5
tremendous *(adj.)*	ungeheuer	15	wary *(adj.)*	vorsichtig	15
trust *(v.)*	vertrauen	13	watchful *(adj.)*	aufmerksam, wachsam	13
trustworthy *(adj.)*	vertrauenswürdig	6	watchword *(n.)*	Parole, Schlagwort	13
turn full circle *(v.)*	den Kreis schließen; hier: seinen Zweck erfüllen	4	wealth *(n.)*	Vermögen	15
			well-being *(n.)*	Wohlbefinden	12
turnover *(n.)*	Umsatz	1; 3; 7; 9	well-established *(adj.)*	gut etabliert, bewährt	9; 13
			whereas *(conj.)*	während	11
U			whiz-kid *(n.)*	Senkrechtstarter	1
unanimous *(adj.)*	einstimmig; sich einig	1	wholly *(adv.)*	gänzlich	12
unauthorised *(adj.)*	nicht autorisiert, unberechtigt	13	wind power *(n.)*	Windkraft, -energie	14
unconstitutional *(adj.)*	verfassungswidrig	15	with a view to *(prep.)*	mit der Absicht um	10
underestimate *(v.)*	unterschätzen	12	with due prominence *(adv.)*	entsprechend hervorgehoben	5
underground *(adv.)*	unterirdisch	14	with the aid of	mit Hilfe von	14
underground carpark *(n.)*	Tiefgarage	1	within *(prep.)*	innerhalb	15
			within easy reach *(adv.)*	leicht erreichbar	10
undermine *(v.)*	unterminieren	8	without prejudice to *(adv.)*	ohne negative Auswirkung auf	5
undersigned *(n.)*	die Unterzeichnenden	5	work *(v.)*	funktionieren	11
undisclosed *(adj.)*	geheim	9	workforce *(n.)*	Mitarbeiter(stab)	9
unexpectedly *(adv.)*	unerwartet	11	worth *(n.)*	Wert	4
unions *(n.)*	Gewerkschaften	9	worthless *(adj.)*	wertlos	8
unit price *(n.)*	Stückpreis, Einzelpreis	6	worthwhile *(adj.)*	lohnend, wertvoll	11
unite *(v.)*	vereinen		wrestling *(n.)*	Ringkämpfe	15
university graduate *(n.)*	Hochschulabsolvent(in)	2	wrongdoer *(n.)*	Missetäter	13
unjust *(adj.)*	ungerecht	15	**XYZ**		
unlike *(prep.)*	nicht wie, anders als	15	yearly *(adj.)*	jährlich	6
unreachable *(adj.)*	unerreichbar	14	youth market *(n.)*	Jugendmarkt	9
Unrelated Business Income Tax *(n.)* AE	etwa: Nebenerwerbssteuer	15			
unrest *(n.)*	Unruhe	9			